God's

Sovereignty

Elisha Coles

BAKER BOOK HOUSE
Grand Rapids, Michigan

Reprinted 1979 by Baker Book House
from the edition issued in 1831
by D. & M. Maclean

ISBN: 0-8010-2429-3

PHOTOLITHOPRINTED BY CUSHING - MALLOY, INC.
ANN ARBOR, MICHIGAN, UNITED STATES OF AMERICA
1979

PREFACE

CHRISTIAN READER,

THE doctrines of GRACE, of which this book treats, are the truths of GOD: Our Author has defended them in a masterly manner. He has not only proved them to be plainly revealed in the scriptures, but has also shewn that they are of such constant use to the children of God, that without the steadfast belief of them, they cannot go on their way rejoicing. It is from these doctrines only that settled peace can rule the conscience, the love of God be maintained in the heart, and a conversation kept up in our walk and warfare, as becometh the gospel. It is from them that all good works proceed, and that all fruits of holiness abound, to the praise of the glory of the grace of God.

In the PRACTICAL view of these points ELISHA COLES is singularly excellent. He has brought these deep things into daily use, and has proved them to be absolutely necessary in daily experience. They are truths, and useful truths. On these two accounts his book has been greatly esteemed by real Christians: And on these I would recommend it, as approved in mine own judgment to be agreeable to the oracles of God, and found to be of such constant use, that until I received them, I could not enjoy the blessings and comforts of the precious gospel.

Opposition to these doctrines will be made so long as there are people in the world, who place some confidence in the flesh; such as are pleased with their own works, and fond of taking merit to themselves. But the word of God is not of doubtful interpretation to those who rejoice in Christ Jesus. They are thankful for a FREE GRACE salvation, and while they enjoy the things which accompany it, with their lips and lives they desire to bless the God of all their mercies.

A *new* edition being called for, I was requested to recommend it to my friends, which I do from my heart. I wish it may be as useful to all who read it, as it has been to me. May the Lord bless it, and render it the means of building up his people in their most holy faith!

WILLIAM ROMAINE.

TO THE CHRISTIAN READER

THIS excellent treatise, containing divers prime points of our religion, which believers' souls do live upon every day, and in the liveliest sense whereof, with application to themselves, they enjoy and exercise sweet communion with God the Father, and his Son Jesus Christ, the Mediator of the new covenant, upon those better hopes, and surer promises, of the doctrines here treated of; doth sufficiently commend itself to such as are thoroughly acquainted with, and experimentally exercised in these things.

I have known the Author long (full twenty-eight years) to have had a spirit greatly addicted to, and affected with, the savory knowledge of the truths here delivered. And though he hath not had the use and help of foreign languages, wherein these points have been mostly written; yet I may say of him (as 1 Tim. 4: 6.) " He hath been long nourished up in the words of faith and good doctrine;" and thereunto he hath so far attained, as to be able to cut the strongest sinews of the principal objections which the adversaries have invaded these truths with. And further, to establish the positive truth, hath backed and confirmed the same by solid arguments, and pertinent scriptures genuinely explained and opened. And, which to me is yet more, he hath extracted the most spiritual, quickening cordials, which the doctrine of grace and election affords plenty of, whereby to comfort all sorts of believers; exhorting and directing the whole company and body of them, how to manage their faith between God and their own souls, in point of election: persuading them all to commit and betake themselves wholly to God's carrying on their salvation, in the way of election: and all along hath strewed his discourse with useful exhortations and applications of the doctrines he does deliver; mixing uses for practice, with the rational discussions, and the ruggeder controversials; which hath been a defect complained of in others, to the reproach of the doctrine itself; and made an argument, that the doctrine is not true, seeing *omne verum est bonum*, and both are inseparable affections of being. Upon these and like considerations, I do heartily commend this treatise to the judicious reader, nothing doubting, but that it will satisfy the weakest Christians, as it hath approved itself to several divines; hoping also that this edition will do as much good to men's souls as the former editions have done. The blessings of heaven go with it.

THOMAS GOODWIN

April 12, 1678

TO THE CHRISTIAN READER

THE doctrines in this treatise declared and vindicated, have exercised the thoughts and best abilities of many learned men. The opposition made against them by the Pelagians of old, excited divers of the ancients to their just defence; whereby they received that light and establishment, as for many ages the church remained in a quiet possession and belief of them; until (of late) the Jesuits, and Socinians, and some others, conspired against to supplant them; and therein had (probably) prevailed ere now, had not the Lord stirred up the spirits of many and great persons to stand on his side, and help to maintain that quarrel of his covenant. It is not unworthy our notice, and deepest resentment, how zealously affected some men are in behalf of such tenets as stand in direct opposition to the grace of God, and their own eternal happiness; how they spare neither arts nor calumnies to disgrace the assertors of those very truths that make up the mystery of godliness; yea, to scandalize and suppress the truths themselves; as if reason and learning were given to no better ends, than to vilify religion. And further, how pronely addicted men are, having imbibed the Arminian points, to take in those that are of most fatal consequence: so far are those principles from yielding any effectual influence towards holiness, or well grounded peace, notwithstanding their pretended adaptedness to promote them, which might be largely insisted upon, but that the designed brevity of this address forbids it. But whatever the ends of men are, or their interest, in defaming the wisdom, sovereignty, and grace of God, and that in a method more arrogant and daring, than persons of the same principles have hereofore ventured to do; the Lord's ends in permitting them are holy and good: and we are assured, that he would not have suffered those dangerous errors to re-invade his church, and his glorious truths to be so coarsely and contumeliously treated, but in order to their further illustration and conquest: and that therefore, as he hath, so he will, of his abundant goodness to the world, and faithfulness to his elect, raise up such as with meekness, light and power, shall withstand their furious torrent, and transmit to the following generations, those blessed and greatly important truths which the world are so implacably bent against, and seek to eradicate.

It is somewhat perceptible of itself, and so acknowledged by the author, that in writing this treatise he had little or no intercourse with books, but those of the holy scripture: which is here mentioned to magnify the grace of God that was with him. And by this may be gathered that a serious and diligent consulting the sacred oracles, with an humble dependance upon God for teaching and success, as they are duties of great importance, so of answerable improvement; the properest and surest means of instruction, touching the mystery of his will, with that orderly and harmonious connexion of the divine attributes for recovering apostate creatures from their dreadful lapse, and placing them in a condition transcendently better than their primitive state: all which, by the Pelagian articles, are reduced to nothing. Yea, there are some peculiar advantages which accompany this discourse. 1. That it is founded and built on the testimony of God alone; whose authority and truth are the only unerring rule, and immoveable basis of divine faith, and its properest touchstone; and the lesser diversions there are to other ways of proof and argumentation, in things of this nature, the more convincing, and free from retortion; and the sooner will our souls be brought to acquiescence and settlement. 2. That the doctrines being declared and vindicated, there is all along a useful improvement made of them, to excite and influence our hearts and lives according to the genuine tenor and import of those truths, very much beyond what the contrary doctrines have ever pretended to. It may be a supplement to other books, where the same truths are worthily contended for, but yet defective in this particular: and so it is not only a work of good use in itself, but it also relieves these doctrines from one of the worst aspersions they have been calumniated with. Divers other things might be mentioned, which reflect a worth upon the ensuing discourse, and bespeak an esteem for it, which, for brevity' sake, are referred to the reader's judicious observation.

That the book may be entertained by men according to its deserts, and blessed of God for the ends it is designed and suited unto, is, and shall be the desire of,

JOHN OWEN.
S. ANNESLEY.

EXTRACT OF A LETTER FROM A LEARNED DIVINE, UNKNOWN TO THE AUTHOR

Sir,

Although I am a stranger unto you, yet having read your excellent book (which I did but borrow) I thought good to let you understand, with how great delight I did read it; and also how great satisfaction and comfort I received by it. I studied these points several years ago very hard; being then put upon it by a strong adversary, one of subtle wit, though otherwise a very common and mean man. But I have said often, that I was much beholden to him for his opposition; for I would not, for much worldly substance, be without that knowledge, which, I hope, through the grace of God, I then attained in those great points by reason thereof. I think that then, and since, I have read most of the best books that have been written upon those points; but especially that book of books, the Bible: yet after all those other books, I must confess, that yours hath given me the most content and satisfaction. For you have most nervously and judiciously laid open the truth, and as strenuously refuted the objections. I bless and adore that divine grace of the Lord, who of his rich goodness and mercy to his poor distressed and distracted church in this nation, hath raised you up, in an especial manner, to be such an instrument of his glory, in vindicating its sovereignty, especially in these high and mysterious points of predestination, particular redemption, the efficacy of grace in conversion, and the perseverance of the saints in holiness. As touching the absoluteness of the covenant of grace, I cannot but admire to see how you coincide with me. I used to say often several years ago, what I find now in your book, that if the covenant of grace were not absolute, salvation would be as difficult by it, as by the covenant of works; because it is as hard for a natural man to *believe* and *live*, as it is for him to *do* and *live*. Well you have, in my judgment, performed your business most piously, practically, and strongly; and your arguments are invincible; many of which yet I had never met with: and I doubt not but you do return the praise and glory of all unto our great and gracious Lord, who by his mere free grace hath enabled you to perform this work; which is so much for the glory of his holy name. I commend you, with your labors, to the grace of our merciful Father, and rest,

Your most affectionate friend,

October 16, 1667   W. W.

THE AUTHOR'S PREFACE

AN ACCOUNT OF THE TREATISE AND PUBLICATION

The principal heads of the following discourse, (generally owned by the churches of Britain,) the author was somewhat instructed in from his childhood; having heard, till a few years since, but little concerning the general point: that, he means, which is commonly so called, as holding the grace of God in Christ to be generally designed and dispensed alike to all; suspending the whole virtue and success thereof on the human will; without peculiar respect or assistance afforded to any, but what is given in common unto men. Which doctrine might rather be termed general, as the generality of men, in nature, are patrons and abettors of it. Not that he thinks all who hold it to be in their natural state; for, as of most, their judgment is better than their practice; so, of some, he hopes their practice may be sounder than their judgment: but so, to hold and practise accordingly, he cannot but think extremely perilous to the souls of men. Divers conferences (accidentally) he had with those of that way: in all which he found it their drift to insinuate that principle; not caring much to discourse of any point else, how useful soever, and importantly needful to be known; but still diverting into that channel: maintaining also their notions, with that confidence of their own, and contempt of the contrary judgment; such uncomely reflections upon their opponents, and slight regard of the Scriptures brought against them, as did in no wise become a contending for the faith: (which has made him think that ironical speech of Job to his friends, too applicable to these: "No doubt ye are the people, and wisdom shall die with you." Job 12: 2.) He also found their tenets mostly grounded upon words and phrases of a variable construction; as not weighing the scope of the texts, nor how the sense they gave of them might accord with those of a contrary tenor; still citing such as were plain and express, to be tried by those of a doubtful sound; whereas the contrary course would have been more genuine, and nearer to find out the truth. Not that any Scripture is doubtful in itself, or inconsistent with others; nor would seem so to us, if its scope and context were duly weighed; but the same word being used on different occasions to a different purpose a heedless attention to the context induces the loss of its proper intention. That he found among them, a general agreement against our doctrine of election, is true: and no less true, that they differ among themselves as much as they do from us; only they bear each other's dissent more quietly than ours. Some of them hold election upon works foreseen; others, that men are elected when they do actually believe, and not before; others of them, that no man is elected, until he hath persevered in believing to the last moment of his life; and others again, that there is no election at all, of particular persons as such, but of the entire species of men from eternity. This put him upon searching the scriptures more freely touching the doctrine of election; and the farther he went, the more he was confirmed in what he had first received. And as he proceeded, he found those other points of peculiar redemption, effectual calling, and final perseverance, so interwoven with that of election, and dependant upon it, as very naturally drew on a discussion of those also. As preparatory to this, it seemed expedient to preface the whole with the doctrine of God's sovereignty, together with his righteousness; the reasons of which, with its usefulness, you may find in the treatise itself. It also lay before him, to observe what useful instructions arose from these doctrines above those of the contrary side; which he hopes will not prove inconsiderable to those who have their senses spiritually exercised to discern.

This work was frequently suspended and laid aside, with the intention of proceeding no farther; and this not from the want, but the redundancy of matter, which he found in the scriptures for it, but himself much too weak to comprehend, and to make it out: partly, also, from the difficulty of reducing his mingling fragments to an orderly consistence. But, by one impulsive occurrence or other,— among which, the inward delight he had in the work, though sometimes intermitted, was not the least,—it still revived and went on afresh, until, by degrees, his gleanings grew into a shock, which he then bound up, designing it only for private use. It so happened, however, that some parts of it (providentially) came to the view and hearing of certain ancient and sober Christians, who, expressing a hearty approbation of it, warmly advised its being printed for more general use, as that which might help at least to confirm the tenure of those already possessed of the truth, but still remain subject to sifting. One who had cast a favorable eye on the contrary points, professed himself well satisfied with what he found in this, touching the tendency of natural free-will, though assisted with general grace, and urged also the publication of it, thinking its plainness might render it more convincing to some, than scholastic disputes, which are found to obscure and puzzle, rather than illuminate and settle the judgment of illiterate persons. Another consideration was, that it might serve as an antidote for young professors; who, being scarcely out of the shell of their natural understanding, are pronely receptive of notions that spring from a covenant of works; which, by means of so plain a discourse on nature's weakness, together with the necessity, constant readiness, and invincible efficacy of divine grace, they might happily be armed against.

Repeated instances induced, at length, a willingness to make it public, provided it should also obtain the approbation of divines to whom he should submit it: their approbation it has received. He yet retains a deep sense of his manifold insufficiency for such a work, and prays that his personal meanness and obscurity may not prejudice the truth.

This being the account formerly given, some later occurrences have induced this farther addition. After the first impression, the author was frequently encountered by persons of the contrary persuasion; by which he came to know more of their spirit and principles than before, but not to his better liking of either. He speaks but of such as he himself conversed with.

Some he found to cry up that excellent creature man; and the great things he is able to do: a taking lure! and consequently the more dangerous to such as are not well settled in principles, because of the marvellous aptness there is in nature to be taken with its own commendation, and to fancy itself considerable in procuring its own happiness; as well as from the difficulty of taking up our rest in the will of another, whose wisdom and love we are little acquainted with, nor can be, until we are pitched upon it. But, for the present ability of this once excellent creature, we have but verbal report, and must therefore suspend our belief, until they produce some credible evidence for it. If those who assert it, have such a talent, it ought not to be hid in the earth: they should be still turning the penny; and the greatness of their stock should be seen by the richness of their effects. It is no point of honor or prudence to boast of possessions, and all things at will; and yet live at the rate of an underling tenant, who holds his all at the will of another. It is surely a rational thing, that, "to whom much is given, of him the more should be required." It behooves, therefore, to ponder these serious questions, What singular thing do ye? and, "What do ye more than others?" That is, What earnings have ye made of those larger talents ye profess to be endowed with? This they should give some tolerable account of, or else they will be thought to boast of a false gift; for it is not words, but performances, must justify abilities, and make out the virtue of principles. Their fellow-christians are, "of themselves, not sufficient to think;" how then will those answer it, with all their florid endowments, to be found even as they?

And because scriptural deductions are most pressing, some have a device to put by their force without resistance: what they cannot answer, they will not understand: it must bear the name of unintelligible notion. The vanity of this evasion is obvious to any that will but consider it; since the rudiments of any science, which by instruction and use are familiar to one, may be strange and uncouth to another, though of more pregnant parts than he, and better skilled in other faculties.

Another thing is, their needless commixing, and consequently perplexing, secret things with those revealed: while they cannot be ignorant, that the decree is God's rule, (which cannot be known to us but by the event,) the law and the testimony ours, by which alone all doctrines are to be tried, and our whole course, both of judgment and practice, to be regulated here, and judged at last. We

acknowledge dark sayings in scripture, and things hard to be understood. But the difficulties rise not so much from the word, as a natural unbelief, prejudice, and darkness within; with those crooked,
wrinkled, or discolored mediums, men commonly look through at
spiritual things, and which must needs render the objects they look
at unlike to themselves.

There is also another snare, as catching as any other, and as
worthy to be cautioned against. The doctrine of free grace, being
so illustrious in the scriptures as not to be spoken against, they will
talk as highly for it in general terms, as any other, and tell us what
great pretensions their doctrine hath to magnify grace, and that they
design nothing more than the honor of it; while, indeed, it is not
grace, but a contrary thing set up with that name; for, follow the
stream, either upward or downward, and as it all rises from, so it all
runs into, freedom of will, and advancement of self, as is obvious to
any impartial observer.

I shall further only notice at present, certain seemingly accidental
queries, modestly pretended, for argument's sake, to clear up obscu-
rities, and reconcile contradictions; which, though a good work in
itself, if orderly managed, they follow so far, and in such manner,
that they do, in effect, bring principles into question, and erase the
very groundworks of religion.

These things are mentioned, not to uncover the weakness of persons, but of principles, and that only as they derogate from the honor
of free grace, and tend to subvert the soul; and the end of it is, to
prevent such as may be hovering about, as not knowing where to
settle, from being caught by the enticingness of words, contrary to
the simplicity of the gospel.

What remains then, but that we bless God, adoring his glorious
wisdom and grace, that matters of present duty, and greatest importance to us, are so plainly revealed, and eternal salvation so little
concerned in the present conciliating of seeming discord? There is
enough manifested to take up our time and strength; and our living
up to that we know, is the readiest way to know more. "He that
will do his will, shall know of his doctrine." And, in the fulness of
time, those seeming discordances shall have an illustrious reconcilement; and they that have most firmly believed now, against all their
carnal reasonings, and unreasonable contradictions, shall not have
the weakest reflections and rays of glory from the lustre of that day:
and this, I suppose, he had an eye to, (a person of no ordinary rank
for human accomplishments,) who, treating of God's decrees, did
freely confess, " That he could not indeed comprehend them, but
would captivate reason to the obedience of faith." With this I close,
subjoining only a word of religious exhortation; namely, that though
it do not confer grace, it may prove, as it has proved to many, a
good preservative from evils in practice, and errors in judgment,
which others, who had not that gracious privilege, have more naturally fallen into. Besides, when God comes to work effectually, those
notions of sin, of Christ, and of grace, of which before they had but
the form, have proved of singular use to facilitate the work. That
the Lord will vouchsafe his blessing with it, is the prayer of his
servant,   ELISHA COLES.

A

PRACTICAL DISCOURSE

OF

GOD'S SOVEREIGNTY

THIS high and tremendous attribute, being an ocean that has neither bank nor bottom, may not be lightly launched into by *any*, however strongly built and well manned, much less by so weak a vessel, without a divine compass, and an anchor within the veil. That the author of this DISCOURSE came into it, was not of choice or design, but of course and emergent necessity. Could he have found another basis to repose that doctrine upon, which was, at first, his only intended subject, he had not touched upon this. But, apparently to him, no ground would bear the weight of Election, but that of Sovereignty, and there it fixed as on a rock; all the lines of its whole circumference running there, and resting there, as in their centre, where also the scripture had laid it. Rom. 9: Eph. 1: &c. And, however it be a foundation disallowed of men, every observing Christian shall find, that without acknowledging divine Sovereignty, for the original, supreme, and unaccountable disposer of persons and things, he shall want a principal means of supporting his faith, and quieting his understanding, in the course of common providences; much more of those mysterious occurrences, and supernatural truths, which he is certainly concerned about.

In this preface I shall treat first of God's sovereignty, and then of his righteousness, as its natural adjunct. The sum of the first lies in this proposition, namely,

" That the great God, blessed forever, hath an absolute power and right of dominion over his creatures, to dispose and determine them as seemeth him good."

That there is such a power, and that this power belongs

to God, no other reason needs be assigned, but, that " he is God, and there is none besides him:" there can be no more, because, 1. There can be but one infinite; for such a being fills heaven and earth; and so no place or room for another. 2. There can be but one omnipotent; for he that is such, hath all others under his feet: besides, where one can do all, more would be impertinent. 3. There can be but one supreme; supreme power may reside in many, as in mixed monarchies and commonwealths; but as law-makers and supreme, they are but one. 4. There can be but one first cause, from which all beings else derive their original; " of whom, and for whom, are all things," 1 Cor. 8: 6. And if he be the Author of all, he needs must have a sovereign right and power to determine all; both as to their being, order, efficacy, and end.

"That sovereign power belongs to God," is a truth so natural, and obvious to reason, that other proof seems as needless, as that the sun is the fountain of light: nor shall I suppose that any who will read this discourse, can so far forget themselves to be creatures, as to seek a proof of their Creator's sovereignty; " the things that are seen so loudly proclaiming his eternal power and Godhead." But since, with our easy admitting the notion, it is none of the smallest difficulties to own it in our practice, and bear ourselves answerably towards him: since also so huge a weight is borne on the shoulders of this divine attribute, and our souls are so highly concerned in the interest and influence of it, it needs must be our duty, and well worthy our time, to look over the instances of it, and to mark and consider them well, as things greatly importing our instruction; whereby we may know something of the greatness of that God in whose hands our souls are; as also of our infinite distance from him, and nothingness to him; and so, with the more humbleness of mind, and self-abasement; as also with the more faith, and creature-like affiance, submit to him, and bear ourselves upon him. To this end, the scriptures have enrolled several ensigns of sovereignty; by which, as by so many footsteps, we are led to the absolute will and power of God, as the supreme cause and disposer of all.

The great act of sovereignty was God's decree for making the world; and of doing, or permitting to be done, whatever should be in it, to the folding of it up. The heavens and the earth, and all the hosts of them, as yet had no being: it was at his pleasure, whether he would make them or not: and if he would, what being he would give them; to what end, and how that end should be accomplished. And that these were all ascertained by the decree is evident; for " known unto God were all his works (which he would do in time) from the beginning of the world." Acts, 15: 18. The scheme and substance whereof (and I hope without intrusion) may be drawn to this effect: " That the great God, most high and holy, being infinitely good, happy and blessed in himself, was also infinitely prompt and well-pleased to communicate thereof to others; to which end, he designed to raise up creatures, angels and men: that for the manifestation of his sovereignty, he would confirm a certain number of those angels in their primitive state; leaving the rest to themselves; who falling from that state, should be cast down, and "reserved in chains of darkness, unto the judgment of the great day," that in this lower world, he would set up the first man to be the head and representative of all that should come of him; that this single person should be created in the image of God, fit to enjoy communion with him, and endued with power to abide therein: that to manifest the weakness of creatures, and their perpetual dependance upon God, he would thus leave him to his first stock, with a perfect freedom of will, to retain, or lose at his own choice; but not without setting before him the happiness or ruin that would certainly follow his well or ill using that freedom; and, being so left, the fallen angel tempting him to disobedience, and also prevailing, both himself and all his posterity should by this revolt fall under the curse: that, for the declaration of his sovereign grace, he would, and accordingly did, choose a certain number of Adam's posterity (in themselves all alike depraved and lost), and ordain them to eternal life; and to make known the power of his wrath, and his just displeasure against sin, he would leave the rest in that state of perdition they would bring themselves into: that of those vessels of wrath, Satan himself (whom they chose to follow) should be the head and ruler: as also over them that were elected, for a time, namely, until the Messiah, their true and proper Head, and into whom he had chosen them, should rescue them out of his power: that to this end, and that he might be known to be just, as well as merciful, in justifying of them, the Son of God should take on him the place of a second Adam, and come into the world with a human body; in which he should fulfil all righteousness, and, by the infinite virtue and merit of his death, should satisfy the law in all its demands, destroy the devil, dissolve his works, and reconcile the elect unto God: that he should be raised again from the dead, and invested with all power befitting the Captain of their salvation; so that he might effectually minister to them whatsoever should be requisite for bringing his sons to glory." This I take to be the sum of God's decree; the great ensign or standard-royal of sovereignty, of which all the others are but consequents, and to which they are subordinate.

The first visible ensign of sovereignty, was creation, or God's giving the world an actual existence in time, according to his decree from everlasting; bringing that huge, yet void and formless mass, at first out of nothing; and then, this glorious fabric out of that confusion: his hanging the earth upon nothing: his assigning to every sort of creatures such form and station, to order, use, and efficacy, and impressing on them such laws and instincts of nature, as seemed to him good, (but all in a regular subserviency to the good of the whole,) which also was effected by his word. What he would, was done with such immediate suddenness, as if the things themselves had proceeded with his breath: " For he spake, and it was done; he commanded, and it stood fast," Psal. 33: 9. The instant production of light, Gen. 1: 3 and 9. The waters separating from the other elements, and gathering into a body, and their going up and down to the place he had founded for them, Psal. 104: 8. with many others, of which you have an index in the first of Genesis, are witnesses of it: as also his so fixing this establishment, that they continue to this day according to that ordinance, Psal. 119: 91.

Consequent to this, as a second ensign of sovereignty, is that universal providence, by which the creation is sustained, and all inferior causes guided to their designed end; and this, notwithstanding all supposable accidents, which might possibly happen, to obstruct or divert them.

And that the creatures have at times deviated from their first rules and settlement, is no derogation from the doctrine of God's sovereignty, but rather an illustration of it; as shewing, that the creatures are still in his hand, as clay in the potter's. Hence we find their innate propensities to be sometimes suspended; at other times overacted; and at times, again, quite contrary to the law of nature: and this, not casually, nor by the force of created powers, nor yet for any private or self-concern, but to serve some special and superior end, which their Lord had to be done. To instance a few; and,

1. Of the creatures without life: As the windows of heaven opening, and the fountains of the great deep breaking up, notwithstanding the firmament above and the bounds beneath, to drown the world of ungodly men, Gen. 7: 11. The Red Sea's dividing, and standing up as a wall, to make way for his people's escape, Exod. 14: 22. The sun and moon's standing still till they were avenged of their enemies, Josh. 10: 13. The stars to the same end fighting against Sisera, Judges 5: 20. The sun's going back in Ahaz's dial, to help Hezekiah's faith, 2 Kings 20: 11. The fiery furnace devouring those at a distance, who cast in the holy confessors, and not so much as touching them that were cast into it, Dan. 3: 22, 27. The winds and seas, which are such impetuous, and, one would think, even lawless, creatures, stir not, nor breathe, but to fulfil his word, Psal. 148: 8. Mark 4: 30, 42.

2. Of living creatures, that have not the use of reason. How readily went they by pairs into Noah's ark, at God's appointment! Gen. 7: 8, 9. The frogs, lice, locusts, &c. with what supernatural boldness did they assault and perplex the Egyptians! so that the magicians themselves confessed that the finger of God was in it, Exod. 8: 19. and as strangely withdrew when their work was done, verse 13. Witnessed also by the dumb ass's reproving the prophet's madness, 2. Pet. 2: 16. The lion's killing the seduced prophet for breaking God's command, yet not eating the carcass, nor tearing his ass, 1 Kings 13: 26, 28. A ravenous bird bringing Elijah food in his solitary condition, 1 Kings 17: 6. The whale's receiving Jonah, and, at God's command, casting him on dry land, without harm, Jonah 1: 17, with chap. 2: 10. The lions' also not hurting Daniel

in their den, yet greedily devouring his accusers, Dan. 6: 22. 24. It must needs be a sovereign power, which thus superintends, restrains, and inverts the course of nature at his will.

Thirdly. Another ensign, asserting God's supremacy, and rightful dominion, is the general vote and subscription of men, especially the most knowing, and such as best understand him. 1. They own it in their practice or actions. Abel offers the firstlings of his flock to God, Gen. 4: 4. Abraham leaves his native country at God's command, to go " he knew not whither," Gen. 12: 4. He also offers his only and innocent son Isaac, in whose life and " posterity all nations were to be blessed," Gen. 22: 2. 10. Job, when stripped of all, falls down and worships, Job 1: 21. When Aaron's two sons were destroyed by fire from heaven, he held his peace, Levit. 10: 2, 3. Eli, when the tingling sentence was denounced against his house, said, " It is the Lord, let him do what seemeth him good, 1 Sam. 3: 18. David, when driven from God's sanctuary, and his throne was usurped by Absalom, said, " Behold, here I am, let him do to me as seemeth good to him," 2 Sam. 15: 26. The men of Nineveh, their destruction being pronounced positively, of which they had no promise of remission, and consequently no visible ground of hope; yet believed God, fasted, " lay in sackcloth, and turned from their evil way," Jonah 3: 5. 8. 2. They likewise own it in their confessions and attestations. Melchizedek and Abraham do both style him " The Most High God, possessor of heaven and earth," Gen. 14: 19. 22. Job professeth, that though he were righteous, yet if God will contend with him, " he will not contend with him, but make supplication to his Judge," Job 9: 15. " The Lord hath made all things for himself," Prov. 16: 4. " For his pleasure they are and were created," Rev. 4: 11. " We are the clay, and thou our potter," Isa. 64: 8. " He worketh all things after the counsel of his own will," Eph. 1: 11. " He giveth not account of any of his matters," Job 33: 3. " In his hand is the soul of every living thing," Job 12: 10. " He is the God of the spirits of all flesh," Num. 16:22. " All nations before him are less than nothing and vanity," Isa. 40: 17. " He stills the tumult of the people," Psal. 15: 7. " If it be of God, ye cannot overthrow it," Acts 5: 39. " The coun-

sel of the Lord, it shall stand," Prov. 19: 21. Psal. 33: 11.
"The lot is cast into the lap, but the whole disposing
thereof is of the Lord," Prov. 16: 33. "The kingdom is the
Lord's, and he is Governor among the nations," Psal. 22:28.
Nebuchadnezzar, that proud and potent monarch, whose
"greatness reached unto the heaven, and his dominion to
the end of the earth, Dan. 4: 22. all nations trembled before him: whom he would he slew, and whom he would
he kept alive, Dan. 5: 19. who said in his heart, I will
ascend into heaven, I will exalt my throne above the stars
of God, I will be like the most High: and who is that God
that shall deliver out of my hand?" Dan. 3:15. Yet even he,
this child of pride, is made to confess One higher than
himself, and to bow before him; proclaiming to the world,
that "the most High doth according to his will, in the
army of heaven, and among the inhabitants of the earth,
and none can stay his hand, or say unto him, What doest
thou? and those that walk in pride he is able to abase,"
Dan. 4: 37. "For thou hast said in thine heart, I will ascend into heaven, I will exalt my throne above the stars of
God: I will also sit upon the mount of the congregation, in
the sides of the north: I will ascend above the heights of
the clouds; I will be like the most High." Isa. 14: 13, 14.
It might further be instanced in Cain, Pharaoh, Balaam,
and other wicked men, how they were even constrained to
acknowledge the sovereignty of God; as appears by comparing Exod. 5: 2. with 9: 27, 28. and Num. 22: 18. Darius, also, in Dan. 6: 26—28.

Fourthly. Another evidence, or witness, we have from
the angels, who are "great in power;" notwithstanding
which, they do perfectly own and submit to the sovereignty
of God. Where subjects are numerous, wise, and magnanimous, and withal perfectly submit to the will of their
Lord, it argues their Lord is an absolute sovereign: and
such subjects are the angels. 1. The elect or good angels:
these show it by their ready submission to any service their
Lord is pleased to appoint them. They are his intelligen-
cers in this lower world. "And the angel answered and
said unto me, These are the four spirits of the heavens,
which go forth from standing before the Lord of all the
earth. The black horses which are therein, go forth into
the north country, and the white go forth after them;

and the grisled go forth toward the south country. And
the bay went forth, and sought to go, that they might walk
to and fro through the earth: and he said, Get ye hence;
walk ye to and fro through the earth. So they walked to
and fro through the earth." Zech. 6: 5, 6, 7. " There was
a day when the sons of God came to present themselves before the Lord." Job 2: 1. Not that he needs their advice,
but to show a little of the majesty of his kingdom. They
are also his messengers: he sends them on his errands, to
negotiate his affairs among men, and to reveal his purposes,
both concerning his church and the world. Dan. 2: 19. and
8: 13, 16. chap. 1: 21. chap. 11: Ezek. 1: 4. They are his
chariots, Psal. 68: 17. His reapers, Matt. 13: 39, 49. The
executioners of his judgments, 2 Sam. 24: 16. 2 Kings 19:
35. And Christ's attendants at his coming, Matt. 25: 31.

2. The apostate angels, or wicked spirits. Though the
testimony we have from these is not from love or good will,
yet it is as great an evidence of God's sovereignty as the
other; in that, being enemies to God, proud and imperious,
they are yet overawed, and compelled to submit. And
hence it was, that the devil dared not to answer again,
when that fatal sentence was pronounced upon him for se-
ducing our first parents, Gen. 3: 15. We have him also
presenting himself before the Lord, to give account of his
actions; and to touch Job, or any thing he had, he durst not,
without leave from God, nor vary a jot from the rule pre-
scribed him. " There was a day when the sons of God came
to present themselves before the Lord, and Satan came also
among them, to present himself before the Lord. And the
Lord said unto Satan, Behold, he is in thine hand; but
save his life." Job 2: 1, 6. In the Evangelists are many
instances of Christ's commanding them forth with authority;
yea a whole legion at once, Luke 8: 30, 33. Nor could
they so much as enter into the swine without his leave,
Mark 5: 12. And, which is more, they were subjected to
the apostles, who had but a delegated, or second-hand power
over them, Luke 10: 17.

Fifthly. We have the Lord himself asserting his sovereign prerogative. In how lofty a style, and with what
imperial authority, doth he utter himself to Pharaoh! " And
in very deed, for this cause have I raised thee up, for to
show my power on thee," Exod. 9: 16. The apostle

quotes the place to prove, that God may raise up men, and appoint them to what use and service he will: " For the scripture saith unto Pharaoh, Even for this purpose have I raised thee up, that I might show my power in thee, and that my name might be declared throughout all the earth," Rom. 9: 17. " Who hath made the seeing, or the blind? have not I the Lord? Exod. 4: 6, 11. " I kill and I make alive," Deut. 32: 39. " I will shew mercy on whom I will shew mercy," Exod. 33: 19. " I am the first and I am the last, and besides me there is no God: and who, as I, shall call, and shall declare it, and set it in order before me? since I appointed the ancient people, and the things that are coming, and shall come," Isa. 44: 6, 7. " My counsel shall stand; I will do all my pleasure," Isa. 46: 10. " My word shall accomplish all that which I please; it shall prosper in the thing whereto I send it," Isa. 55: 11. " And if the prophet be deceived, I the Lord have deceived that prophet, and I will destroy him," Ezek. 14: 9. A remarkable story is that of the lying spirit, and the effectual commission he had from God, to persuade, and also to prevail: " And the Lord said, Who shall persuade Ahab, that he may go up and fall at Ramoth Gilead? And one said on this manner, and another on that manner. And there came forth a spirit, and stood before the Lord and said, I will persuade him. And the Lord said, wherewith? And he said, I will go forth, and I will be a lying spirit in the mouth of all his prophets. And he said, Thou shalt persuade him, and prevail also: go forth and do so." 1 Kings 22: 20, 21, 22. How should we tremble before God, at the hearing of such a word! But yet, I do not reckon the last two as acts of pure sovereignty, but rather of his justice; as punishing one sin, by leaving to another; according to that in Rom. 1: 21. 28. " Because that when they knew God, they glorified him not as God, nor liked to retain him in their knowledge, God gave them over to a reprobate mind." And yet there is here an impression of sovereignty, in that he deals not so with all who are alike obnoxious to it.

Sixthly. Another ensign of sovereignty is formed of those several acts and institutes, which cannot be derived (at least not so immediately) from any other attribute than that of sovereignty. I shall instance a few, namely, The putting of man's everlasting condition upon his eating or non-eating the fruit of such a tree, Gen. 2: 17. In not destroying Adam presently upon his disobedience; and in the free promise of a Saviour, unsought unto for it, Gen. 3: 15. In protecting Cain when he had forfeited his life to justice, Gen. 4: 15. In preserving Ham from the deluge, though as wicked as those that perished, Gen. 7: 13. In ordering the blessing to Jacob, who sought it unduly; and denying it to Esau, who sought it diligently, and to whom it belonged of natural right, Gen. 27: 19. 34. 38. In the sudden turning of Esau's heart to love Jacob, whom he had inveterately hated, and came with full purpose to destroy; yet in a moment his heart is melted; he weeps on his neck, and offers himself and soldiers to be his convoy, Gen. 27: 41. with chap. 32: 6. and 33: 4. 12. In causing a fear to be on the Amorites, that they did not pursue Jacob, when highly provoked by his sons' cruelty on the men of Shechem, Gen. 35: 5. In sending a message of peace to Sihon, whom he had determined to destroy; and to that end had hardened his spirit, and made him obstinate, Deut. 2: 26. In causing those nations to destroy one another, who came leagued to destroy his people, 2 Chron. 20: 1. 22, 23. In destroying Esau's mount irreparably, and for ever; while Israel, whose land also was full of sin, shall not be forsaken, Obad. ver. 9. 16. 18. 21. Mal. 1: 4. especially considering that these were the several effects of his loving the one, and hating the other, and that " before they had done either good or evil," Mal. 1: 2, 3. Rom. 9: 11. 13. In sending Ezekiel to a rebellious house, that " would not hear;" and not sending him to them that would: " Not to many people of a strange speech, and of an hard language, whose words thou canst not understand: surely, had I sent thee to them, they would have hearkened unto thee. But the house of Israel will not hearken unto thee; for they will not hearken unto me; for all the house of Israel are impudent and hard hearted, Ezek. 3: 6, 7. and Matt. 11: 21. In hiding the mysteries of his kingdom " from the wise and prudent, and revealing them unto babes, Matt. 11:25. and speaking in parables to the multitude," lest they should be converted," Mark 4: 11, 12. Acts 16: 6, 7.

It is further manifest, by the Lord's punishing sometimes lesser trespasses, and that severely, and in his own; while winking at those of a greater magnitude in other men. Moses is excluded Canaan for a hasty word, though smartly provoked, Deut. 32: 51, 52. when Jonah is but mildly reproved for passionately expostulating, Jonah 4: Uzziah dies for but touching the ark, 1 Chron. 13: 9, 10. while the Philistines bore it away in triumph, 1 Sam. 5: 1. Hezekiah but shows the ambassadors from Babylon his house and treasures, and for this his sons and all must go into captivity: "And Hezekiah hearkened unto them, and shewed them all the house of his precious things, the silver, and the gold, and the spices, and the precious ointment, and all the house of his armor, and all that was found in his treasures: there was nothing in his house, nor in all his dominion, that Hezekiah shewed them not. Behold the days come, that all that is in thine house, and that which thy fathers have laid up in store unto this day, shall be carried into Babylon: nothing shall be left, saith the Lord," 2 Kings 20: 13. 17. Not that any sin is little in itself, or punished beyond its demerit; but the Lord is pleased thus to do, partly to show his displeasure against sin, and that he will not bear with it, even in those that are dearest to him; but partly also, if not chiefly in such like cases, to set forth his sovereign greatness, and the uncontrolableness of his matters. "Why dost thou strive against him? for he giveth not account of any of his matters," Job 33: 13. The seventy-third Psalm is full to the same purpose. That also of Job, and the manner of God's dealings with him, is much to be remarked: he had lived a very strict and holy life; ("not a man like Job in all the earth;" the Lord himself seems to glory in him;) unto which all outward blessings were promised, and freedom from such sufferings; and when bereft of all, "held fast his integrity," Job 1: 8. and 2: 3. yet the Lord goes on to afflict him, and leaves him wholly (saving his life) in Satan's power. Had he been a wicked man, as his friends objected, those sufferings had evidenced the justice of God; but now his sovereignty: which also seems to be intended by that speech of God to Satan, "Thou movest me against him, to destroy him without cause," Job 2: 3.

Seventhly. There are yet other footsteps of sovereignty, by which that high and holy attribute is further illustrated to us; as, namely, "The Lord's over-ruling the designs

and actions of men, to bring his own counsels to pass;"
although improper in their own nature, yea, disservient
thereto; and sometimes by men contrived on purpose to
prevent them. The project of building Babel's tower, to
keep that rebellious rout together, is turned to their utter
dispersion, Gen. 11: 4. 8. Jacob's dissimulation, and palpable abuse of his father's infirmity, proved the means to
obtain his blessing, and that contrary to his settled intention, Gen. 27: 18. 29. Laban dealt hardly with Jacob, to
keep him low, and to serve himself of him, but God takes
occasion thence to give him Laban's substance, and that
by Laban's consent and agreement, Gen. 29. To obviate
Joseph's dreams, his brethren sell him into Egypt: and by
this means the Lord keeps them all alive, and accomplish-
eth that honor to Joseph, which they intended to prevent,
Gen. 37: 9. 20. 28. 42: 6. 1: 18. 20. Pharaoh lays insuperable burdens on the people, to diminish them; and the
Lord multiplies them under it. "The more they were oppressed, the faster they grew," Exod. 1: 12. Moses, a
keeper of sheep, a man of slow speech, and one that had
no mind to the work, Exod. 4: 10. 13. yet he shall be
God's ambassador to Pharaoh, (the proudest and most inflexible monarch upon earth,) and bring Israel out of
bondage. And who shall be his commander in chief, to
deliver his people from their potent oppressors, but Debo-
rah, a woman? Judges 4: 9. At another time, Gideon,
"whose family was poor in Manasseh, and he the least in
his father's house," Jud. 6: 15. and though he had a numerous and powerful enemy to deal with, and, one would
think, had need of all the hands he could make to fight
them, yet his army of two and thirty thousand, must be
reduced to three hundred men, and they to have no other
arms but trumpets, and lamps in their pitchers; and by
these he delivers them from that huge host, Judges 7: 3.6,7.
And much like unto this was Shamgar's killing six hundred
men with an ox-goad, Judges 3: 31. and Samson a thousand
with a jaw-bone of an ass, chap. 15: 15. It may further be
traced in his producing contrary effects by the same cause;
and then again the same effects by causes contrary, Exod.
4: 6, 7. So Daniel and his fellows had a fairer countenance
with pulse and water, than those who eat of the king's own
provision, Daniel 1: 15. It is further evidenced, by his

causing the wrath of man to turn to his praise; which, in the nature and tendency of it, is to destroy them that praise him, Psal. 76:10. By his catching "the wise in their craftiness, and causing them to fall by their own devices," Job 5: 12, 13. Psal. 5: 10. Witness Ahab, 1 Kings 22: 20. 22. and Haman, Esth. 7: 10. The persecution of the saints at Jerusalem was designed to suppress the doctrine of Christ; which yet was thereby dispersed into many countries, and caused "to grow mightily," Acts 8: 1. 4. So the preacher's imprisonment proved to the furtherance of the gospel, Phil. 1: 12. 14. And since the Scriptures were finished, human stories, and our own observation, do abundantly prove the matter in hand. Do but consider how it prevailed to the dethroning of Satan, and turning the world upside down, and this by means of the weakest and most unlikely, to reason, that could be pitched upon: not by the sword and spear, the bow and battle-axe, the barbed horse, and the martial heroes of the earth; but by the bare word of God: and this, not by the hand of learned scribes and pharisees, lawyers, doctors, poets, philosophers; but by poor illiterate fishermen, carpenters, publicans, tent-makers. And who shall be the subjects and party militant of this never to be conquered kingdom? Not "the wise and prudent, mighty and noble; but babes, the poor, weak, despised, and things that are not; and by these he confounds the things that are," 1 Cor. 1:27. And by what arms? "patience, and faith in the blood of the Lamb," Rev. 12:11 and 14:12.

Consider, also, the constant persecution of the church, and that by men of all sorts, especially those of greatest power and policy; the barbarous devastations that have been made upon it; and with what implacable enmity the world is edged against it; and that yet it stands invincible, and is still getting ground: you cannot but acknowledge the evident footsteps of sovereign power; "that the most High beareth rule over all, Dan. 4: 25, 26. and as for the counsels of the wise, he turneth them backward," Isa. 44: 25.

Eighthly. An especial ray of this glorious power shines forth in God's actual predominating over and subduing the spirits of men, in calling and converting whom he will. One would think that a rational being should better discern

his own interest, and out of choice comply with the will
of his Maker, as who must needs know what is best for
his creature, and who in reason can have no other design
upon him but his good: but we find otherwise; the best
things degenerated turn the worst, and are hardest to reduce. Of all creatures, man fallen, doth most avert, im-
pugn and resist, when God would turn him out of his
natural course; notwithstanding the sorest of evils do attend
his present state, and all desirable happiness would apparently follow his change; yet so wedded is he to his lusts,
and headstrong in his own will, that none of these things
move him: but on he goes, and on he will, yea, though an
incensed angel with a drawn sword should withstand him.
To crush them to nothing, or break them to pieces, were
easily effected; a little of divine power would do that. But
to humble a proud and lofty spirit; to soften and melt an
obdurate heart; to tame, meeken, and reconcile a sanguin-
ary rebel; to change the very inwards of one habituated in
sin and enmity against God, and make him pliable to divine
impressions: this highly proclaims the exceeding greatness
of his power; it is a glorious trophy of divine sovereignty.
Which is also farther conspicuous, and greatly illustrated,
in maintaining the work begun, and bearing it on through all
opposition. For there needs the same Almightiness of
power to preserve the new creation, as at first to raise it.
The way of God being altogether upwards and supernatural,
there is a great proneness in creatures to revolt from it,
like a rolling stone on the steep of a hill. The remains of
old nature would, torrent-like, bear down all, if sovereign
power did not bar up the one, and sustain the other. For
a spark of divine nature to live in the breast of a lapsed
creature, is as great a miracle, and as high an effect of
sovereign power, as all the instances before enumerated,
and more.

Ninthly. The sovereignty of God displays itself with a
yet more astonishing glory, in his eternal disposure of men's
everlasting condition. To show, or not to show mercy, to
persons equally dignified, (or rather undignified,) in themselves; to make of the same lump one vessel to honor, and
another to dishonor, is the sublimest act, and most apparent demonstration of sovereign power concerning men.
The reason of which, and that to satisfaction, might have

been given, and would, had it befitted the greatness of
God, or the trust and reverence we owe him; but for the
present he is pleased to give none other but that of his
right; he may do what he will with his own, Rom. 9:18.

Lastly. Most transcendently glorious, and for ever
adorable, is the sovereignty of God, in his ordaining the
man Jesus, " who was holy, harmless, undefiled, and separate from sinners," and was also united to the second
person, " to make his soul an offering for sin." That the
Lord of glory should be made sin, and a curse; that was
such a tremendous act of divine sovereignty as never shall
be paralleled, and should therefore for ever seal up our
lips from replying against God, about his disposing of
sinful worms; which thing, whenever we hear or think
upon, we should put our mouths in the dust.

Before I come to the inferences, I would add a caution
or two, to prevent those sinister deductions which our de-
ceitful hearts may be ready to draw from this sovereign
truth.

Caution I. See that you make not God the author of
sin, by charging his sacred decree with men's miscar-
riages, as if that were the cause or occasion of them;
which we are sure it is not, nor can be, any more than the
sun can be the cause of darkness. Be it always remembered, that the Lord's rejecting of men puts nothing of
evil into them, nor necessitates the will; it only leaves
them to their own ways, which they freely choose; yet
banking them in, and stopping them up, as he did the
fountains of the great deep, lest they deluge the world
with sin.

Caution II. Go not about to palliate, nor think to ex-
tenuate your sin, by arguments fetched from God's decree. That sin of the Jews, in " crucifying the Lord of
glory," was in no wise lessened beecuse the counsel of
God had determined the thing to be done, for they perpe-
trated it with wicked hands. Nor is men's unbelief ever
the less culpable, from God's eternal disposement of their
conditions; for it is not upon that consideration that they
stumble at the word, or turn the deaf ear to it, or resist
it, but from their own natural blindness, and enmity
against it.

And so I come to the inferences of this greatly important doctrine; and,

First. From the scriptures so copiously holding it forth, I infer that the doctrine of God's sovereignty is a very teaching doctrine, and full of instruction; and, consequently, that it is both a duty, and much for our profit, to be well acquainted with it. And great confidence I have, that the farther you go in an humble fiducial disquisition and contemplation of it, the clearer will be the reason thereof, and the more usefulness will still appear to be in it. Let reason but keep its own place (that is, let it go by the rules of right and reason,) and nothing will be more consonant thereto, than that "the most High should bear rule over all, and do according to his will;" and that men, who are atoms of clay animated by his breath, should own him for their sovereign lord, and accordingly submit to him; yea, though so it were that our own personal welfare were not concerned in it, it will be of singular use and moment to us in the whole of our lives. Nothing like this will allay those carnal reasonings, which are so unreasonably prone to put in their verdict of spiritual things, which yet carnal reason hath no cognizance of, and will indeed be silenced by nothing else: the apostle, therefore, thinks them not worthy a further reply, whose captious inquiries the sovereignty of God will not satisfy: "Thou wilt say then unto me, Why doth he yet find fault? for who hath resisted his will? Nay, but, O man, who art thou that repliest against God? Shall the thing formed say unto him that formed it, Why hast thou made me thus? Hath not the potter power over the clay, of the same lump to make one vessel unto honor, and another unto dishonor?" Rom. 9: 19, 20, 21. O that the glory of this high attribute might hide pride from men!

A *second* inference, which naturally flows from this doctrine, is that of the psalmist: "O come, let us worship, and bow down, and kneel before the Lord, our maker." Psal. 95: 6. Let us give him the glory of this great attribute, by a real and practical owning that indispensable bond of obedience which it lays upon every creature: we are highly obliged by it, both in point of subjection, and in point of faith.

First, In point of subjection, to his laws, ordinances, and providences.

1. For the laws of God, and his appointments. These we are to attend, observe, and obey; I cannot say, " For the Lord hath need of them;" for neither can our righteousness profit him, nor our wickedness impair him. Job. 22: 2, 3. chap. 24: 7. " He is the Lord thy God, and worship thou him." Psal. 45: 12. This is that strong reason by which he hath backed both commands and prohibitions: " I am the Lord thy God." Exod. 20: 2. Thou shalt do thus: and thus thou shalt not do, " I am the Lord:" this he sets in the front of all; and with this he closeth the rear, and guards them on every side. Moses brings it in as a convincing reason why we should love God with our whole heart, and keep his commandments, namely, because he is the Lord, and he only. Deut. 6: 4. No one, therefore, may pretend to a right of giving laws to men, or to an interest in their love and obedience, save with respect to God, and the authority they have from him. And though he sometimes is pleased (and it is a great condescension in the great God,) by arguments taken from our own good, to draw us to obedience: " Do it, for it is for your life." Deut. 32: 37. Yet in our spirits, that of his sovereign glory should have the preference. To cast out Ishmael was a thing grievous to Abraham; but being commanded of God, he " debates it not, nor delays to do it." Therefore hold on your way, though never so great obscurity be upon it at present: mind your duty in the midst of discouragements; go as Peter, who, though he had labored all night, and caught nothing, yet says, " Master, at thy command I will let down the net again." Luke 5: 5.

2. Be subject to his ordinances. If he please to command the using such means as have no natural virtue towards such an effect, as in Moses stretching his hand over the sea, and smiting the rock with his rod; so water in baptism, and bread and wine in the Lord's supper: presume not to say, " What is there in these?" Godliness is a mystery, which only faith can understand: there is no divine institution but hath meat in it that you know not of, which, if rightly used, will speak for itself. If he please to make clay of dust and spittle, contemn it not, but submit to his will and way, and be thankful for thy cure.

Samson's hair was an ordinance to him, which when he slighted, the spirit of God left him, and he became as other men, and recovered not until it was grown again: " Lo, thou shalt conceive, and bear a son; and no razor shall come on his head; for the child shall be a Nazarite unto God from the womb; and he shall begin to deliver Israel out of the hands of the Philistines," Judges 13: 5. " And Delilah made Samson sleep upon her knees; and she called for a man, and she caused him to shave off the seven locks of his head; and she began to afflict him, and his strength went from him. Howbeit the hair of his head began to grow again after he was shaven," chap. 16: 19. 22.

3. As touching the providences of God: observe them, and submit to them. Look not on them as empty things; the least may yield you instruction, as also the most unlikely: " Out of the eater comes forth meat, and out of the strong, sweetness," Judges 14: 14. though the thing be a riddle to a heart uncircumcised, plough with his heifer, and ye shall find it. Neither look on them as things impertinent; but say rather, " Is there not a cause," though I see it not? the Lord does nothing in vain. Neither yet look on them as things contingent: a sparrow falls not without his will, and " the hairs of your head are all numbered," Matt. 10: 29, 30. David was " dumb, and opened not his mouth." Why? " Because thou, Lord, didst it," Psal. 39: 9. and Shimei's cursing he bears patiently on the same account, " The Lord hath bidden him," 2 Sam. 16: 10, 11.

There may be such a mixture and confusion of things, and your expectation so delayed and frustrated, that your froward untamed heart may be ready to wrangle it out. " Why falls it alike to all? why to the just according to the work of the wicked; and to the wicked according to the work of the righteous?" Eccl. 8: 14. or, " Why one event to them both?" This is not to inquire wisely; you should rather conclude, " The Lord hath need of them;" that is, he hath occasion to use such a providence to fulfil a word, or purpose; and that of greater importance than to satisfy your private concern, or present expectation. If you would cast, so as to lie by your mark, this attribute of sovereignty gives you the best ground. Search and observe as much as you will, so you take faith along with you, without which you can do nothing warrantably. Faith is a sworn officer to the great king, and has a key for every lock that is fit to be opened: it forces nothing; but where it cannot enter, it stays without, and waits a better season. Let faith also be chief speaker in all your debates; and then the result will be, that carnal reason and present sense (though very tenacious and stubborn) shall yield the cause, and let you go.

The sum of all this is, that though you be not conscious to yourself of any particular cause or miscarriage, besides what is common to men (which was the case with Job,) " Lay your hand upon your mouth," as Job did, Job 40: 4. " The most High doth according to his will:" this even the proudest of kings acknowledged, Dan 3: 34, 35. " when his understanding returned to him;" and so will you: and know, that if your spirit be out of frame in your present condition, it would not, at present, be better in any other.

Secondly, Our faith also is highly concerned in the sovereignty of God: for it both obligeth to believe in him, and also affords matter for faith to work upon. To these ends the Lord holds it forth to Abraham; " I am the Almighty God; walk before me, and be thou perfect," Gen. 17: 1. This was what enabled him to believe he should have a son; even while the deadness of his own body, and of Sarah's womb, wrought strongly against it, Rom. 4: 19. This also was what made him so readily assent to the offering up of his son, when he had him. He had as much to say against it, as could well be supposed; for the promise was, that " in Isaac all the families of the earth should be blessed," Gen. 28: 14. which promise, and this command, Abraham's reason could not reconcile. The contradiction would surely have run him down, had not his faith in this great attribute held fast, and guided the reins; suggesting to him, that he who gave Isaac a being from a withered stock, was also able to raise him from the dead, Heb. 11: 19. Abraham therefore disputes it not; stands not so much as to consider of it; but up he gets early to do it, Gen. 22: 3. and hence he obtained that honorable title, to be called " the friend of God!" James 2: 23.

Ye have seen now what Abraham did; " Go ye and do

likewise;" take hold of God's sovereignty as your own, engaged by a covenant of grace, and so to be exerted for your good. Faith gives a propriety in any attribute it looks upon, and draws out the virtues thereof for itself. And therefore, whatever difficulties are in your way, be not disheartened at them; but call in this sovereign power, by faith, to your help. Remember the ready subjection which all creatures do pay to his word; by which alone (without creatures' service) he can level the mountains, and make crooked things straight; restrain, alter, invert, and turn upside down the very course of nature; so that which is death in itself, shall be life to you. New cords and withes, when touched by his word, are as flax and tow when touched by the fire; iron shall be as straw, and brass as rotten wood, Judges 16: 7. Job 41: 27. Therefore lengthen the cords, and strengthen the stakes of your faith; you cannot believe greater things, or better than God can do for you. Even sin itself, which is the great (and really the only) evil; it is his enemy as much as yours: and you may be sure he would not have suffered its being in the world if he had not a power to correct and curb it, yea, and to destroy it too, at his pleasure: take hold of his sovereign strength, and your work is done.

But here also a caution or two may seasonably be added, for such reasons as are mixed with them.

1. If death in the pot hath once been healed, and your borrowed axe-head (sunk once, past hopes of recovery) brought again to your hand, 2 Kings 6: 6. see that remissness grow not upon it, lest at another turn the handle drop after the head. Gather not wild gourds a second time, 2 Kings 4: 39, &c. lest your prophet be absent, or meal denied you. Presume not to dally with temptations (as Samson did,) and then think to go out and shake yourself, as at other times, Judges 16: 20. The divine power is too great a thing to be trifled with, or made to serve with the follies of men.

2. Never look on this great attribute of sovereignty without your mediator. As without him, it cannot but be matter of terror and amazement to sinners; it is he only can render it propitious to you. As nothing is pleasing to God but in and through Christ, so nothing in God is comfortable to men, or for their eternal good, but as it comes

to them through him: as waters out of the sea immediately are not potable, unless they be first decocted by the sun, or pass through some vein of earth, to make them congruous to our nature.

I shall here mention two particulars of nearest concernment to us, wherein we are in a special manner to have respect unto the sovereignty of God.

1. As touching your own condition, (your everlasting condition,) submit to mercy, to sovereign mercy; that is, yield yourself to God without capitulating, or making terms with him. Those Syrians well understood the meaning of this; they put ropes on their heads, and themselves in the conqueror's hands, upon an uncertain conjecture, [" peradventure they will save us alive,"] 1 Kings 20: 31. So do ye, although ye have but a [may be] " we shall be hid," Zeph. 2: 3. mind your duty, and leave the issue to God; believe above hope, and against hope: follow God in the dark, as your father Abraham did, not knowing whither he would lead him: thus to do, is to give glory to God. Therefore, " fear the Lord, and obey the voice of his servant;" even then, " when ye are in darkness, and have no light," Isa. 50: 10. (namely, of his special favor and love to you in particular.) And though never so great discouragements are before you, from the guilt of sins committed, the power of in-dwelling corruptions, and your present averseness to believing; and here withal, that faith is the great commandment; let your heart answer, Is it my duty [my duty] to believe? Nay, then I must. Remember his greatness, his absolute dominion, the uncontrolableness of his matters; that " he hath concluded all in unbelief, that he might have mercy upon all," Rom. 11: 32. (that is, that the salvation of those who shall be saved might appear to be of mercy, and to be so acknowledged:) to him therefore commit your cause, and commit it to him as your sovereign lord, and so leave it with him; and see that you take it not out of his hand again, by your doubting the issue of it: and know, that then is your soul nearest to peace and settlement, when brought to this submission. " Be in subjection unto the father of spirits, and live," Heb. 12: 9.

But let not the word be misconstrued. I do not mean, by submission, that you should be satisfied under a denial of mercy, on the account of God's absolute dominion: I cannot think that a necessary term or qualification in your treating with God for salvation: for, 1. I do not find that God requires such a submission, as the condition of obtaining mercy; nor that he hath made any promise to give such a submission, in order to that end; nor any instance in scripture of the saints having or endeavoring such a frame of spirit in that business; nor yet that men are any where taxed for not attaining to it. They are blamed, indeed, and that worthily, for not submitting to the righteousness of God; (that is, for not renouncing their own, and flying to that of Christ;) and this blame-worthiness you cannot escape, if finding yourself lost and undone, you will not presently run to Christ, without first finding in yourself something that may seem to commend you to him. 2. Such a submission seems repugnant to God's revealed will. For, if this be the "will of God, even our sanctification," that we should believe on his Son, and love him with our whole heart, then it cannot be his will that we should be willing to remain in an unsanctified state, in unbelief and enmity against him; which are the inseparable conjuncts of willingness to be separated from God. 3. Because the promise of ease and rest is made to the weary and heavy laden, coming to Christ; not to a contentedness to be divided from him: and the promise of satisfaction is to your hungering and thirsting after righteousness; not to the cessation of your desire, without the thing which only can satisfy. 4. Because, to be satisfied without obtaining mercy, is to be satisfied with an utter incapacity to glorify the grace of God, and to enjoy communion with him, which are the principal end and duty of men. 5. It is cross to the genius and concreated principle of the reasonable creature, which is, to seek its own happiness: in any thing short of which it ought not to acquiesce. 6. Such a submission cannot be requisite in preparatory work; because that would suppose the highest pitch of grace attained (if it yet be a grace, and attainable,) before you believe; and consequently, that it is not a grace out of Christ's fulness; for ye are supposed to have it before ye go to him. And therefore, when I say, ye must submit, without capitulating or making terms, my meaning is, ye are not to treat upon terms of your own making, nor propound any thing to God, but what sovereign mercy propounds to you, as the way and means of obtaining your great end: and great reason ye have for this submission; for herein lies your interest; those being, in truth, the only terms by which a lost and sinful creature can be rendered salvable, or capable of being saved; as will further appear in the sequel of this discourse.

I think, with humble submission, that if any point of time may be supposed before the decree, it was then that absolute dominion bore sway; but ever since election came in, it is grace that reigns: not that sovereignty is ceased, but transferred: before it was in power, but now in grace; in grace, as touching the elect, and in justice, respecting the rest. Grace is the attribute God delights to honor, and all the other are, if I may so speak, as subjects of this: even Christ himself was made a servant, to perform the pleasure of his grace: "Behold my servant, whom I uphold; mine elect, in whom my soul delighteth: I have put my spirit upon him: he shall bring forth judgment to the Gentiles," Isa. 42: 1. So then, that you are to submit unto, is the good pleasure of God's will, as held forth in the covenant of grace, undertaking for, and perfectly able to save you; and as having his sovereign power engaged to make it good. Which seems the scope of that passage in Moses' prayer for the people, when they had highly provoked God: "Let the power of my Lord be great, according as thou hast spoken," &c. Numb. 14: 17, 18, 19. It was to pardon, and still to own them for his people. And to this agree all those scriptures which hold forth the power of God as the ground of faith; as that by which he is able to pardon sin, to subdue iniquity, and to hold your souls in life. You are therefore directed, if you will have peace with God, "to take hold of his strength," Isa. 27: 5. which cannot be meant of a contentedness in having that strength put forth to destroy, but as being perfectly able and engaged by his covenant to save you. As to the time when the Lord will manifest his love to you; as also the manner and measure of his dispensing it; the good pleasure of his will is expressly, and with all quietness of spirit, to be submitted unto: but as to the thing itself, you ought not to be said nay; but do as he did, who had power with God, and prevailed. "He wept, and made supplication," Hos.

12: 4. but still resolved, " I will not let thee go, except
thou bless me," Gen. 32: 26.

2. As for the other nearest concernment, touching your
children, deal in like manner for them, by submitting them
to the same mercy. It is true, that next to your own personal salvation, there cannot be a greater evidence of God's
love to you, than to choose your children after you, nor
any thing more desirable to you: therefore, " command
them, and instruct them to keep the way of the Lord,"
Gen. 18: 19. that he may bring on them the blessing you
most desire for them: but be not over solicitous, and cast
down, because you see not yet the marks of election upon
them. The Lord doth not indeed bind himself to take all
a believer's children, nor doth he limit himself from taking
any others. There is nothing declared touching his purpose to take all the one, lest they should thence take occasion to be remiss in their duty (which, till conversion, is
very natural to us:) nor doth he exclude the children of
others: for that might discourage, and weaken their hands
to that which is good. In this various dispensing of his
everlasting love, he is pleased so to reserve his liberty and
sovereign prerogative, that he greatly manifests his love
to believers, in so frequent choosing of their seed; and the
freeness of his grace, in not rejecting wholly the seed of
others.

Infer. 3. How happy and sovereignly blessed are those
who have an interest in this great and sovereign Lord! Be
the earth ever so unquiet, and the tumult of it ever so
boisterous and unruly, the Lord is above them. He sits
on the waters, as a prince in his chariot, guiding all as he
will; he is that great dictator, whose word is the law indeed:
if he but say, Come, Go, Do this, there needs no more.
Who would not be the subject of such a prince? and much
more his favorite? and yet, this high privilege every soul
is blessed with, that has in truth taken hold of his covenant: for that takes in all between the two eternities, and
eternity itself withal; and the spirit or strength of the whole
lies in those few (but very compendious) words, " I will
be your God." When the Lord would comfort his people
to purpose, and put on their eagles' wings, what a glorious
narrative doth he make of his power and sovereign great-

ness, in Isa. 40, from verse 12 to verse 26! And then tells them, that all this is theirs, verse 27. And if God be yours, all things are yours. Who, and where is he that can supplant you of his blessing? you may rejoice in his highness, the thoughts whereof are matter of terror to other men. After the rehearsal of all the happiness and glory that men or angels are capable of, it shall all be comprised in this, as the original thereof, and sum of the whole, " Happy are they whose God is the Lord," Psal. 144: 15.

Infer. 4. We may see here the reason why God doth sometimes defer to answer the doubts and queries we stick at, and most desire to be resolved about: it is not only to shew his sovereignty, but to bring our hearts to a practical acknowledgment of it. Moses was very unwilling to go on this message to Pharaoh: many pretences he had to put it by: while the danger he might be in for killing the Egyptian was the bottom objection, though he speaks it not out. Indeed, the men who sought his life were now dead, which if he had known before, all those excuses had probably been spared: but the Lord was pleased to conceal it from him until he had brought him to a full compliance with his will, and then reveals it to him unasked, Exod. 3: 11. and 4: 10. 13. 19. So, likewise, he would not take off his hand from Job, until he had well learned him this lesson, Job 42: 2, &c. Say not therefore (because you have not returns so soon as you would,) " The Lord hath forsaken me; my Lord hath forgotten me," Isa. 49: 14. But follow that great resolution recorded of old, " I will wait upon the Lord, who hideth his face (at present) from the house of Jacob, and I will look for him," Isa. 8: 17.

Infer. 5. Let no man, then, who will say, " the Lord he is God," presume to intrench on his sacred royalty, by seeking a reason of his decrees, beyond or besides the good pleasure of his will. Even sovereigns of dust will not admit it in subjects, though of the same mould with themselves. It is an imperial secret, " the chief of the ways of God;" it belongs to himself alone to know it; and the knowledge thereof would not profit us now. Besides, there is enough revealed, of great importance to us at present, on which to employ the utmost of our time and strength. By over-grasping, we may sprain our hands, and unfit them for service, otherwise within their compass, but we gain

nothing. Therefore go not about to fathom this great deep.
Who, but one of shallow understanding, would think to
measure the sea by handfuls? or to give a demonstrative
reason of its various and convertible courses! Remember
that you may magnify his word, Job 36: 24. But lessen
it not, by pretending to comprehend it, Eccles. 8: 17.
"Sanctify the Lord in your hearts, and fear before him,"
Isa. 8: 13.

Infer. 6. This gives a reason, why men of the largest
capacity, for learning and natural understanding are so
mightily puzzled and labyrinthed in spiritual matters, particularly the doctrine of election: why they do so strongly
oppose it, and are so hardly reconciled with it. They are
not, in truth, subdued to the doctrine of God's sovereignty:
and therefore, while in discussing those points of faith,
they judge as their natural optics represent them, they lose
both themselves and the truth; which yet, in some degree,
"is made known unto babes," (men of low stature to them)
whose spirits the Lord hath subdued to rest contented with
what their Father is pleased to tell them; and for the rest
(as namely, the manner and reason of God's disposements
and dispensations) they live by faith in his righteousness;
waiting for the day that shall reveal all things, when the
tabernacle of God, which yet is in heaven, shall be let
down among men, or they taken up into it, and these
hidden things of sovereignty shall be more openly known
among them.

Lastly, This doctrine of God's absolute dominion, clears
away all that made-ground and rubbish, which the principles of free-will grace do found their election upon; and
shews us the only true and proper foundation of scripture-
election; with those other important truths which hold
upon it, or are consequents of it: all which have their head
in the sovereignty of God, and are derived thence, as rivers
are from the sea: as through his blessing and grace may
appear afterwards. And so I shall close up this first part
of the preface, with that holy rapture of the Psalmist: "Be
thou exalted, Lord, in thine own strength; so will we sing,
and praise thy power," Psal. 21: 13. "The Lord hath prepared his throne in the heavens, and his kingdom ruleth
over all. Bless the Lord, ye his angels, that excel in
strength! Bless the Lord, all ye his hosts, ye ministers of

his that do his pleasure! Bless the Lord, all his works, in all places of his dominion! Bless the Lord, O my soul," Psal. 103: 19, 22.

RIGHTEOUSNESS OF GOD

HAVING founded this discourse on the Sovereignty of God, as the best and most natural ground of satisfaction (or captivation) to reason, touching Election, now as a means to qualify our spirits, and reconcile them with the doctrine of Sovereignty, it seemeth expedient to annex that of his Righteousness: and, I think, there is not a more rational proposition, or one more clearly requiring submission, than

"That there is no unrighteousness with God."

This is the natural adjunct of divine sovereignty, which, as we are indispensably bound to believe, so to be well grounded in the faith of it, will be of exceeding great usefulness to us in every condition; especially under those darker administrations, of which we do not see at present the cause, reason, or tendency; when matters of great importance seem to be confused or neglected; when all things in view fall out alike to all; and you cannot know either good or evil, by all that is before you. I shall therefore collect some of those considerations, from which you may find some light and influence in a dark and cloudy day; and by which, as a means, I myself was drawn in and guided to this determination, before I had searched the scriptures expressly concerning this subject: and they may serve, both as arguments to demonstrate the proposition, and as antidotes against those poisonous contradictions, which carnal reason and unbelief will be too often forging and flinging in upon us. And,

Argument I. Is founded on that infinite blessedness, which the most high God was possessed of in himself, before the world, or any creature was made. He did not make them for any need he had of them, but for his pleasure, Rev. 4: 11. and if he needed them not, there could be no need, or reason why he should make them such, or to such an end as not to be wisely overruled, and their end attained, without doing wrong to any. The motives by which men are swayed to wrong-doing, are chiefly two, 1. To obtain something they have not. Ahab slew Naboth for his vineyard, 1 Kings, 21: and Athaliah all the seed royal, to get the throne, 2 Kings, 11. Or, 2. To secure what they have. Pharaoh oppressed the people, lest growing mighty they should shake off his yoke, and get them out of his service, Exod. 1:10. Jeroboam set up his calves to keep the people at home, and firm to himself, 1 Kings, 12: 27, 28, and the Jews put Christ to death, lest the Romans should come and take away their place and nation, John, 11: 48. These two have shared the parentage of all the oppression and wrong-doing that have been in the world: neither of which is compatible with our great and blessed God: for all things are his already; he possesseth the heavens and the earth, and all the hosts of them, with an absolute power and right to dispose of them. And as for securing what he hath, of whom should he be afraid? for, 1. "There is no God besides him;" the Lord himself, who needs must know it, if there were another, professeth solemnly, that "he knows not any," Isa. 44: 6, 8. And, 2. As for creatures, they are all more absolutely under his subjection, than the smallest dust under our feet is to us. "The nations are to him less than nothing and vanity." Isa. 40: 17. He needs not so much as to touch them, to bring them down: it is but "gathering to himself his spirit and his breath, and they perish together," Job 34: 14, 15. If the Lord but withhold his sustaining influence, they fall of themselves; but he remains the same to all generations.

Arg. II. Another argument is founded on the infinite perfection of his nature. This those seraphic heralds proclaim under the notion of holy, holy, holy, Isa. 6: 2. Its reduplication imports the highest perfection. And Moses, who of all mortals, had nearest access to God, puts it in the front of his triumphal titles, Exod. 15: 11. "Glorious in holiness!" It is that whereby all the divine excellencies are summarily expressed. The righteous Lord will do no iniquity: he is of purer eyes than to look upon it. It is an high demonstration of his excellency, that he cannot deny himself: that is, he cannot do any thing that is in the least degree contrary to his holy nature; nothing that needs to be retracted, or to alter his mind about it. His will is the rule of righteousness, and righteousness is the rule of his will. The saints of old were perfectly of this mind: "Shall not the Judge of all the earth do right?" Gen. 18: 25. And the apostle puts it as a question not to be answered, that if God were unrighteous, "How then shall he Judge the world?" Rom. 3: 6.

Arg. III. It is also apparent, from the constant rule and measure of God's dispensements, which are not done fortuitously, nor rashly, but with deliberation and exactness. "He lays judgment to the rule, and righteousness to the plummet," Isa. 28: 7. He will not punish without a cause, nor more than is deserved. Touching the sins of Sodom, "I will go down," says God, "and see whether they have done, [altogether] according to the cry of it," Gen. 18: 21. "He renders to every one according to their deeds," Rom. 2: 6. "and gives them [a just] recompence of reward," Heb. 2: 2. "He will not cast away the perfect man, nor help the wicked," Job, 8: 20. Eliphaz puts the question with great confidence, (as well he might,) "Who ever perished being innocent?" Job, 4: 7. His righteousness is such, that it even holds his hands until the innocent be out of danger. The angels were straightly commanded, not to begin the execution of God's wrath on the wicked world, "until his servants were marked out," Rev. 7: 3. and when the Lord came to destroy Sodom, he hastens righteous Lot to Zoar, with this only argument, "I cannot do any thing until thou be come thither," Gen. 19: 22.

Arg. IV. It is further evidenced, by the laws he hath given unto men; the sum of which is, to do righteously; and the end of them, the good and welfare of the creature. After a thousand years' experience of these, compared with the issue of men's inventions, they are acknowledged to be "right judgments, good statutes, and laws of truth," Neh. 9: 3. What an admirable catalogue have we in Romans 12: 12. and Gal. 5: 22!

1. Of such as concern our duty towards himself immediately, this is the sum; "Thou shalt worship the Lord thy God, and him only shalt thou serve," Matt. 4: 10. There is nothing more equal and just than to worship and serve him, whose we are: to love and to live to him, from

whom we have our life and breath; especially considering that "his commandments are our life," Deuteronomy, 16: 18, 19.

2. Such as refer more immediately to ourselves, as temperance, chastity, moderation, sobriety, &c. These, as is evident to all, do greatly conduce to our outward welfare, both in point of health, estate, prosperity, &c. And what evil consequents do attend the contraries of those virtues, might be every day's observation; more especially such as relate to our spiritual state and welfare: of which more particularly under the next argument.

3. Such commands also as respect our duty towards men; as to do justly; to shew mercy; to "follow peace with all men," every one to mind his own business, and not intermeddle with others: so, "to be subject to the powers that be;" and to "pray for those in authority," (the neglect of which duty may be a cause of our disquietment from them, at least it may prove an eclipse of our joyfulness in suffering under them, &c.;) the sum of this kind of duties we have in that standing uncontrollable rule, of "doing to others as we would they should do unto us." On the contrary, there is nothing forbidden but what tends to our hurt; as if it were needful, might be demonstrated by instances innumerable.

4. To this also might be added, the strict injunctions that God hath laid upon the subordinate dispensers of his law; as, namely, "to judge the people with just judgment; not to wrest judgment, nor respect persons," Deut. 16: 18, 19. "yea, he curseth them that pervert judgment," chap. 27: 19, "and will surely reprove them that accept persons," Job, 13: 10, &c. And "shall mortal man be more just than God?" chapter 4: 17. Will he, under such penalties, command men to do thus, and not much more do so himself?

Arg. V. Another beam of the righteousness of God, shines forth in his putting the matter of our duty into such a way and method, as renders it more facile, and mostly conduceth to our chief end.

As, 1. "To remember our Creator in the days of our youth," Eccl. 12: 12. For the work of conversion, and turning to God, must needs be much easier then, than when habituated in an evil course: for long impenitency (besides the provocation it is to God,) estranges the mind more from him: makes the spirit more inflexible, and harder to be wrought upon; it multiplies our work, and subtracts our strength: for one accustomed in evil to learn to do well, and for a black-moor to change his skin, are things of a like possibility: it is a very rare and difficult thing for " a man to be born again when he is old."

2. To watch against, and suppress the first motions of sin, and to avoid whatever might be an occasion, or have tendency towards it.   And in order thereto, to " take heed to our spirit," Mal. 2: 15.   " To keep the heart with all diligence," Prov. 4: 23:   " To abstain from all appearances of evil," 1 Thess. 5: 22.   " To hate the garment spotted by the flesh," Jude, ver. 23.   " And to make a covenant with our eyes," as Job did, Job, 31: 1.   For the professed practice of some saints is directive to others, and equivalent to a command.   To keep an enemy from rising, is much easier than to quell him when he is up; yea, to nip sin when it is young, is the ready way, not only to keep it low, but to kill it; as the continual plucking off buds from a tree or plant, destroys the root.

3. Not to do any thing, the lawfulness whereof is dubious to us; which, as it is a sin in itself, (as every thing is which is not of faith,) Rom. 14: 23, so it tends to obscure to us the true sight of other things, and emboldens to further attempts.   Yea, farther, not to mind only the lawfulness of things, but their expediency, 1 Cor. 6: 12, the not heeding of which proves often an occasion of sin to others, whereof we cannot be guiltless.   So, likewise, to cherish all motions to good; not to quench the Spirit, 1 Thess. 5: 19. and to hearken, or listen diligently what the Lord God will speak, Exod. 15: 26. who oft-times delivers his mind with " a still and small voice," 1 Kings 19: 12. which doubly obligeth our attention.

4. In his pressing, with so much weight and necessity, those great duties of faith, love, patience, self-denial, &c. (1.) Faith, which consists in submitting to the " righteousness of God," taking hold of his strength, and following the conduct of his wisdom: and in order thereto, shewing us our own sinfulness, weakness, and folly, with the vanity of all created bottoms, which have always failed at the greatest need; and so drawing our hearts to lean on himself only,

in whom alone we have righteousness and strength, Isa. 45: 24. (2.) Love: this is a powerful, active, candid, and obliging principle: it bears all things; thinks no evil; takes all in good part, 1 Cor. 13: 5. makes that both portable and pleasant, which without love, would be both harsh and burdensome. (3.) Patience, and meekness of spirit; these mitigate the dolor of any suffering, and often prevent or allay the storm that is rising. " A soft answer turneth away wrath," Prov. 15: 1. Judges 8: 3. It also breeds experience; 1. That any afflictions may be borne through him that strengthens us, 2 Cor. 12: 9. 2. That afflictions are all for our profit, Heb. 12: 10. 3. That we could not well have been without them, 1 Pet. 1: 6, 7. 4. It also gives to understand the Lord's meaning in them, which the noise of tumultuous passions would drown in us. And, as a means to work this patience, the Lord sets before us, 1. That there is a cause of every chastening; and that cause is from ourselves; and therefore no cause to complain. 2. That he afflicts not willingly, but only when there is need, and no more than needs must. 3. That he hath many gracious ends in afflicting: as, (1.) To humble for sin committed; as in Joseph's rough dealing with his brethren, Gen. 42: 21. (2.) To purge out dross; as in the case of Manasseh, 2 Chron. 33: 11. 13. and the whole church, Isa. 27: 9. (3.) To prevent sins we should otherwise fall into: thus he kept Paul from being exalted above measure, 2 Cor. 12: 7. (4.) To wean us from the world; this he expected from Baruch, Jer. 45: 4, 5. and this effect it had upon Asaph, Psal. 73: 35. (5.) To exercise our graces; as Abraham's great faith, by his various temptations; and Paul was much under infirmities, that he might " magnify the power of Christ," 2 Cor. 12: 9. (6.) By lesser temptations, and deliverances from them, we are fitted for greater, and our faith strengthened, both to bear and to get through them; which greater had they come before, might have overturned us. 4. Self-denial: this is a duty of nearest concernment to us, since we have no enemies so great as self-love, and fleshly lusts to war against our souls. These things considered, will shew that David's conclusion is right and genuine; " Good and upright is the Lord, therefore will he teach sinners in the way," Psal. 25: 8. Even reason itself might tell us (to be sure sanctified reason and experience will,) that thus to command and direct, is to lead in the right way; and it highly commends to us the righteousness of God.

Arg. VI. The righteousness of God is farther made out, by his affixing rewards and punishments, to good and evil works respectively, according to what is the proper result and natural product of them: " Whatsoever a man sows, that shall he reap," Gal. 6: 7. " Every seed shall have its own body," 1 Cor. 15: 38. "He will give to every one according to his ways, and the fruit of his doings," Isa. 3: 10, 11. Jer. 32: 19. Holiness hath in it a natural tendency to life and peace: it is a tree of life, Prov. 3: 18. Grace and glory grow from the same root: salvation is the end of faith; the flower that grows upon it, 1 Pet. 1: 9. " The work of righteousness is peace, and the effect thereof quietness and assurance for ever," Isa. 32: 17. It is sometimes called, " the way of life," Prov. 12: 28. Sometimes " the fountain and well-spring of life," Prov. 14: 27. And it tendeth to life," Prov. 19: 23. For if the root be holy, the branch cannot be otherwise, Romans, 11: 16.

It is so likewise with sin: death follows sin, not only as a punishment for delinquency, but as its natural offspring, Prov. 23: 29. Original corruption is the root; sin the stalk that grows next upon it; and death the finishing, or full corn in the ear, James, 1: 14, 15. If there be no justice to revenge sin, sin would be vengeance to itself: " Sinners lie in wait for their own blood," Prov. 1: 18. "It is their own wickedness that corrects them," Jer. 2: 19. " The way of sin inclineth to death, and its footsteps to the dead: its steps take hold on hell," Prov. 2: 18. and 5: 5. Unbelief may be an instance for all; as out of which all sins else are derived: this was the root of Adam's apostacy, Gen. 3. of all that people's rebellions in the wilderness, Numb. 14: 11. of the Jews' rejecting the Messiah, John, 19: 7. 12. Faith is that which holds the soul to God, its life and blessedness: unbelief is departing from him, or letting go its hold; the loosing of the knot, upon which the soul falls off of its own accord: and the first step from God sets in a way of death: as a branch breaking off from its stock dies of itself. This was Adam's unbelief: in all men since, it is a refusing to return.

Arg. VII. This doctrine is further confirmed, by the general unanimous consent and affirmation of those best able to judge. (1.) They assert it. Job, a man of great wisdom and integrity, "not his like in all the earth," Job 1: 8. and none so sorely afflicted; yet, says Elihu to him, by way of counsel (as what himself would do in like case), " I will ascribe righteousness to my maker," chap. 36: 3. and " surely God will not pervert judgment," chap. 34: 12. " God is known (that is, he is known to be God) by the judgments which he executeth," Psal. 19. 6. " The Lord is upright; there is no unrighteousness in him," Psal. 92: 15. " He loveth righteousness, and hateth iniquity. The sceptre of his kingdom is a right sceptre," Psal. 45: 6, 7. " Righteousness and judgment are the habitation of his throne," Psal. 97: 2. Deut. 32: 4. That " true and righteous are his judgments," is the voice of those in heaven, Rev. 19: 2. (2.) They submit to it, even then when most provoked by men's injurious dealings with them for his sake; and when the Lord's own hand hath been most severe towards them. " Aaron held his peace," Lev. 10: 3. " It is the Lord," saith Eli, " let him do what seemeth him good," 1 Sam. 3: 18. Hezekiah also, " Good is the word of the Lord," 2 Kings 20: 19. Yea, they have done thus, when by the light of natural reason they could see no reason for it; witness Job; who, when plundered of all, because " he feared God, and eschewed evil," and could justify himself to the height, as to any hypocrisy; yet, says he, " I will make supplication to my judge," Job 9: 15. Look on our Lord and Saviour himself, and see his confession: " Our fathers cried unto thee, and were delivered; but I, though day nor night I am not silent, thou hearest me not." How does he close his complaint? Not, Thou dealest more hardly with me, who less have deserved it; but, " Thou art holy," Psal. 22: 2, 3, 4. Jeremiah, indeed, began to object, because the " way of the wicked prospered, and they were happy that dealt treacherously:" but he presently bethinks himself, withdraws his plea, and yields the cause: " Righteous thou art, O Lord, when I plead with thee," Jer. 12: 1. I might instance the suffrages of wicked men, and of the most obdurate among them, whose consciences, at times, have enforced their confession of this truth; and the testimony of an adversary proves strongly. Pharaoh subscribes to it: " The Lord is righteous, I and my people are wicked," Exod. 9: 27. As also doth Adoni-bezek, and Saul, Judges 1: 7. 1 Sam. 24: 17. 19. (3.) the saints triumph in the righteousness of God, as well they may, and call upon others to do the like: " The Lord reigneth, let the earth rejoice," Psal. 93: 97. 99. " O let the nations be glad, and sing for joy; for thou shalt judge the people righteously," Psal. 92: 4. " Let the heavens rejoice, and the earth be glad before the Lord: for he cometh to judge the earth," Psal. 96: 11. 13. &c. And hence it was that Paul, and the rest of them, though the present sense of their sufferings was grievous, yet they gloried in them, and rejoiced greatly in hopes of that glory and " crown of righteousness, which God, as a righteous judge, had prepared for them," 2 Tim. 4. 8.

Arg. VIII. The righteousness of God is yet farther illustrated, by the issue and event of his darkest dispensations. " The consumption decreed shall overflow with righteousness," Isa. 10: 22. and nothing else shall be in it. His people, though long under oppression, he brought them forth at last, with the greater substance. His leading them about in the wilderness, as it were in a maze, forty years together; and bringing them back to where they had been many years before; yet proved it to be the right way, Psal. 107: 7. and it was for " their good in the latter end," Deut. 8: 16. David's long persecution by Saul, made him the fitter for the kingdom, and adapted him for the office of principal secretary to the great King; opportunely acquainting him with all the affairs of the heavenly state and council, that are fit to be known upon earth: and by his hand and experience they are confirmed to us; and this among the rest. " Blessed is the man whom thou chastenest, and teachest him out of thy law," Psal. 94: 12. We see it also by the end the Lord made with Job; " he brought him forth like gold," and doubled his blessings upon him, Job 43: 12. The basket of good figs were sent into captivity for their good, Jer. 24: 5. Paul's afflictions turned to his salvation, Phil. 1: 19. Even the temptations, sorrows, and sufferings of Christ himself, which were such as never were known by men, were intended, and accordingly did, perfect and enable him for his office of mediator: " Wherefore in all things it behooved him to be made like unto his brethren, that he might be a merciful and faithful high priest in things pertaining to God, to make reconciliation for the sins of the people. For in that he himself hath suffered, being tempted, he is able to succor them that are tempted," Heb. 2: 17, 18.

Arg. IX. Another great instance and evidence of the righteousness of God appears in the manner of his procedure in reference to the elect. Those precious souls, whom he loved from everlasting, and determined to bring to glory: yet, having sinned, not one of them shall enter there, without satisfaction made to his justice; even those he will not justify, but so as to be just in doing of it, Rom. 8: 3. 3: 26. The mercy-seat being sprinkled with blood, Lev. 16: 14. was evidently a shadow of it; for the glory of God does not consist only in shewing mercy, but to do it in such a manner as not to clash with his justice. It is a part of his name and glory, that " he will by no means clear the guilty," Exod. 34: 7. but who then shall be saved, since " all the world is found guilty before God?" Rom. 3: 19. Yea, there is yet a way to shew mercy (which is ever adorable,) and therein is shewn the manifold wisdom of God, as well as his righteousness, in the contriving a way for " mercy and truth to meet together," Psal. 85: 10. which was done by transferring the guilt of his chosen upon another, who was able to bear it, and to give a more adequate satisfaction to his justice, than they ever could have done by their personal sufferings: this also was typified by the law of the scape-goat: " And Aaron shall cast lots upon the two goats, one lot for the Lord, and the other lot for the scape-goat. But the goat, on which the lot fell to be the scape-goat, shall be presented alive before the Lord, to make an atonement with him, and to let him go for a scape-goat into the wilderness. And he that let go the goat for the scape-goat, shall wash his clothes, and bathe his flesh in water, and afterward come into the camp." Lev. 16: 8. 10. 26.

Arg. X. Consider especially that great instance of Christ himself, the first elect, and head of all the family; and the compact made with him; who, though he were a son, " His beloved son, in whom his soul delighted:" yet if he will undertake for sinners, he must stand in their stead. " All their sins must meet upon him," and he must bear the punishment due unto them, Isa. 53: 4, 5. It was not " possible that cup should pass from him:" no, " though he sought it with strong cries and tears;" and that of him who was able to save him from death, who also loved him as his own soul: he was not, he might not be released, until he had paid the utmost mite. For although grace is perfectly free to men, in pardoning and saving of them; yet justice must be satisfied, and Christ was abated nothing. This last unparalleled instance of incomparable justice doth highly illustrate the point in hand, namely, " That our great and sovereign Lord cannot but do right."

Inferences from the Righteousness of God

Infer. 1. May this doctrine prove an eternal blast to the vain and presumptuous confidence of impenitent sinners, who, " because vengeance is not speedily executed, have their hearts fully bent and set in them to do evil," Eccles. 8: 11. Because the Lord (at present) holds his peace, they think he is like themselves, Psal. 50: 21, &c. Let them certainly know, that he is able to deal with them: and, further, that his righteousness obligeth him to vindicate himself: he will by no means clear the guilty, nor be always silent: though slow, yet sure; and strikes home at last, Psal. 2: 9. " He will arise to judgment, and set their sins in order before them," and reckon with them for all the hard speeches which they, ungodly sinners, have uttered against him: the sight whereof shall strike their trembling souls (notwithstanding their stoutness now) with horror and amazement; and make even all their bowels ready to gush out. " He will wound the hairy scalp (the proud and presumptuous head) of every one that goes on in his wickedness," Psal. 68: 21. " A dart shall strike through his liver," Prov. 7: 23. and down with him to hell, the nethermost hell, in a moment. Why then will you " run against the thick bosses of his bucklers?" Job 15, 26. " and set briers and thorns in array against a devouring flame?" Isa. 33: 14. Can dried stubble dwell with " everlasting burnings?" Did " ever any harden himself against God and prosper?" Job 9: 4. No, nor never shall. Where will

his hope be, when God taketh away his soul! Job 27: 8.
Therefore take up betimes, leave off, and know that he is
God, Psal. 46: 10.

Infer. 2. Let this doctrine for ever vindicate the holy
and good ways of God (both those he walks in towards us,
and those he commands us to walk in towards himself,)
from all those senseless imputations of harshness, morose-
ness, nicety, preciseness, or whatever else the profaneness
or ignorance of men can tax them with: for, as it is said,
so it is found by the certain and sober experience of all
that fear him (and against such experience no reason is to
be admitted;) I say, it is a general infallible experiment,
that " all the ways of wisdom are pleasantness to him that
walks in them," Prov. 3: 17. which argues, that those who
think otherwise, are ignorant of them, and therefore not
competent judges. It is granted, indeed, that those whose
hearts are in these good ways of God, have their steps too
often turned aside, and go haltingly in them: but, in truth,
the fault is not in the way, but in the men. There is some
fracture in their bones, dislocation of joints, or evil tumor;
something is out of order, and needs looking to. A cripple
will limp in Solomon's porch, on the smoothest pavement,
when one that is sound in his limbs will walk with delight
on rougher ground. The law, and our hearts, were once at
perfect agreement; the discord came in by our free-will de-
viations, and swerving from our first make. Therefore
admit not the least motion that looks but awry on the commands or disposements of God; but justify them to the
height, and take shame to yourself, as Paul himself did,
" The commandment is holy, but I am carnal," Rom. 7:
12. 14.

Infer. 3. If the Lord cannot but do right, then let us all
(and every one) take heed of sin, which the holiness and
justice of God are so inexorably bent against: he will not
pardon without satisfaction. Yea, beware of little sins
(little, I mean, in esteem with men, or in comparison of
some others.) Your nearness to God will not excuse you;
for, you " have I known, [therefore] you will I punish,"
Amos 3: 2. Even Moses, his servant, for once speaking
unadvisedly, was shut out of Canaan, Numb. 20: 10. 12.
and though he would fain have gone into that good land,
and solicited the Lord much about it, as if he would have

no denial; yet the Lord would not hear him: "Speak no more to me of this matter," Deut. 3: 26. To make light of the least sin, because grace abounds, is to sin against your own soul, and to make the precious blood of Christ a common thing (the least is the price of blood.) Although he love thee, and that so as never to take his loving kindness from thee, yet he will not let thee go altogether unpunished; yea, the Lord may hide from thee the sense of his love, and make thee feel his displeasure, even to the breaking of thy bones, &c. For he must discountenance sin, and that for our good, as well as to vindicate the honor of his righteousness.

Infer. 4. You that acknowledge God's uprightness, and profess to be his children, convince the world of the truth of your principles by your practice. Shew yourselves to be his offspring, by your likeness to him: " do justly, love mercy, walk humbly." To " be blameless, and harmless, and without rebuke," Phil. 2: 15. is your best argument to refute the world's calumnies, and to prove yourselves to be the sons of God. Shew it also, by your justifying God, even while " he wraps himself in a cloud," Job 22: 13, 14. " and his footsteps are not known," Psal. 77: 19. He that owns not God's hand in every dispensement, disowns his sovereignty; and he that repines, denies his righteousness: acquit yourself in both.

Infer. 5. Then let none stumble at present administrations, nor admit of a sinister or suspicious thought touching this holy Lord God. The reason of his ways may be unknown, but cannot be unjust: he sees through the dark cloud, though you and I cannot. We know " the Lord doth not afflict willingly," Lam. 3: 33. and his people are in heaviness but for a season, and if need be, 1 Pet. 1: 6, then, surely, " it is meet to be said unto God, I have borne chastisement," (that is, my sin procured it for me, and I have no cause to complain;) " I will offend no more," Job 34: 31. Acknowledge his uprightness, and he will be " gracious unto thee," chap. 23: 24. And do it when thou canst not see the reason of his judgments, nor their tendency; taking it still for a rule, " That all the ways of God are perfect: nothing can be put to them, nor any thing taken from them," Eccles. 3: 14. It was a good resolution in Job, that, " though he were righteous, yet would he not answer God; but make supplication to his judge," Job 9: 15. and though he should slay him, " yet will he trust in him," chap. 13: 15. and this would he do, even while he thought he might maintain his own ways before him.

Be patient, therefore: " the coming of the Lord draweth nigh," James 5: 7. " who will judge the world with right-eousness," Psal. 9: 8. Let neither the wicked's prosper-ity, nor the daily chastenings of his own people, be an offence to thee; go up " into the sanctuary of God," Psal. 73: 17. there thou shalt know the end. It shall not always be carried thus; there will be a reckoning for the good things they had in their life-time; when those that have lived in pleasure, will wish that their souls had been in thy soul's stead, under all its pressures: and it shall be no grief of heart to thee, to remember thy mortal and momentary suf-ferings, Rom. 8: 18. when thou seest such peaceable fruits of righteousness brought forth thereby, Heb. 12: 18. when thou shalt be wrapt up with holy amazement, and shall say in thine heart, " I lost my children, and was de-solate; a captive, and removing to and fro (had no abiding place,) who hath begotten me these?" Isa. 49: 21. chap. 60. Whence came they! what root sprang they from! my light afflictions were not worthy to be compared with this glory! 2 Cor. 4: 17. He will never repent that he sowed in tears, who brings home his sheaves with such joy. But as you go along to this your blessed home, and sweet place of eternal rest, it may be worth the while to ruminate such scriptures as these: " Though a sinner do evil a hundred times, and his days be prolonged (he goes unpunished,) yet surely it shall be well with them that fear God: but it shall not be well with the wicked," Eccles. 8: 12, 13. " Verily, there is a reward for the righteous: Verily, he is a God who judg-eth in the earth," Psal. 58: 11. " And his judgment is according to truth," Rom. 2: 2. " and blessed are they that wait for him," Isa. 30: 18.

Infer. 6. *Lastly,* All the objections that are brought against the doctrine of election's absoluteness, personality, and eternity; the peculiarity of redemption; the efficacious predominance of grace in calling; and believers' invincible perseverance in faith and holiness, would all be disbanded, and sent to their own place, were this one truth (which none in words will deny) but truly believed and received in love; namely, " That God hath an absolute right of dominion over his creatures, to dispose and determine of them as seemeth him good; and that in the doing thereof he cannot but do right."

And so I come to the matter first intended.

ELECTION

THE doctrine of Election containeth the whole sum and scope of the gospel; and our minds, if honestly subdued to the doctrine of God's sovereignty, cannot be employed about a more excellent subject. It is called " The foundation of God," not only because of the supereminency of it, but as a foundation of his laying, which God himself is the author of, and he alone; and the basis whereof is himself: it is that foundation which standeth sure, and keeps all them sure who stand upon it.

Election is the pitching of everlasting love, or the good pleasure of God, choosing and decreeing to eternal life: it is the great charter of heaven, God's special and free-grace deed of gift to his chosen ones, made over in trust unto Jesus Christ, for their use and benefit. Now, in deeds of gift (to make them authentic) there must be inserted the name of the donor, or person that gives; the name of the donee, or person to whom; the quality and extent of the thing that is given; the time when it was done; the consideration that moved thereto; and, in case of impotency, it is usual and necessary to ordain some friend as feoffee in trust, who is to stand seized or possessed of the gift for the donee's use: all which are evidently found in scripture election, and may be summed inot this proposition.

Prop. " That there is a peculiar people, who were personally chosen of God in Christ, according to his own good pleasure, and ordained to eternal life, before the world began."

Before I come to a downright proof of the proposition, I shall first explain the terms, and then produce some instances of a lower kind of election, that is, to matters of a lower concern than that of eternal life; which yet may be reckoned a type and shadow of it.

1. For explanation. This word ' peculiar' denotes the

.emption or privileging of a person or thing from the power of another, in whose jurisdiction it was, or seemed to be: it sometimes signifies riches, or substance, which is of a man's own proper getting, by labor and industry: it is also used to denominate such a part of a man's inheritance as he keeps in his own hands; which our law calls his demesne lands. In all which respects, the elect are aptly termed a peculiar people: for, (1.) Though Satan be prince of the world, and rules on every side; yet, as touching the elect, it is but an usurped and temporary jurisdiction that he hath over them: they do, indeed, belong to another prince, to whom their chief Lord hath given them; who therefore (in the appointed time) will rescue them from that usurpation. (2.) They are the Lord's treasure, or inheritance, obtained by labor indeed, with sweat and blood; than which nothing is more a man's own, nor hardlier parted with; such was the portion bestowed by Jacob on his beloved Joseph, " even that which he got with his sword, and with his bow," Gen. 48: 22. And, (3.) They are the Lord's demesnes: he keeps them in his own hands, tenders them as the apple of his eye, and will not entrust them in the hands of others: no, not of their own selves.

' Chosen or elected:' the proper import of the word is, to select or make choice of one or more out of a greater number. ' Personally chosen,' that is, they were singled forth, or pitched upon by name; and chosen in Christ, or into Christ, as their head and mediator; that being in him, all the grace and glory they were chosen unto might be rightfully theirs, and accordingly applied to them.

' To ordain' is the same here as to predestinate, appoint, prepare, decree, or fore-determine of things to come: which was in such manner done, that the event always has, does, and ever shall, justly succeed according to designment. In this sense men cannot be said to predestinate, because they cannot, with any certainty, determine of things not yet in being: but all things were present with God from eternity, and his decree was the cause of their after-existence.

By ' eternal life' I understand, not only the saints' actual possession of blessedness and glory; which consists in their perfect conformity to God, and union with him (according to the 17th of John,) but also, whatever is requisite thereto, by way of right, preparation, or otherwise; wherein are comprised, the mediation of Christ, effectual calling, and final perseverance in faith and holiness; which are indeed but so many parts or subdivisions of election: you have them all conjoined in one verse, both as appropriate to the same persons, and as being inseparable, in Isa. 62: 12. where those for whom the highway is cast up, are termed " the holy people;" there is their election; the " redeemed of the Lord;" that is plainly their redemption: they are also said to be " sought out;" which imports their effectual calling: and " a city not to be forsaken," which implies not less than perseverance. And they are here put in succession, as they fall in order of time: election is therefore called " a preparing unto glory," Rom. 9: 23.

' Before the world began.' The same thing, for brevity sake, is commonly called eternity; and in Scripture-phrase, from everlasting.

' According to his own good pleasure.' This shews the root of election; the great bottom-ground on which it is founded, exclusive to all things else, as being any way casual, contributary, or motive thereto.

II. For instances of a lower kind of election: consider here God's choosing or destinating certain persons by name (and some of them before they were born,) to signal and eminent service in the world; wherein they were patterns of the election we are treating of, and may well be accounted a collateral proof and evidence of it.

Abraham was pitched upon to be the root and father of God's peculiar people; whom he would own and honor above the nations of the world; and that in him " all families of the earth shall be blessed," Gen 12: 1—3. which contains a promise, that the Messiah, or Saviour of the world, should come of his posterity: a wonderful high honor; but what was there in Abraham, that might move God thus to prefer him above the rest of his kindred? was he any thing more to God? or had he served him better than other idolaters with whom he had lived? No, in no wise; and yet the Lord singled him forth, and called him alone, Isa. 51: 2. And, in truth, no other reason can be given for it, than what is given for his love to Abraham's posterity; " He loved them because he loved them," Deut. 7: 7, 8. Nor was he pitched upon to be the father of many nations,

nor Sarah to be the mother of them, for any natural fruit-
fulness in them above others; for Abraham's body was now
dead; and Sarah, besides her natural barrenness, was past
the age of child-bearing; which occasioned her to laugh at
the promise: for who, indeed, would make choice of a
dried stock, and barren soil, to begin his nursery with? in
such materials there is nothing to induce to it.

The same courses he was pleased to take with Abraham's
immediate seed: he takes not all of them; but, " in Isaac
shall thy seed be called," Gen. 21: 12. Thus, Isaac was
taken, and Ishmael left. And though Abraham's prayer
was heard for Ishmael, so as to have him blessed with outward things; yet, as to the main thing, God rejects him,
and resolves to establish his covenant with Isaac, chap. 17:
9. who was yet unborn.

The like he also doth by Isaac's children. " Jacob he
loved, but Esau he hated," Mal. 1: 2, 3. Rom. 9. which is
both the prophet's and apostle's exposition of those words,
" The elder shall serve the younger," Gen. 25: 23. and
this difference was put before they were born; yea, and entailed also upon their posterities: the one are " the people
of his wrath, against whom he hath indignation for ever,"
Mal. 1: 4. " their captivity shall not return." " When the
whole earth rejoiceth, they shall be dosolate," &c. Ezek.
35: 3. 14. but for Jacob, " the Lord will bring them back
to their own land, and plant them, and build them assur-
edly; and do them good with his whole heart," Jer. 31:
37. 41. But let it be observed, it was not Jacob's more
worthy demeanor, whether foreseen or acted, that procured
him the blessing. Esau did more for it than he, and more
sincerely: he hunted for venison, and for true venison,
such as his father loved; which he also makes ready, and
brings with speed, big with expectation of his blessing;
which also he seeks importunately, " with tears and bitter
crying," Gen. 27: 4, 5. 38. Now, what good things does
Jacob do to inherit the blessing? 1. He goes about to invade another's right; for the blessing belonged to the first-
born. 2. He seeks to pervert the known intention of his
father, which was to bless Esau. 3. He abuseth his father
with counterfeit venison. 4. He takes the name of God in
vain, to make his dispatch the more probable, Gen. 27: 28.
5: He seeks it by fraud, and downright lying: he clothes

his neck and hands with the kid's skin, and roundly affirms himself to be Esau (very improper means to obtain a blessing!) it need not be asked, which of the two's deportment was most deserving? One would easily conclude the blessing to be Esau's: but see the event! he that carries himself so unworthily, carries away the blessing; he that behaves himself dutifully to obtain it, is dismissed without it; and though his father blessed Jacob unwillingly, and by mistake, yet when he came to know it, he was so far from reversing what he had done, that he earnestly affirms it: " I have blessed him; yea, and he shall be blessed," Gen. 27: 33. Would we know, now, the reason of this strange (and according to men) irrational event? it was, " that the purpose of God according to election might stand, (the elder must serve the younger,) not of works, but of him that calleth," Rom. 9: 11. And it is wonderful to observe, how God ordered the whole course of this transaction, as intending it a full and pregnant example of eternal election: for it holds forth plainly the sovereignty of God over his creatures, in taking whom he will; the freeness of his grace in choosing those that are less deserving; the sure effect of his purposes; with his wise and certain ordering of things relating to his end: as also of his using means and instruments therein, quite besides the natural scope of them, and contrary to their own intendment.

Then for the Israelites:—This people the Lord chose in Abraham four hundred years before he publicly owned them: they are expressly termed, " an elect nation," as being separated from the rest of the world; " an holy, special, peculiar people unto God." He took them for " his own portion, the lot of his inheritance:" read his own words (for they are precious words with those to whom they appertain): " Ye shall be holy unto me; for I have severed you from other people, that ye should be mine," Levit. 20: 26. " The Lord thy God hath chosen thee to be a special people unto himself, above all the people that are on the face of the earth," Deut. 7: 6. The Lord this day hath avouched thee to be his peculiar people, and to make thee high above all nations," chap. 26: 18, 19. " The Lord had a delight in thy fathers, to love them, and he chose their seed after them, even you above all people," chap. 10:

15. &c. But were they as far above other nations in goodness, in greatness, or excellent demeanor? had they better improved their part in the common stock? and was that it which entitled them to this honor? No such matter, as appears, (1.) By the reason there assigned; "Ye shall be a peculiar treasure unto me, above all people, [for all the earth is mine,"] Exod. 19: 5. It is as if the Lord had said, there is no difference between you and other nations: all the earth is mine, and I may take where I will: I am not tied to any: I might take of them, and discard you; they cannot carry it more unworthily than you have done, and will do. I looked from heaven, and considered their works and yours, I see that your hearts are fashioned alike. And, (2.) Their after-demeanor did abundantly verify it; and the Lord foresaw it; "I knew that thou wouldst deal treacherously, and wast called a transgressor from the womb; that thou wouldst be obstinate, thy neck an iron sinew, and thy brow brass; and that thou wouldst do only evil from thy youth up," &c. Isa. 48: 4, 8. Jer. 32: 30. What then was the cause and motive of God's choosing them above others? It was his undeserved love and favor to them; "He loved them because he loved them," Deut. 7: 8. and 9: 4.

Come to David: God hath provided himself a king among Jesse's sons, and Samuel must go to anoint him: but it must be "him whom the Lord should name to him:" not the eldest or goodliest person; and therefore, says he (when they pass before him), "The Lord hath not chosen this, nor this, nor these, but David." It is true, the Lord did not mention David's name to Samuel; but he did what was equivalent; for when David comes in, he tells him, "This is he, anoint him." 1 Sam. 16: 1. 12. And observe, this [he] was the youngest, the meanest and most unlikely; scarce reckoned as one of the family; for he was not brought in amongst the rest. Then, note his circumstances; his employment was to keep the sheep: his exercise, what was it but such as is reckoned effeminate? he addicted himself to music. See also his complexion or constitution of body, white and ruddy; no promising character of a martial spirit: and yet this man (or rather this lad and stripling) thus qualified, and thus educated, he must be the captain of the Lord's host; who yet had the greatest enemies to deal with, and therefore had need of a man of courage and conduct to be over them. Well, let David's birth, complexion, employment, education, be what it will, ever so unlikely in all human respects, yet this David is, and must be the man whom the Lord will honor to rule his people, to fight their battles, and to do exploits. In this choice the Lord w, s pleased to set by whatever is taking with men: " he seeth not as man seeth," that is he regards not men for their natural accomplishments: if for any thing, it must be (probably) for some excellent endowment of the mind; and that of wisdom is of as weighty consideration in the choice of a prince, as any other: but this is no inducement or motive to God; " he respects not any that are wise in heart:" Job 37: 24. and if he did, it was not here to be had. David had no prince-like qualities above his brethren, until afterwards; as is plainly intimated in these words, " The Spirit of the Lord came upon him from that day forward," 1 Sam. 16: 13.

Then for Jeremy: The Lord ordains him to be a prophet, sets him over nations and kingdoms, commissionates him to root out and pull down, to build and to plant, &c. why? what had Jeremy done, that the Lord should call him to so imperial a work? Sure no great matter; for this he was ordained to before he was born; " Before I formed thee in the belly, I knew thee; I sanctified thee, and ordained thee a prophet:" it also appears by his own confession, how unfit he was for such a work: and how unwilling; " I cannot speak, for I am a child," Jer. 1: 5, 6.

Another instance may be Cyrus: This man was decreed to a great and noble work. It was, in brief, to destroy the golden monarchy; to break in pieces the hammer of the whole earth, to release God's people out of captivity, and to build his temple: and this was prophesied of him more than an hundred years before Cyrus was born. The Lord styles him his anointed, his elect, his shepherd, and one that should " perform all his pleasure:" and he calls him by his name too; which is twice repeated, as a thing to be remarked: and to enforce it the more, he adds a note of narrower observance; " I have called thee, even thee by name," Isa. 44: 48. and 45: 1, 2, 3, 4, 5, 6. 13.

Was Cyrus thus chosen, because he would be a puissant

prince? or did the Lord make him puissant and victorious, because appointed to such a work? hear what the Lord himself (who best knows the ground of his own designation) says of him: "Thus saith the Lord to his anointed, to Cyrus, whose right hand I have holden," (that is, I gave him strength, and taught him how to use it) " I will loose the loins of kings, and open to him the two-leaved gates; I will go before him:—I will break in pieces the gates of brass and cut in sunder the bars of iron," &c. But what shall Cyrus have done, that the great God should do him this honor? he did not so much as know the Lord; which is also twice repeated, as a matter worthy our observation, Isa. 45: 1—5.

Lastly. PAUL: The Lord from heaven commissions him his preacher-general among the Gentiles; to bear his name before Kings; to maul and ransack the devil's kingdom; and to turn the world upside-down; witness his doings at Ephesus, Athens, and other places. And this he was called to, even while in the heat of his persecuting fury against that name, which he is now sent to preach: and that there was no motive on Paul's part, himself is witness, where speaking of that his call, he ascribes it to the pleasure and power of God, as much as he doth his natural birth, Gal. 1: 15. The original of all which is couched in that word, " He is a chosen vessel unto me," Acts 9: 15.

I might also bring in the stories of Samson, Josiah, John Baptist, and others to the same effect, but that time would fail. Now these instances may not be valued as historical relations only; (that would be too narrow a meaning for them), but according to the scripture way of inferring, and improving to spiritual uses; and so there will be a good preparatory proof of the business in hand: For if there be an election personal unto things of less eminent concernment; and that so long before some of the persons were in being; if also there be an absoluteness in God's decrees concerning these; how much more in matters of eternal weight! And if the Lord did not look out of himself for the moving consideration on which he selected those persons to their several honors, and achievements, (and if he had, he should have found none,) much less an election to eternal salvation, and union with himself, be founded in the creature. Doth God take care for an ox? from the less to the greater is a scriptural way of arguing, and proves strongly.

I come now to a more direct and positive proving the proposition, wherein my present scope is not so much to prove that there is an election, as what this election is; viz. how it is qualified and circumstanced: and this respects the objects of election, with the manner, time, and motives of it. And yet, as introductive to these, it may be expedient to touch on the other; and so, for the clearer discussion thereof, I cast the proposition into six branches.

I. That there is an Election of men to Salvation.
II. That this Election is absolute.
III. That it is personal.
IV. That it is from Eternity.
V. That the Elect were chosen in Christ.
VI. That Election is founded upon grace.

These being made good by positive scripture, or arguments taken thence; it will not much concern us what is alleged to the contrary: They are of the deep things of God, and discoverable only by scripture light; and therefore in vain are they brought to any other touchstone; for who hath known the mind of the Lord, or can, but as himself hath been pleased to reveal it?

I. There is an Election of Men to Salvation.

That is, there are some, a certain remnant, that shall be saved: and this by virtue of election.

This is clearly implied in those noted and compendious sentences, vessels of mercy, afore prepared unto glory, Rom. 9: 23. The election hath obtained, Rom. 11: 7. The Lord added to the church such as should be saved, Acts 2: 47. And as many as were ordained to eternal life, believed, Acts 13: 48. But more expressly in Rom. 11: 5. There is a remnant according to the election of grace, 1 Thess. 5: 9. God hath not appointed us unto wrath; but to obtain salvation: And 2 Thess. 2: 13. God hath from the beginning chosen you to salvation, &c. And these are called the election, or party of elect ones; as those circumcised, are called the circumcision; and the angels that stood, are distinguished from those that fell, by the title of elect. They are also said to be chosen vessels, vessels of mercy; as

those that are left, vessels of wrath, and sons of perdition:
the scripture still sets them forth by distinguishing charac-
ters.

1. As a party separate from the world; I (says Christ)
have chosen you out of the world, John 15: 19. I pray
not for the world, but for them which thou hast given me,
John 17: 9. And they are not of the world, even as I am
not of the world, John 17: 16. Unto you it is given to
know the mystery of the kingdom of God; but unto them
without all things are done in parables, Mark 4: 11. Of
Jacob and Esau, (who were an evident type of this separation) it is said of Rebeckah, "two nations are in thy
womb, and two manner of people," Gen. 25: 23. And of
Jacob's posterity, "the people shall dwell alone and shall
not be reckoned among the nations," Numb. 23: 9. And
this "people (says God) have I formed for myself," Isa. 43:
21. "These are the people of his holiness; the rest are
adversaries," chap. 63: 18. 2 Pet. 2: 9.

2. As men of another race or kindred; and as springing
from another root. "We are of God, and the whole world
lieth in wickedness," 1 John 5: 19. (or in that wicked one
as their root and head:) "He that is of God heareth God's
words; ye therefore hear them not, because ye are not of
God," John 7: 47. The one party are said to be "children of light," the other of the night, 1 Thess. 5: 5. the
one of God, the other of the world, 1 John 4: 4—6. the
one is from above, the other from beneath: John 7: 23.
God is the Father of the one, and the devil of the other,
chap. 8: 41, 42. 44.

3. As men subject to another head. "We are thine,"
says the church to God; "thou never bearest rule over
them," Isa. 63: 19. "all that the Father giveth me (saith
Christ) shall come to me, John 6: 37. my sheep hear my
voice; I know them, and they follow me, and a stranger
they will not follow," John 10: 27. and this, "because one
is their master, even Christ," Matt. 23: 8. Of others, he
saith, that "they will not come unto him," John 5: 40.
The one party are followers of the Lamb, the other of the
prince of darkness, led captive by him at his will.

4. As belonging to another world. "The good seed
are the children of the kingdom," Matth. 13: 38. and they
are distinguished from the children of this world, as a par-

ty " accounted worthy to obtain the world to come," Luke
20: 35. and accordingly we find, that none are admitted
into the new Jerusalem but " whose names are found written in the book of life, Rev. 21: 27. and whose name " soever was not written there, was cast into the lake of fire,"
chap. 20: 15. On the same account Judas is said to go
to his own place, Acts 1: 25. and the elect into " the kingdom prepared for them," Matth. 25: 35. I shall bring but
one only argument for proof of this branch, and it is of such
weight, that there needs not another, namely, that except
the Lord had thus reserved a remnant, no flesh had been
saved: the whole world would have been as Sodom, Isa.
1: 9.

II. Election is absolute.

In this are two things of great import, irrevocable-
ness, and independency. The decree is irrevocable
on God's part, and independent as to human performances.
The Lord will not go back from his purpose to save his
people; nor shall their unworthiness or aversion make void,
or hinder his most gracious purpose. And hence those
various expressions of the same thing, namely, predestinate, ordain, prepare, appoint, have nothing subjoined that
is like a condition. There is indeed a kind of conditions (or rather qualifications) that must, and always do,
precede the final completion of election; as " repentance
towards God, and faith towards our Lord Jesus Christ:"
which therefore may be called conditions of salvation;
but not so to election.

Election is the great fundamental institute of the gospel:
it is that which in human states is called the supreme law;
which is both irreversible in itself, and requires that all
inferior administrations may be accommodated thereto: so
the salvation of God's elect being the highest law of the
heavenly state and kingdom, must on the same (and firmer)
ground remain inviolable. It is that for which all things
else have being; the plot whereby God designs to himself,
the highest glory, and for which he hath been at such cost,
that should his design miscarry, the whole creation could
not countervail the damage. He could not therefore,—for
God cannot deny himself,—I say, he could not so contrive
the grandest design of his glory, as that it should ever need

to be revoked or altered: nor could he leave it obnoxious
to disappointment; as it must have been, if ventured on a
created bottom: yea, it behooved him, as supreme lawgiver,
so to determine and subjugate all, that the great end of all
might not be frustrated.   And thus any prudent founder
of a state would do, if the utmost of his skill and power
would extend to it: but from their defectiveness in these,
the best founded states on earth are subject to mutation:
princes die, and their thoughts perish; their minds alter
and depart from their first intentions; successors drive a
contrary interest; unlooked for accidents entangle them;
foreign enemies encroach upon them, and obstruct their
work: or the people's own folly may be such, as to mar
and defeat the best laid designs for their own good.   Human affairs are exposed to thousand incidents, which human
prudence can neither prevent nor provide against.   But
with God it is not so: no event can be new to him: " He
declares the end from the beginning," Isa. 46: 10. his
judgment and purpose cannot alter, " he is of one mind, and
who can turn him?" Job 23: 13. he is also immortal, and
" the thoughts of his heart stand fast to all generations,"
Psal. 33: 11. no creature can seclude itself from his government; " In his hand is the soul of every living thing,"
Psal. 145: 16. yea, the most casual (to us) and opposite
emergencies, are by his power, and wisdom reducible to
his purpose, and cannot resist their being made subservient
to his will.   And this may be one reason why election is
so often said to be " from the beginning, and from the
foundation of the world," namely, to show that whatever
should be in time, should be subordinate to election, which
is all one as to make it absolute.   And further, this absoluteness may be evinced by such arguments as these:

Arg. I. If election were not absolute, it would be but
after the covenant of works; which being conditional, how
soon was it broken, even by one who had power to keep it!
and if man in that honor did not abide in it, how should he
now, when so strong a bias is grown upon his heart, that he
runs counter ever since? Gen. 6: 5. "If there had been a
law given that could have given life, righteousness should
have been by the law," Gal. 3: 2. which shows, that the
new covenant does more for us than the old; for it
giveth life; and then it must give the performance of the

condition which that life depends upon: it also shows, that the first covenant did not give life, and that it failed because it was conditional. The law shows our duty, but giveth not wherewith to perform it: the new covenant does both, by writing the law in the heart. All under the covenant of works are without God, without Christ, without hope, Eph. 2: 12. and this, because strangers to the covenant of grace, or grace of election. If therefore the elect shall be in a better state than before, their election must be absolute: and that it might be so the new covenant was made with Christ on their behalf; and is, " that grace given us in him before the world began," 2 Tim. 1: 9. Titus 1: 2.

Arg. II. Election must be absolute; because whatever can be supposed the condition of it, is a part of the thing itself: much like that promise of God to Abraham, " To thy seed will I give this land," Gen. 12: 7. In which promise the Lord undertakes as well to give Abraham a seed to inherit that land, as that land to his seed: and accordingly we find that the next head of that seed was born by virtue of the promise, Gal. 4: 23. 28. so the whole course and series of things conducing to the final accomplishment of election, is included in it, and ascertained by it; and that with such firmness and security, as if the end itself had been attained when the decree was made; as, namely, redemption from sin, effectual calling, and perseverance to glory (of which more fully under those heads); which also seems to be the meaning of the apostle, where he makes eternal life itself to be the substance of the promise: " And this is the promise that he hath promised us, even eternal life," 1 John 2: 25.

Arg. III. It must be absolute, because by such an election only can salvation be ensured. This bottom Adam had not in his primitive state; he was made upright, but his continuing in that state, depended upon his well using of what he had, without any additional help. In him may be seen the utmost that created grace of itself can do, even in a state of perfection; unto which being left, how soon did he degenerate, and come to ruin? and all his posterity would have run the same course, if placed in his stead; as we know they have done (one by one) notwithstanding all the helps which are given in common unto men. And it is no wonder, since now they have so strong a bent unto

evil, which Adam had not.   And if there be any advantage
cast in, (which some do affirm, and call it the new covenant,) the more is our doctrine confirmed: for the more
helps they have, if yet they fall short, (as they do,) the
more evident it is, that nothing short of such an election
will secure them.   An example of this we had in the old
world; who, by their natural ingenuity, and long lives to
improve it, together with Noah's six score years' preaching,
and the Spirit's striving, were not led unto God, but still
grew from bad to worse, until all "the imaginations of
their hearts were only evil, and that continually," Gen. 6:
8.   And this was not the case only of some, but of the
whole race universally: "All flesh had corrupted his way,"
chap. 6: 12. It is true, that Noah was found righteous; and
as true it is, that election was it that made him so.   Noah
"found grace in the eyes of the Lord," ver. 8. in the same
sense that Paul obtained mercy, 1 Tim. 1: 16. viz. by mercy's obtaining, or taking hold of him.   It may also be
seen in the people of Israel; who, over and above their
common and natural grace, had many helps and additions
that others had not: "the Lord dealt not so with any nation as with them," Psal. 147: 19, 20. and yet the generality of them so bad, that they justified their sister Sodom,
Ezek. 16: 51.

The first covenant thus failing, such was the grace of
our Lord (foreseeing it) as to determine on a second, or
new covenant; by which he would fix and secure a remnant,
and that infallibly: and hence it is termed, The covenant
of grace, as not depending at all upon works; and this is
that grace that saves, and "reigns to eternal life," Rom.
5: 21. Eph. 2: 5. 8.   And these are the "sure mercies of
David," recorded in the 55th of Isaiah: it is the absoluteness of it that makes it a better covenant.

Arg. IV. There is the same reason for the absoluteness
of men's election, as of Christ's. That man, or human
body, which the second person was to assume and unite to
himself, was not ordained to that union upon any condition
whatever; as, namely, if he should fulfil all righteousness,
destroy the devil, dissolve his works, and make atonement
for sin; for these he could not have done without that
union: and that his ordination thereunto was absolute, appears by Heb. 10: 5. "A body hast thou prepared me;"

and Luke 1: 35. " That holy thing which shall be born of thee shall be called the Son of God," Matt. 1:21. " He shall save his people from their sins." In which places the absoluteness of the decree for that man's being united to the Son of God, is evidently set forth. And that our election (as to this circumstance of it) holds proportion with that of Christ, you shall see more fully afterwards. Take only (at present) those gracious words, which, doubtless, he uttered with great satisfaction to himself in the 17th of John, ver. 21. " Thou hast loved them as thou hast loved me."

Arg. V. It was requisite that election should be absolute, because of the absoluteness of God's decree touching the death of his Son, unto which he was fore-ordained unrepealably, 1 Pet. 1: 20. and all that he saved before he suffered, were saved on the credit of that decree, Rom. 3:25, 26. The scripture also says plainly that he was "the Lamb slain from the foundation of the world," Rev. 13: 8. and that it was not possible that cup should pass from him, Matth. 26: 39. 42. And if it be a thing below the prudence of men to lay down the price without securing the purchase; then, surely, the wisdom of God could not determine the death of his Son for men's salvation, and yet leave the salvation of those very men at an uncertainty: which it must have been, if their election were not absolute.

Arg. VI. *Lastly*, It might also be argued from the nature of divine promises; which are patterns, or declarative copies of the decree. Now the promises touching spiritual blessings are absolute; they are of that word which is "for ever settled in heaven," Psal. 119: 89. See the promises of sending Christ to be a redeemer, Gen. 3: 15. the Holy Ghost to sanctify, and lead into all truth, John 16: 13. to sprinkle clean water upon them; to give them a new heart; to cause them to walk in his statutes; that he will be their God, and they shall. be his people, and shall not depart from him, Jer. 24: 7. Ezek. 36: 26. that if they sin, he will chastise them with the rods of men, but his everlasting kindness he will not take from them, Psal. 89: 30—34. and that at last he will " present them faultless before the presence of his glory," Jude 24. These all, with others of like tenor, are delivered in positive and absolute terms, without any shew of reservation, proviso, or condition. And if these, which are transcripts of the decree, be absolute, it follows that the decree also is the same: and on this ground it is the apostle stands when he challengeth all the world to nullify God's election, Rom. 8: 33, 34. which he could not have done, had not election been sovereignly absolute.

    III. Election is personal: and,
    IV. It is from eternity.

These two I put together in proof, because they are frequently joined in scripture. It was not the whole lump of mankind that was the object of election; neither was election, as some say, a decree to elect such as should happen to be thus and so qualified: but certain determinate persons were chosen by name, or singled out from among the rest, and ordained to eternal life. Our Saviour styles them the " men that were given him out of the world," John 17: 6. and they were given him by name, as well as by number; and by those names he knows them, chap. 10: 3. 14. It is not unworthy our deepest attention, how the Lord takes notice of the names of his people; as intending it, doubtless, a signal token of the special regard he hath to their persons. He therefore tells Moses, " I know thee by thy name," Exod. 33: 17. It is an appropriating of them to himself, Isa. 43: 1. " I have called thee by name; thou art mine." Sometimes also, when he calls to those he eminently owns, he doubles their name by repetition: thus to his friend Abraham, Gen. 22: 11. To Moses, his servant, Exod. 3: 4. and others. But I find no instance of his speaking so to other men: and these, I suppose, are recorded as worthy of special remark; and that it is no light matter (much less to be scoffed at, as it is by some frothy spirits,) that the elect were chosen by name, and that their names are written in heaven. And that it was transacted from eternity, is evident from John 17: 23, 24. Eph. 1: 4. Rev. 13: 8. and 17: 8. and other scriptures.

    The personality of election, with its eternity, may be evinced by such arguments as these:

    Arg. I. From the example of Christ's election. It was not a person uncertain that was to be Lord and Christ; but the second person in human nature: and this capacity he sustained from everlasting, Prov. 8: 23.—31. 1 Pet. 1: 20. Nor was it any body which he might assume, but the very

numerical body that was prepared for him, Heb. 10: 5.
Psal. 40: 7. "And this very person he loved before the
foundation of the world," John 17: 24. It is worthy of
observation, how particular the decree was, even in things
circumstantial, to our Lord Christ; as that he should come
of Abraham's stock, of Judah's tribe, of David's lineage,
be conceived of a virgin, born at Bethlehem; and this when
the sceptre was departing from Judah; that he should be
buffeted, scourged, spit upon, hanged upon a tree, his
hands and feet pierced; that gall and vinegar should be
given him to drink; that a bone of him should not be
broken (even while on both sides of him others' were;) that
his garments should be parted, and lots cast on his vesture;
as also that he should rise again the third day, &c. And
that these were all decreed, appears by the prophecies of
them, which are the decree exemplified, or drawn out of
the register. As touching his resurrection, it is said expressly in Psal. 2: 7. " I will declare the decree:" and the
same is as true of all the rest. And if the election of the
head was personal, and from eternity, why not theirs that
should make up his body, since they did as really exist
then, as the human nature of Christ did? Besides, it was
very agreeable that he and they should both be appointed
together: for he could not be a head, but with respect to
a body: and that they were expressly determined of, appears by Psalm 139: 16. " In thy book were all my members written, when as yet there was none of them." If
you say, that was meant of David's members; I answer,
that if God thought the members of an earthly body worthy
his registering, he could not be less particular and exact
about the mystical body of his son: besides, David was his
type.

Christ also was ordained to be a Saviour, and that by his
death, and both " from the foundation of the world,"
1 Pet. 1: 20. It was therefore expedient then also to be
determined how many, and who in particular, should have
salvation by him. He was not to die for himself; but for
those whose security he undertook. Now it is not a thing
proper to speak of security, or bail, but with respect to a
debtor, or offender; and that debtor or offender must be
known too, and named, or else the entering of the bail is
an insignificant act; especially where the surety hath no

debt or default of his own to be charged with. Our Lord
and Saviour did not make his soul an offering for somebody's sins, but uncertain whose. Aaron knew whose
trespasses he offered for: their names were graven on his
breast-plate: not their national name or qualification (namely, Israelite, or believer,) but their personal names, Reuben,
Simeon, Levi, &c. So had our great high priest, or he
could not have made atonement for us: and that place, Rev.
13: 8. points at the same time for both. Those words
" from the foundation of the world," do refer as well to
the writing of their names in the book of life, as to the
lamb's being slain; as is evident from the 8th verse of the
17th chapter, where, deciphering those ".who shall wonder
after the beast," he says, they are such whose " names
were not written in the book of life, [from the foundation
of the world,"] as were theirs who followed the Lamb, and
whom " God had from the beginning chosen to salvation,"
2 Thess. 2: 13.

Arg. II. The design of God, in the death of Christ,
could not otherwise be secured. Had the design been, to
purchase salvation for believers, without ascertaining the
persons that should believe, it had been uncertain whether
any would be saved, because uncertain whether any would
believe. If certain that some would believe, this certainty
must be decreed: for nothing future could be certain otherwise. And if it was decreed that some should believe,
the individuals of that some must be decreed also: for faith
is the gift of God, and could not be foreseen in any, but
whom he had decreed to give it unto. Which laid together,
are a good demonstration, that those Christ should die for,
were as well pre-ordained, as that he should die for them;
and that definitely, and by name.

Arg. III. It may be further argued, from the Father's
" preparing a kingdom from the foundation of the world,"
and mansions or places in it. To prepare the way of this
argument; consider the punctuality of God's disposements
in things of a lower concern: he did not create the earth
in vain (that is, to stand empty and void, as at its first formation;) nor the several quarters thereof to be inhabited indefinitely, by some nation or other, who should happen to
get possession of them, but " he divided to the nations
their inheritance, and the bounds of their habitation,"

Deut. 32: 8. Acts 17: 26. Mount Seir was given to Esau, and Ar to the children of Lot, chap. 2: 5. 9. each nation had its limits staked out, and this from the days of old. And if we may distinguish of acts in God, and of time in eternity; his purpose to form and bring forth those nations, must needs be as early as to create and furnish those parts of the world which they should inhabit. Now, earthly settlements being of trivial moment to the heavenly mansions; it seems a good consequent, that if yet particular nations were fore-appointed for particular provinces on earth; much more should particular persons be designed for those particular mansions in heaven: and if either were appointed first, it must be the person: for, " the sabbath was made for man, and not man for the sabbath." Heaven was made at the beginning of the world; but election was before.

The domestics of God's house, or place of glory, are a sacred state or order of kings and priests; and each individual person hath his place or apartment set out for him. Those glorious places were not prepared for believers indefinitely; but for certain determinate persons particularly: the twelve apostles shall have their twelve thrones, and each one his own. This is evident by our Saviour's answer to the mother of Zebedee's children: " To sit on my right hand, and on my left, is not mine to give; but it shall be given to them for whom it is prepared of my father," Mat. 20: 23. If for believers indefinitely, why not for these two brethren, especially since they first made request for them? The truth is, those places were not now to be disposed of; it was determined who should have them long before, even " from the foundation of the world," chap. 25: 34. The scope of this answer was not to shew that the places requested were prepared for believers indefinitely (for these were believers who made request for them;) but that they were appointed for certain particular persons, and they must have them. Much might be added, in confirmation hereof; but by these (I hope) it is clear, that election is personal, and from eternity.

V. Election is in Christ: or, the elect were chosen in Christ.

It was requisite the new covenant should have a head

and mediator, as well as the old; that righteousness and
life might flow from him into all the elect seed, as sin and
death had done from Adam: in which respect, Christ and
he are set forth as parallels, in Rom. 3: from verse 12. to
21. The benefits which the elect were chosen unto, they
are made partakers of, by their union with Christ: he is
the root, in whom all fulness dwells. Not only the foundation on which the church is built; but the rock which affords all the spiritual materials of the heavenly temple;
even the cement that holds one part to another, and the
whole to himself: and this by virtue of the decree. For
we are to consider that there is a decretive union before
the actual; and the one influenceth the other into being;
and that as really, as the determined death of Christ did
the salvation of those who died before him. Though Christ
be not the cause of election, yet he is the grand means,
by whom we obtain the blessedness we were chosen unto:
by him it is, that " we have access unto that grace wherein
we stand," Rom. 5: 2. And we shall find, that the epistles generally, when they speak of the great things relating
to salvation, do still bring in Christ, as the person principally concerned about it. Salvation, indeed, is a gift; it
is perfectly free; yet not to be had, but in Christ: " It
comes upon us through his righteousness; as by one man's
disobedience many were made sinners; so by the righteousness of one (by means of their oneness with him) shall
many be made righteous," Rom. 5: 18, 19. Mankind (by
their apostacy in Adam) had destroyed in themselves the
whole of that principle which would have led them to God,
as their life and blessedness: and had, withal, contracted
such an enmity against him, and repugnancy to all over-
tures for returning to him (and this gulph was so fixed,) as
would for ever have kept God and us asunder, had not that
blessed project of choosing in Christ been set on foot to
dissolve it. It could not be done by any created power;
nor could creatures so much as propound a way for it: and
if they could, who durst so harden himself, as to mention
the thing which only could do it! But the great God,
blessed for ever, he finds out a way for it: and the same
love that ordained to eternal life, would also put it in such
a way, as should surely take effect. And to this end
(namely, that those ordained to salvation might be both

rightfully entitled thereto, and successively brought into it,) they were put into Christ by election: he was the chief and eminent elect one; the first-born, and prince of the family: and all the elect besides were given to him, as younger brethren, to be maintained upon his inheritance. It is plain to him that reads, that the whole of salvation was laid upon Christ; that he bears up the pillars of it, and that all shoulders else had been too weak: he is both the means and centre, by whom, and in whom, God will have all things gathered together in one. He was made " God with us," that we might be made one in God; as appears by the scope of his prayer in the 17th of John. In him the father is well pleased; and out of him there is nothing pleasing to God, or eternally good for men: we are therefore said to be chosen in him, Ephes. 1: 4. to be called in him, Phil. 3: 14. to be created in him, Ephes. 2: 10. to be preserved in him, Jude 2. and in him to be blessed with all spiritual blessings, Ephes. 1: 4. Blessings in themselves would not be so to us, if not in Christ; and being in him, all things are turned into blessings to us: for now nothing can come at us, but as coming through him: and whatever so comes, is tinctured by his divine excellence, and made propitious to us: and hereby it is, that the thing we were chosen unto, is effectually and infallibly provided for. There are divers good reasons and ends for God's choosing the elect in Christ. As,

Arg. I. That by bringing in man's restoration this way, he might, as it were, baffle his great adversary, and out-shoot him in his own bow: and it well became the wisdom and grace of God thus to do. The devil thought, by poisoning the root, to vitiate and ruin the whole stock and progeny; and he failed not of his design. The Lord would therefore retrieve that ruin, by putting his elect into an head incapable of degeneracy; and not only recover them, but bring them into a better estate than they had lost: he would set up a man that should be too hard for the devil, and be able both to destroy him, and dissolve his works; and he hath accordingly done it. In which method of man's recovery, is a great answerableness to the method of his ruin: and it is a thing the Lord would have us to mind, as appears by the parallel before mentioned, Rom. 3: 12—21.

Arg. II. That by shewing us his righteousness in the way and manner of our recovery, we might the more readily subscribe to his righteousness in the imputation of Adam's sin: for, without a sight and knowledge of the one, we cannot, with any heartiness, submit to the other. Hence, some, in their too bold arguings against election, have alleged, that what Adam did was without their consent: but will they abide by this allegation? In the matter of Achan, each single person stood in the place of the whole nation; and so on the trespass of one, wrath came upon all; yet had not that confident people the hardiness to plead, that Achan's act concerned not them; they did not consent to it: but let them take heed, lest while they thus excuse themselves from Adam's sin, they do not, by parity of reason, seclude themselves from the righteousness of Christ: since the setting up the second Adam was as much without their consent as the first.

Arg. III. If the elect had not been in Christ, the satisfaction he undertook for sinners could not have availed them. As Adam's sin could not have been ours, if not in him; so neither the righteousness of Christ, if not in him. Divine justice could not have punished him for us, nor absolved us through him; we could not have been justified and reconciled by the blood of his cross, had not he sustained our persons, and stood in our stead; another's act cannot be mine, either in profit or loss, if there be not a legal oneness between us.

Arg. IV. If not in Christ, we could not have been sanctified. The lump was sanctified in the first-fruits; and so is the church in Christ, 1 Cor. 1: 2. The wild olive-nature could not be suppressed and changed, but by grafting into the true: " For if the first fruit be holy, the lump is also holy: and if the root be holy, so are the branches," Rom. 11: 16. A man cannot be naturally born, but from Adam, as his natural head; and as impossible it is to be born again, without a like relative union to Christ, as our spiritual head. There is no being a new creature, but by being in Christ: " They that are joined unto the Lord (and they only,) are one spirit with him," 1 Cor. 6: 17. 2 Cor. 5: 17. The branch must be in the vine, before its sap can be derived into it: he that sanctifieth, and they that are sanctified, must be one. There must be a contact (a touching of him,) before this virtue can come from him: for the promises being all made to Christ, Gal. 3: 16. cannot descend to us, but as being in him; it is that makes us heirs of promise: the Holy Ghost, in whom all promises are virtually contained, " is shed upon us through Jesus Christ," Tit. 3: 10.

Arg. V. *Lastly*, By this choosing in Christ, salvation itself is invincibly secured; and could not otherwise be. The first Adam had but a conditional life; it depended on his own personal obedience, and therefore subject to losing: and had he kept it, he could have derived to us but the same that himself had; which still must have been a mutable state (for this Adam, while a public person, and as such could not be said to be in Christ; if he had, he should not have fallen:) but the second Adam hath life in himself: " For as the Father hath life in himself, so hath he given to the Son to have life in himself," John 5: 26. and that absolutely: he is the " prince of life," Acts 3: 15. and implantation into him inspires his branches with his own life. And " the law of that spirit of life in him, makes free from the law of sin and death," Rom. 8: 2. " He that thus hath the Son, hath life," 1 John 5: 12. " and shall have it more abundantly," John 10: 10. " Because he lives, they shall live also," chap. 14: 19. It is a bottom that cannot miscarry; as they are sanctified in Christ Jesus, so in him they are preserved, Jude 1. To this end, " it pleased the Father, that in him all fulness should dwell," Col. 1: 19. and to put those he would save into him as their head; that being incessantly influenced from an immortal root, they might effectually be kept from withering and falling off; and grow up to that state and glory they were designed for by election. This is the grand record, and ground of our safety, " that God hath given to us eternal life, and this life is in his Son," 1 John 5: 11.

Having gone these steps towards the compass and extent of election, it concerns us to know where this broad river hath its head; what rock it is that this immense fabric is built upon; lest we give the honor of it to another; or endanger ourselves by settling on a wrong foundation: to shew which is the scope of the last particular under this general head: namely,

VI. That election is founded upon grace; or, the good
pleasure of God's will is the only original cause and
motive of election.

Election is a " promotion that cometh neither from the
east, nor from the west, or south," but from God; who,
as he puts down one, and sets up another: so some he
chooseth, and others he passeth by, as seemeth him good;
and none can say to him, What doest thou? or, Why hast
thou made me thus? for election, as it always supposeth a
greater number out of which the choice is made, so an
arbitrary power in him that chooseth, to choose whom he
will, without giving account to any for what he doeth. But
the ground or motive of divine election is very different
from the manner of men; for they commonly pitch upon
things for some natural aptness of them for their works:
they will not take a knotty, cross-grained, or wind-shaken
piece of timber, to make a pillar of state: but the Lord
pitches upon such (and such to choose,) the poor, base,
weak, foolish things of the world; the worst of men, and
chief of sinners: the instances of Paul, Manassah, Mary
Magdalen, and others, make it evident: and of these he is
pleased to make lively images of his son, and pillars for
the house of God (columns of state indeed!) whereon to
write his own name; to manifest thereby his sovereignty,
holiness, wisdom, power, righteousness, and free grace to
eternity.

The Lord's way and method in bringing his sons to glory,
is the best demonstration of the right order of causes; for
though there be a concurrence of many things, as causes
and effects, one of another, yet, if observed in their order,
they will still lead us up to the good pleasure of God, as
first and supreme, and perfectly independent. And this I
term the only original cause of election, to shut out all
works and worthiness of men from being any way causal,
influential, or motive thereto; and so from sharing in the
glory of God's grace, which he is very jealous of, and will
not impart to any. The New Testament current runs evidently this way, making the whole of salvation, both means
and end, to depend expressly on the divine will. " It is
your Father's good pleasure to give you the kingdom," Luke

12: 32. " Thou hast hid these things from the wise, and revealed them to babes; for so it seemed good in thy sight," chap. 10: 21. " A remnant according to the election of grace," Rom. 11: 5. " Predestinate to the adoption of children, according to the good pleasure of his will," Eph. 1: 5. " Redemption also, and forgiveness of sins, according to the riches of his grace," Eph. 1: 7. (the same grace that elected:) the making known the mystery of his will: this also is according to that [his good pleasure] " which he hath purposed in himself," ver. 9. Yea, all the operations of God, whether for us, upon us, or by us, they all have their rise from the same spring, and are carried by the same rule: " He worketh all things after the counsel of his own will," ver. 11. And for the Old Testament, you have it sufficiently exemplified there in the instances before given, and especially touching the ground of God's love to the people of Israel (who, in that respect, were the archetype of the spiritual election;) namely, that " his own good pleasure" was the only cause of his choosing them above other nations: " He loved them, because he loved them," Deut. 7: 8. and 9: 4. and 10: 15. And, which is yet more, the election of Christ himself was of grace: " It pleased the father, that in him (the man Jesus) should all fulness dwell," Col. 1: 19.

And good reasons there are, why election should be founded on grace; and why it could not, with respect either to God's glory, or the elect's security, be founded otherwise. And

Arg. I. Is from the sovereignty of God; whose will being the supreme law, admits not a co-ordinacy, much less will it stand with sovereign power to be regulated by the will of another. That would be a contradiction to sovereignty; for that which regulates, must be superior to that which is regulated by it. Sovereign princes, to shew their prerogative, affirm their acts of grace to be of their own mere motion: and their grants are reputed the more authentic, being so expressed. The like we find in scripture frequently ascribed to God; that " he will have mercy on whom he will have mercy," Rom. 9: 18. that " he worketh all things," (not by motives from without, but) " after the counsel of his own will," Eph. 1: 11. that " it is not of man's willing or running; but of God, who sheweth

mercy," Rom. 9: 16. and, indeed, his own mere motion
was both a nobler and firmer consideration than any desert
on the creature's part. When the world had been drowned
for their obdurate impenitency, the few that remained were
as bad as before; and those that should come after, the law
foresaw would be the same. One would think, now, the
natural result of this experiment should be, " I will utterly cut them off, and be troubled with them no more;"
but the Lord's thoughts are not as our thoughts; he argues
and concludes in another mode: " I will not again any
more curse the ground for man's sake." And he is pleased
to give the same reason here why he will not, as before
why he would; as is seen by comparing Gen. 6: 5. and 7.
with chap. 8: 21. See also the instance of God's dealing
with Ephraim; he was wroth with him, and smote him; and
Ephraim, so far from relenting, that " he went on frowardly," (that is, stubbornly, as resolved in his course;)
" I hid me (says the Lord,) and was wroth," Isa. 57: 16.
this, one would think, if Ephraim had had in him but a
spark of ingenuity, or love to himself, should have moved
him to alter his course: but what cares Ephraim? he still
kept the same way; and it was the way of his heart: not
an inconsiderate pet, or sudden temptation, but natural
and fixed: all which the Lord sees and considers; and having laid all together, resolves to heal him, and " restore
comforts to him," Isa. 57: 18. On the other hand, those
good souls " who feared the Lord, and obeyed the voice
of his servants, they yet walked in darkness, and had no
light," Isa. 50: 10. Ye may be sure, they would gladly
have understood their condition, namely, that they were
such as " feared the Lord;" their will could not be wanting to a thing so greatly importing their comfort; nor were
they idle in seeking for it; they walked, though in the dark,
but could not walk themselves out of it; they are still as
they were; they had no light. By these different examples
it is evident that the sovereignty of God still keeps the
throne, and his dispensations of mercy, whether in purpose or in act, are not governed by the wills of men: they
are things too low to be counsellors to God. And if it be
thus in things of a lower concernment, much more in that
great business of eternal election, which is the sublimest
act of sovereign power: for non-election is not a punish-

ment, but the withholding of a free favor, which God, as a sovereign lord, may justly deny to one sinner, while he gives it to another. And yet this hinders not, but that every man, at last, shall be judged according to his works.

Arg. II. Election must be founded only upon grace, because grace and works are inconsistent in the cause of salvation. The scripture is very cautious of admitting any thing as a concomitant with grace in this matter; yea, although it be a thing that doth always accompany grace, and that without which a man cannot be saved. The apostle puts them in opposition, and is very intent upon the argument, as a thing of great moment, in Romans 11: where, first, he shews, that amidst the general defection of the Jewish nation, there still was a remnant whom God had reserved: these he terms " the foreknown," ver. 2. and in the 7th verse he calls them plainly, " the election;" and then, lest any should ascribe it to a false cause, as in that parallel case he resembles it to, namely, that " they had not bowed the knee to Baal," but stuck to the true religion, when others fell off; he tells us, No; their election was founded upon grace: and as for works, they had no place in the causing of it. By grace, he means the free favor of God, who is not moved by any thing without himself; but what he does he does freely, without respect to men's desert: nay, their undesert rather, is an expedient consideration in this act of grace. By works, I understand all that self-righteousness, goodness, conformity to the law, or whatever else is performable by men. These (namely, grace and works) he proves as inconsistent as contraries can be; and that the least mixture would vary the kind: if but a scruple of works be taken in, grace is no more grace; for, " to him that worketh, is the reward not reckoned of grace, but of debt," Rom. 4: 4. Grace and faith are well agreed; these both have the same scope and end: but grace and works have always clashed: the setting up of the one, is the deposing of the other: either the ark must be out, or dagon down; one temple cannot hold them both. To the same effect is the drift of that discourse in Gal. 5. It appears from Acts 15: 1. that some there were who taught a necessity of circumcision; as without which they could not be saved: seemingly willing they were to admit of Christ, so they might join circumcision with him, and keep-

ing the law of Moses: but this dangerous daubing with
things unmixable, our holy apostle could not brook; both
as reflecting on the honor of his master, and undermining
their only foundation; and therefore to keep them from, or
bring them off that perilous quicksand, he tells them expressly, these two cannot stand together in that matter; for
if they be " circumcised, they are debtors to the whole
law, and Christ is become of none effect to them," because " they are fallen from grace." It is as if he had
said, If you take in any part, though never so little, of
legal observances, as necessary to your being justified, ye
forfeit the whole benefit of gospel grace: the grace of
Christ is sufficient for you; he is a Saviour complete in himself; and if you look, though but a glance, at any thing
else, it is a renouncing of him: he will be a Saviour altogether, or not at all; and therefore he tells them again,
and that with a kind of vehemency, that " if they be circumcised, Christ shall profit them nothing," Gal. 5: 2.

And as a man may not put in his claim for justification
on account of his works, so neither of his faith, as if that
were materially, or meritoriously, causal of justification:
for faith itself, as it is the believer's act, comes under the
notion of a work. Let us therefore consider what part it
is that faith holds in this matter; lest, while we cast our
works, as not standing with grace, we make a work of
faith. It is faith's office to make the soul live wholly on
the power and grace of another; which is to renounce self-
ability, as much as self-desert: to apprehend that righteousness by which grace justifies: not only to be justified
thereby upon our believing, but to work in us even that
faith by which we apprehend it, Rom. 5: 2. He that will
be saved, must come, not only as an ungodly person, but
as a man without strength, chap. 5: 6. and as such, in himself, he must come to be justified freely by the grace of
God, chap. 3: 24. For in him, only, can he have strength
to believe, even as righteousness upon his believing, Isa.
45: 24. he must reckon himself an ungodly man, to the
very instant of his justification. " The just indeed shall
live by faith;" but it is not his own faith, or act of believing, that he lives by, though not without it; which also
seems to be the apostle's meaning, where he says, " The
life that I now live, I live by the faith of the son of God:

and I live, yet not I, but Christ liveth in me," Gal. 2: 20. Where note, that as faith is the life of a believer, so Christ is the life of his faith; and he lives on Christ, by virtue of Christ's living in him.

Notwithstanding all which, it is evidently true, and must constantly be affirmed, that grace and works will still be together in the way of salvation (the one doth not exclude the other;) only not as colleagues or joint causers thereof; but rather as a workman and his tools, which himself first makes, and then works with them. "By grace are ye saved, through faith; and that not of yourselves, it is the gift of God." Eph. 2:18. Even this believing or acting faculty is a creature of grace's raising up; and therefore, in the throne it is meet that grace should be above it. Works, therefore, how good soever, are not the cause of salvation: and if so, not the cause of election; for this, indeed, is the cause of them both: and works, if right and truly good, will always be ready to own their original, and to keep in their own place; where also they will be most considerable, and do the best service.

Arg. III. That election has no other foundation but the good pleasure of God's will, is further argued, from man's incapacity to afford any ground or motive to God for such a gift. Adam stood not so long as to beget a son in his own image: it is seen by his first born Cain, what all his natural seed would naturally be. And though some do presume to magnify man, and to speak of him at another rate; yet evident it is by scripture light, and the experience of those renewed, that man fallen is poor, blind, naked, and at enmity with all that is truly good; and that he is never more distant from God and his own happiness, than while in high thoughts of himself, glorying in his own understanding, strength, worthiness, freedom of will, improvement of common grace, and the like; for these make him proud and presumptuous, and to have slight thoughts of that special and peculiar grace, by which he must, if ever, be renewed and saved. But the Lord himself, who best knows him, reports the matter quite otherwise, and we know that his witness is true; namely, that "all the imaginations of their hearts are only evil continually," Gen. 6: 5. that "their inward part is very wickedness," Psal. 5: 9. that "every man is brutish in his knowledge; altoge-

ther brutish and foolish; yea, even their pastors," Jer. 10:
8. 14. 21. that is, the very best and most intelligent among
them: that "their hearts are full of madness," Eccl. 9: 3.
"wise to do evil, but to do good have no understanding,"
&c. Jer. 4: 22.   And it was not thus only with the Gentile
nations, who were left to walk in their own way; but even
with the Jews who had all the means of becoming better
that could be devised, Isa. 5: 4. excepting that of electing
grace, which took in but a remnant: "they were called
Jews, rested in the law, made their boast of God, knew
his will, approved the things that were excellent; were
confident that they were a guide of the blind, and a light
to them that were in darkness, instructors of the foolish,
teachers of babes," Rom. 2: 7. 21.   And yet all this while,
and in the midst of all these high attainments, did not teach
themselves: and where they are ranked together, he proves
them to be "all under sin, none righteous, none that understandeth, none that seeketh after God, none that doeth
good, no, not one, chap. 3: 10—18.   Yea, this depravity
of nature was so deep and indelibly fixed, that the Lord
himself tells them, "The Ethiopian might as soon change
his skin, as they learn to do well," Jer. 13: 23.   All which,
with abundantly more, bespeaks a condition extremely
remote from yielding a cause or motive for this blessed
election.

   Arg. IV. If God's love to men had its rise from their love
to him, it would not have that singular eminency in it, that
is justly ascribed to it: "God so loved the world," John 3.
16.   So as not to be expressed; so, as not to be paralleled;
so, as not to be understood, until we come to that state
wherein we shall know as we are known; nor then neither
fully, because it is infinite.   By this it is that God's love
to man is so highly celebrated; "Herein is love; not that
we love God, but that God loved us," 1 John 4: 10.   And,
"Behold what manner of love the Father hath bestowed
upon us!" chap. 3: 1. which surely then is not after the
manner of men; for even publicans do so, Matth. 5: 46.
and "sinners love those that love them," Luke 6: 32. but
to love enemies, and while enemies (as to love a wife that
is an adultress; and so to love her, as to win her heart back
again;) this is God's love to his chosen.

   But, notwithstanding these scriptures, with many others,

seem purposely written to obviate such conceptions as would feign our loving of God to be the ground and motive of his love to us; yet, great endeavors there are to father election upon foreseen faith and works, which that they call the covenant of grace, has, they say, qualified and capacitated all men for; and which certain more pliant, ingenious, and industrious persons (as they speak) would attain unto, by the helps they have in common with other men: but this pedigree of election is excepted against, as being not rightly induced: for, 1. Men having (in Adam) divested themselves of all that was holy and good, the Lord could not foresee in them any thing of worth or desirableness, but what he himself should work in them anew, and that of pure grace and favor; for sin and deformity could not be motives of love. And that the elect, of themselves, were in no wise better than other men, is evident by the scriptures late quoted; where the Holy Ghost asserting the universal depravity of human nature, exempts not one. But if such excellent and distinguishing qualifications as faith and holiness had been foreseen, and so imputable to them, the spirit of truth would not have ranked them even with the children of wrath, Eph. 2: 3. as he doth. But, 2. If they were otherwise, what could they add unto God? or whereby could they oblige him? " He respecteth not any that are wise in heart," Job 37: 24. " If thou be righteous, what givest thou him?" chap, 35: 7. and, " who hath prevented me, (says the Lord,) that I should repay him?" chap. 41: 11. that is, who is he that is beforehand with God, in doing aught that might induce his favor? " He regardeth not persons, nor taketh rewards," Deut. 10: 17. he is not propitious to any for what they can do for him, or bring to him. Take Paul for an instance: he walked up to the light he had; was blameless; lived in all good conscience; knew no evil by himself,—a rare degree of legal righteousness!— but that it was not this moved God to make him a chosen vessel, he thankfully acknowledgeth, with self-abasement, upon every occasion, Tit. 3: 5. 1 Tim. 1: 14. 2 Tim. 1: 9. 3. Faith follows election: God respects the person before his offering. But was not Abel respected as a believer, and his offering for his faith? yea, but that faith of his was not the primary cause of God's respecting him. If Abel's person had not been respected first, Abel had never been a

believer: for faith is the work and gift of God; and, according to the course of all judicious agents, he that will work,
must first pitch on the subject he will work upon; and he
that gives, on the person he will give unto.　Besides, Abel
could do nothing before he believed, that might move God
to give him faith; for, till then he was in the flesh, and they
that are in the flesh cannot please God," Rom. 8: 8. Heb.
11: 6. therefore it could not be Abel's foreseen faith that
was the cause of God's respecting him.　The scripture
speaks often of iron-sinewed necks, and brazen brows;
and of men's being in their blood, when the Lord said, they
should live: as also that God loved Jacob before he had
done any good thing; and that the saints love God because
he loved them first: but no where of foreseen faith and
holiness, as the cause and ground of God's love to men.
4.　Faith and holiness are middle things: they are neither
the foundation nor top-stone of election.　They are to
sovereign grace, as stalks and branches are to a root: by
which the root conveys its virtues into its principal fruit.
Eph. 2: 8. "By grace are ye saved, through faith." 2 Thess.
2: 13. "Chosen to salvation, through sanctification of the
Spirit, and belief of the truth."　They are no more the
cause of election, than the means of an end are the first
cause of purposing that end: nay, no more than Tatnai's
propensity (or aversion rather) to build the temple, and to
provide sacrifices for the God of heaven, was the cause of
Darius's decree, that those things should be done, and that
by him. Ezra 5 and 6. chapters.　5. If men be predestinated to faith and holiness, (as they are,) Rom. 8: 29: 30.
1 Pet. 1: 2. then they were not seen to be so qualified before that predestination: or if they were, then their election, as to that particular, would seem impertinent.　There
can no rational account be given, why men foreseen to
be such, should be so solemnly predestinated thereto.
Besides, if salvation be the inseparable product of faith
and holiness, according to John 5: 24. "He that believeth
hath everlasting life, and shall not come into condemnation," 1 Pet. 1: 9. "Receiving the end of your faith,
the salvation of your souls;" then to ordain to salvation
those foreseen to be so qualified, would seem a thing
both needless and insignificant: it would look like the
sending of men where they would have gone of themselves.

Such sapless, irregular, and injudicious notions, are very unworthy that celebrated and ever adorable act of predestination: and if duly weighed, would set us farther off from the doctrine of self-advancement, which stands in point-blank opposition to the doctrine of God's grace.

Arg. V. It could not stand with the wisdom and goodness of God, to found the salvation of his people on a fallible bottom; which it would certainly be, if dependant on any thing besides his own immutable will. For whatever it was that election had being from, by that also it must be maintained: what, then, would become of it, if built on that goodness which is as the morning cloud and the early dew? Hos. 6: 4. The creature's will, even in a state of perfection, was too slight and fickle a thing to build this eternal weight upon: and if a man at his best estate was vanity, how much more afterwards, when so strong a bent of vanity came upon his will?

Arg. VI. To derive election from any root besides the good pleasure of God, is to frustrate the principal end of man's salvation, namely, " The glory of God's grace," Eph. 1: 6. and 2: 7. This attribute, of all the rest, he will not have eclipsed, nor entrenched upon: it is so divinely sacred, as not to admit the least human touch; for which very cause, the Lord hath so contrived that blessed design and plot of his glory, that all " boasting is excluded; and no flesh shall glory in his presence," 1 Cor. 1: 29. But if any thing in the creature be entitled to the causality of election, flesh will glory; and instead of excluding man's boasting, grace itself will be excluded, Rom. 11: 6. which is far from a glorifying of it. I would here resolve a query or two, which some have urged from scripture: as,

1. How can this doctrine stand with the [general] love and good will of God towards men; who, it is said, will have all to be saved? 1 Tim. 2: 4. 2 Pet. 3: 9.

Answ. 1. If the word [all] be taken universally, it takes in unbelievers as well as others; (which cannot be the meaning:) therefore, the literal sense of words is not to be rested on, when the like phrase of speech elsewhere used, or evident scope of the same or other scripture, agrees not to it: the design and current of the whole must guide the construction of particular parts. 2. Though the doctrine of general love will not stand with that of special

election; yet the doctrine of special election will not stand
without that, and against it: for, there is nothing more
plain, than that there is an election of men to salvation; as
also, that the genuine import of election, is, to choose one
or more out of many:. which necessarily implies the leaving
or not choosing of some; and consequently the not willing
of salvation to all universally.   3. The will of God cannot
be resisted; because with his willing the end, he wills
also the means; 'and those such as shall compass his end;
Isa. 46: 10.   " My counsel shall stand, I will do all my
pleasure;" i. e. What I please to will, that I will have
done.   4. The apostle is not here discoursing the extent
of God's special love; whether all men universally are interested in it: but exhorting believers to a general duty;
namely, to give thanks for kings and all in authority; because of the benefits we have by government: and to pray
for them; not only for their peaceable governing of us; but
if otherwise, that God would turn their hearts and make
them nursing fathers to his church. And to enforce the duty,
tells us, there is no degree nor state of men exempted from
salvation; God hath chosen some of every sort; and therefore we ought not to shut any out of our prayers.   5. The
word [all] is often used, when but a part and sometimes the
lesser part, of the thing spoken of, is intended by it: as on
the contrary, when the universality of the subject is intended, it is expressed by singulars; as, he that believeth shall
be saved; and him that cometh unto me, I will in no wise
cast out.   It sometimes signifies all of such a sort; so Eve
was said to be the mother of all living; not of all living
creatures, but all of her own kind.   It other times intends
some of all sorts: as where it is said, all the cattle of Egypt
died, Exod. 9: 6. " and the hail smote every tree and every
herb," ver. 23.   And yet other cattle are mentioned after,
and a residue of trees are said to be escaped, ver. 19. 25.
and 10: 5.   So here, God will have all men to be saved;
that is, some of every sort and degree; Gentiles as well
as Jews; kings and men in authority, as well as those of a
meaner rank; as is evident by comparing the 1, 2, and 4
ver. together.   The same in Joel; " I will pour out my
spirit upon all flesh," &c. Joel 2: 29. that is, upon some
of every age, sex, and degree, without distinction; young,
old, masters, servants, sons, daughters, &c. as it follows
there.   6. To these universal terms do belong divers re-

strictions, which must be gathered from the scope and context: as, where the gospel is said to be preached to every creature under heaven, Col. 1: 23. and yet men only are intended, and not all of them neither: for the gospel had reached but a small part of the world at that time, and not the whole of it yet. So, Moses is said to have in every city them that preach him, Acts 15: 21. it must be understood only of cities where the Jews dwelt, and had synagogues; which were but few in comparison. Those also that were scattered abroad, went every where preaching the word, Acts 8: 4. i. e. they avoided no place nor person, but preached wherever they came. At first it was confined to the Jews, but now without limit. "Every man shall have praise of God," 1 Cor. 4: 5. it can be meant only of good and faithful servants; which are but a remnant to the whole piece. So, God is said to be the Father of all, Eph. 4: 6. and yet Satan, we know, is the father of the far greater part of the world. And Christ is said to reconcile all things, Col. 1: 20. and yet all the angels must be exempted: the good angels, because they never were at enmity; and the evil ones, because not reconcilable, Eph. 1: 10. "That he might gather together in one, all things in Christ:" This all things seems plainly to intend the elect; for they are the subject discoursed of in the whole chapter: and in Matthew, those gathered together are styled the elect, chap. 24: 31. In Heb. 12: 8. all are said to be partakers of chastisements; and yet sons only can be intended: for bastards are not partakers of it, as it follows there. "They shall be all taught of God," John 6: 45. It respects only the sons of the church, (i. e. such as are elected,) whose iniquities are forgiven them, and their sins remembered no more, Jer. 31: 34. It is the tenor of the new covenant, which is made with the house of Israel, that is, Jews in spirit, or the elect nation, Heb. 8: 10, 11. And if these terms universal, *all* and *every*, are sometimes applied to the elect, exclusive of others, why not as well in the place whence the query is taken? I have instanced these, to show what contradictory notions would follow should the vocal sound of words be adhered to: what a sandy foundation universal election is built upon: and how likely we are to lose the truth, while we listen to an uncertain sound; the meaning whereof may yet be had from the context, and general current of scripture.

2. How shall this kind of election be reconciled with Acts 10: 34. "That God is no respecter of persons?"

Answ. 1. This shows the inconvenience of minding the literal sense of the words above the scope: the former exception takes in all; and now this excludes all: for, if literally taken, God should have respect to none. 2. The Jews were an elect nation; and so, this objection will lie against their election as much as this we are upon. 3. The scope of the place plainly intends, that God respects no man's person, either less or more, for his outward condition, or carnal privileges. Till then the partition was up, and the Lord seemed only to regard the Jewish nation, suffering all besides to walk in their own ways, Acts 14: 16. But now had God to the Gentiles also granted repentance unto life, Acts 11: 18. You will say, perhaps, they were fearers of God whom he thus accepted. True; but that was not it which first induced his acceptance, or entitled them to it; although it was their inlet into it, and evidence for it. If men fear not God till he hath put his fear within them: then their fearing of him doth not precede his respect towards them: but follows upon it, and this is the favor which he bears to his chosen, Psal. 106: 4. But,

3. If men be ordained to salvation absolutely, what need or use is there of good works?

Good works have divers good uses and ends, and good reasons there are for God's ordaining them to be walked in: without supposing our walking in them to be the ground, condition, or motive of our election: as, 1. To testify our love to God; of which we have no such evidence, as the keeping of his commandments, 2 John 5: 3. 2. To show forth his virtues, whose offspring we profess ourselves to be, Matth. 5: 45. That ye may be (i. e. ye may appear and approve yourselves to be) "the children of your Father which is in heaven." 3. To convince those without, that they, by our good conversation, may be won over, and learn to do well; or else be compelled to glorify God in the day of visitation. 4. For encouragement and example to weaker Christians; who are yet children in the good ways of God, and are more aptly led by example than precept. 5. That by having our senses exercised about holy things, we might become more holy, and so, more capable of communion with God here, and prepared for our heavenly inheritance. 6. Good works are a part of election, and the elect are as absolutely ordained to them, as to salvation itself, John 15: 16.

Objections I did not intend to meddle with: but considering that that which follows of this kind (though done for another occasion) may help to discover the lightness of what is alleged against our doctrine of election, I have therefore inserted it here; and hope it shall prove to its further confirmation.

Object. There is no election, nor decree of election, of particular persons as such: but of the entire species of men from eternity.

Answ. Election is the choosing of some from among others, and it always supposeth a greater number out of which the choice is made; and, consequently, the taking (or choosing) of all is quite besides the notion of election: the scripture says, they are chosen out of the world, John 15: 19. then the world is not chosen: that is, the entire species of men is not the object of election.

Object. God hath not decreed from eternity to elect any person of mankind upon any terms, but that in case he liveth to years of discretion he may possibly perish.

Answ. This is excepted against: 1. Because the person of Christ himself is not exempted. 2. Because as possibly the death of Christ might be in vain. 3. It makes the decree and election two things, and divers in respect of time. That election was from eternity, is proved before, Eph. 1: 4. and that the elect shall not perish, is absolutely promised, John 16: 28.

Object. Threatenings of damnation are absolutely inconsistent with a peremptory decree to confer salvation.

Answ. No more than the threatening of death upon Adam was inconsistent with God's purpose to send him a Saviour, Gen. 2: 17. with chap. 3: 15. That caution also, that " except the mariners staid in the ship, they could not be saved," as well consistent with that peremptory promise, " that there should be no loss of any man's life," Acts 27: 22. 31. The promise of safety was absolute, but their actual obtainment of it was conditional. Yet so, as that the performance of the condition on their part, was as certain by the decree, as safety upon their performance of it: for he that determined the safety of their lives, determined also, that it should be effected by their abiding in the ship; and that this caution, or threatening of danger, in case they went out, should be a means to prevail with them for that abiding; and so it did. In like manner, that saying of the apostle, that " if they lived after the flesh, they should die, Rom. 8: 13. was very consistent with what he had said before, namely, " that sin should not have dominion over them," Rom: 16: 14. and that " nothing should separate them from the love of God," chap. 8: 39. For as the Lord deals with reasonable creatures, so he makes use of rational arguments, motives, and cautions to work upon them: both end and means, and inducements to the use of those means, were all determined together.

Object. We judge it a very senseless part in a father, to give his child complete assurance, under hand and seal, that he will make him his heir, against all possible interveniencies; and yet presently threaten him, if he be not dutiful, to disinherit him.

Answ. Undutiful children may dare to judge thus of their father's actions; and children, that otherwise are dutiful and good, yet, while children, may have childish conceptions of what their elders do: but men grown up, and acquainted with their father's prudence and goodness, will lay their hands upon their mouths. The promise and purpose of God, to give Canaan to Abraham's seed, was so absolute, that, by the objector's own confession, all their unworthiness could not deprive them of it: it is also evident by their demeanor, and the event at last: yet how often does the Lord threaten to disinherit them? and to " blot out their name from under heaven," Exod. 32: 10. Numb. 14: 12. Deut. 9: 14. Did Moses now go and " charge God foolishly?" did he tell him, It is a senseless part thus to threaten, after so absolute an engagement to the contrary? No; he puts the Lord in mind of his promise to their fathers; of his mercy in pardoning them afore-time; what reflection it would have on his honor among the Egyptians, if he should now destroy them, &c. Not a word of complaint, that first to promise, and then to threaten, is a senseless thing: it had been senseless in Moses thus to do, and in no wise consistent with his duty. But more directly; it were no senseless part in a father, to purchase an office for his son, and so to settle it on him, that it shall not be in his own power to reverse it; and yet, keeping to himself the knowledge of that settlement, propose the enjoyment thereof conditional, namely, upon terms of obedience to his father's command: the tendency of all which is but to prove himself the son of such a father, and to prepare him for his place: and, the more to oblige his son to a studious preparing himself for it, to lay before him the evil and danger of a negligent course; by which, if persisted in, he might render himself incapable. But, surely, supposing this father to have the same power over his son, as God hath over the heart and spirit of his people; he will so order him by instruction, discipline, and good principles, that he shall not run into a forfeiture. Besides, threatenings of damnation are not properly applicable to believers, who know themselves so to be: for " he that believeth, is passed from death to life, and shall not come into condemnation, John 5: 24. however, at times, for want of a thorough knowing their state, unthankfulness for it, or some other miscarriage, they bring themselves under doubtings of it: but for such as have complete assurance under God's hand and seal (as the objection speaks,) they are " sealed up to the day of redemption," Eph. 4: 30. Rom. 8: 15. with a seal that never shall be loosed.

Object. In case any person were so adjudged to eternal life from eternity, that there is no possibility of miscarrying, then there was no necessity of Christ's dying for him.

Answ. The asserters of absolute election do hold, with the scriptures, that election is " in and through Christ:" the same decree that ordained to salvation, ordained also the mediation of Christ in order thereto: that God might be " just in justifying, he hath appointed us to obtain salvation by our Lord Jesus Christ," 2 Thess. 5: 9. Ye might, with as much shew of reason, infer, that if such an end be appointed to be wrought by such a means, then that means is unnecessary to that end: that if God had chosen men to salvation through sanctification of the Spirit, and belief of the truth, then holiness and faith are needless things. These are absurd reasonings, which the truth neither owns nor needs.

Object. We judge such an election to be an open enemy to godliness: for who will strain and toil himself for that which he knows he shall obtain by an easy pace?

Answ. The doctrine of conditional election can be no

friend to godliness, whatever it may pretend to; since all
that a man doeth on that account terminates in self. Godliness is to aim at God as our chief end in all that we do:
now one that holds the elect sure of salvation, and believes
himself to be one of them, and yet goes on to fear God,
and obey him, glorifies God more than he that performs the
same duties for kind (and perhaps greater in bulk,) in expectation of life thereby. The Pharisees fasted oftener
than Christ's disciples; but were not such real friends to
godliness as they. Long prayers, fastings, and alms-deeds,
are all nothing without love: and who, do you think, will
love God more, he that believes himself sure of God's love
unchangeably, or one that holds that, after all his toiling
and straining, he may possibly run in vain, and lose all at
last? If ye speak thus, ye cross the experience of God's
children; yea, and of nature too; for who counts it a toil
to eat his meat when nature requires it, especially when it
is most agreeable both to his palate and constitution? "All
the ways of God are pleasantness to them that walk in
them:" and these would not leave them again, although
their future happiness were not concerned in it: if they be
grievous to any, it is from their unacquaintedness with his
love, 1 John 5: 3:

Object. It must needs make men very remiss and loose
in the service of God.

Answ. A strange assertion! that the assurance of God's
love should make men careless in serving him: they that so
judge, can never be over diligent to make their calling and
election sure. Christ knew that the " angels had charge
over him," and that " he should not dash his foot against
a stone;" yet was nevertheless careful of his own preservation. Paul was sure of the crown of righteousness; and
yet as diligent in beating down his body, and strained as
hard in running his race, as any of those who lay the stress
of salvation upon their works.

Object. Such a notion of election lays the honor and
necessity of that great ordinance of preaching the gospel
in the dust: for if the elect (so called) shall as certainly be
saved by a weak, simple, or corrupt ministry, and this, it
may be, enjoyed but a day or two in all a man's life, or
loosely attended upon, wherein is the ministry of the gospel
to be esteemed?

Answ. That peremptory decree, that "summer and

winter, day and night, shall not cease," takes not away
the necessity of the sun's being in the world, nor of its
daily rising, setting, and various revolutions; for by these,
as the necessary means thereof, must the decree be made
good.   So the absoluteness of that other part of the promise,
that " seed-time and harvest shall not cease," doth not a
whit discharge the husbandman either of his usefulness or
duty; but evinceth the one, and enforceth the other;
giving also encouragement to him in his work.   The force
of this answer will not be evaded, by alleging, that God
affords them means proper and sufficient for seed-time and
harvest, (that is, they have fitting seasons, with seed corn,
horses, ploughs, and other utensils of husbandry;) and that
is all the promise intends; and if they improve them not,
the fault is their own.   True, it is so, and they shall smart
for their neglect: but what will become of the promise, and
sureness of the covenant?   Therefore this is not all that
God doeth for men in this point.   He that decreed how long
the earth shall endure, and what number of men he will
raise upon it, did also decree his own upholding thereof
during that time, and by what means those men should be
propagated, and kept alive; and did accordingly put into
them the principles of self-preservation; by which they are
naturally prompted to use them, as they are to eat, drink,
and sleep: " He hath set the world in their hearts," Eccl.
3: 11.   As the elect shall certainly be saved, and also prepared for that salvation; so hath the Lord appointed them
such a ministry, and for so long a time, and their attendance thereon in such a manner, as best agrees with his
own intention, and which he will bless and make effectual
for that end; as is seen by his sending Paul to certain
places where he must preach, and not hold his peace:
Why? Because God had much people there, (that is, of
his elect ones,) who must be brought in by Paul's ministry.
Bythinia, and other places, he is not suffered to go into,
though he would; God had not yet any work for him there.
Those that are to be taken, the Lord will bring them under
the means, as he did that shoal of fishes under Peter's net,
John 21: 6.   Witness the eunuch, Cornelius, the jailer,
and others.   And this means, whether powerful or simple
in man's esteem, it is all one to God; his word shall accomplish that he sends it for; and the weaker the means
are, the more is the power of God magnified.   See Acts,

chapter 2, how by illiterate men's ministry, he took them by thousands, and "added to his church daily such as should be saved," Acts 2. 9, 10, 11. 47. So, then, the ministry of the gospel is in no wise made useless or disestimable by the doctrine of absolute election, but is rather heightened thereby, as being the "power of God to that salvation he hath chosen us to."

Object. Of what great consequence to the world are the richest gifts of wisdom, knowledge, utterance, &c. if all those who are in any possibility of being saved by them, may and shall as certainly be saved without them?

Answ. That the richest gifts of wisdom, knowledge, utterance, are of no great consequence to the world, is no consequent of the doctrine of absolute election; for they are given " for the perfecting of the saints, and edifying the body of Christ," that is, the elect: and all the diversities of gifts, manifestations, and operations, do concur to the same end, since it is the same God who worketh all in all: That is, he appointeth men to salvation, these gifts, as a means to prepare them for it, and makes them effectual thereto. But that those richest gifts of wisdom, knowledge, and utterance, are of no great use or consequence to the world, is a very natural consequent of that doctrine, which tells the world that the sun, moon, and stars, do preach the gospel sufficiently for salvation: which if they do, wherein, indeed, are those richest gifts to be esteemed, and to what end is this waste? Why should the best of men suffer stripes, imprisonments, and death, for doing that which might be done by those above the reach of danger? And, withal, it is too well known and obvious, that men of greatest knowledge, utterance, and depth of reason, such as are styled the princes of this world, are not always, nay, are very rarely, the fastest friends of truth and godliness; and those few that are, are not always most successful in their work, Eccl. 9: 11. while some others, meanly furnished in comparison, have turned the world upside down, 2 Cor. 12: 10. Acts 17: 6. 2 Cor. 10: 10. The Lord oft-times rejects the wise and prudent, and reveals himself by babes, to take from men occasion of boasting, and to make it appear, that the faith of his people does not stand in the wisdom of men, but in the power of God, 1 Cor. 2: 5. " Whose weakness is stronger than men, and his foolishness wiser," chap. 1: 25.

Object. Upon what account can men be pressed to a frequent, diligent, conscientious attendance upon the ministry, if salvation, and consequently preparation, and meetness for salvation, shall as certainly be had by a broken, careless, superficial attendance in this kind?

Answ. On what account did the Lord so frequently admonish his people, " to keep the law, without turning aside; to circumcise their hearts; and to be no more stiff-necked;" and this, as the condition of their obtaining Canaan? if all their unworthiness could not deprive them of Canaan, which the author of this objection elsewhere affirms they could not. But further, as men are creatures, it is their duty to serve and honor God; and, in order thereto, to wait upon him in his ordinances, and that with all diligence, although the business of their salvation was not concerned in it, but much more since it is, if any thing of self-concern may enforce a duty: and truly the present sweetness that is in the good ways of God, is argument sufficient to induce our most serious attendance thereon. But that salvation or meetness for salvation, may as certainly be had by a careless attendance, it is far from the doctrine of absolute election to assert: for it presseth it still as an important duty, to " give all diligence to make our calling and election sure." But, really, remissness in duty is the natural result of that doctrine which teacheth That a man possibly may lose all he hath run for at the last step: for who will strain and toil himself, as they term it, for an uncertainty? And if there be any such who neglect their duty, because if elected they are sure to be saved, they give but a sorry evidence of their state; and are, commonly, such as oppose the doctrine of election, and not of those who hold for it.

Object. Such an election as we contend against, we judge to be the most unworthy the most excellent nature of God; and to be at manifest defiance with his wisdom, holiness, mercy, justice, &c.

Answ. If the election contended against be such as the objector's arguments are pointed at, it is such as I suppose never was held by any; and then it is ill-spent time to set up counterfeit notions, and make a great business of confuting them. But it is absolute election, without respect to men's works, that is striven against: and for this we say, 1. Absolute election is no way contrary to the wisdom

of God, but most consonant thereto; for how can it stand
with his wisdom, to determine the death of his Son for the
salvation of men, and leave it undetermined, and consequently uncertain, whether any one person shall have salvation by it? For so it must be, if election be not absolute.
2. It is so far from being at manifest hostility with the
mercy of God, that it is most congruous and suitable to the
very nature of it.   To shew mercy, is to open the heart to
one in distress; to love and do good to enemies, whom he
might as justly have destroyed, and was no way obliged to
spare, much less to advance them: nay, perhaps they were
deeper involved in guilt than other men, even the chief of
sinners; which is, certainly, the highest illustration of
mercy, and far from a manifest defiance of it.   3. It doth
not oppose the justice of God; for, to whom is he debtor,
or can be?   All had a stock in Adam; and having lost it by
their own default, God is not obliged to restore it; therefore no injustice to repair one, and not another.

Object. Doth it argue any sovereign or high strain of
grace, when ten thousand have equally offended, to pardon
one or two, and implacably resolve to punish and torment
all the rest to the utmost extremity?   And this against all
possible interveniency of sorrow and repentance for their
faults?

Answ. It were very desirable that men, while they
pretend to argue for the truth, would order their speech as
becomes the gravity of such a subject, Eccl. 5: 1. and
much more, that they come not so near a downright re-
proaching that glorious grace, of which we cannot have
apprehensions awful enough.   The men who thus speak,
had need to try their spirits, whether they be of God; since
from the same premises they draw conclusions quite contrary to those, who, we know, " spake as they were moved
by the Holy Ghost."   In scripture account, it is no derogation from the grace of God, that he called Abraham alone,
leaving millions beside to their perishing condition.   Nor
can I believe that Moses understood it as disparaging God's
love to mankind, when he tells us, that he chose the people
of Israel for his own peculiar people; who yet were the
fewest of any people, Deut. 7: 7.   One of a city, and two
of a family, were less in proportion than one or two of ten
thousand; yet no complaint upon it, by those interested in
that grace.   It is the property of God's children to admire

that he loves any, and especially themselves; and not to find fault because he loves not all alike. "Who am I, (says David,) that thou hast brought me hitherto!" And Christ's disciples, "Lord, why wilt thou manifest thyself to us (us twelve) and not to the world?" John 14: 22. It is therefore strange to consider, why and how, any that call themselves of the brotherhood, came so to espouse the quarrel of those without; and that with such eagerness, as to strive and fall out among themselves about the other's concerns. It were more advisable to leave off disputing, and fall to practice. But, to answer more directly: 1. This remnant is not so contemptibly to be spoken of; they are "Ten thousand times ten thousand, and thousands of thousands," Rev. 5: 11. And how small soever the number be, (if it were but one, it were more by one than the whole creation could deserve,) I say, how few soever they are, no man knows but himself may be one of them; unless by despising the grace of God in election, he hath proved it otherwise to himself. 2. To pitch on a few while in their blood and enmity against God, and resolve even then to make them everlastingly happy, and that against the natural bent of their own will, was a grace much more high and sovereign, than to save them for their own better improvement of what they have in common with other men; for that would not be of grace, but of debt. Or if the Lord should bring ten thousand times that number into a salvable state, (as they speak,) but so as, very possibly, not one of them shall ever be saved, it would not bring the thousandth part of that glory to his grace, as to save a few invincibly. 3. If the Lord did foresee that but few would believe, and yet resolve to save none but such as should believe; then the objection, as to fewness, falls on the objector's doctrine as much as ours. 4. As for godly sorrow, faith, and repentance, they are the gift of God, and proper to the elect: and so, no reason to suppose the interveniency of these in them that are left; or to fear an implacable resolution to punish and torment any in whom these possibilities go forth into act.

Other allegations they have against the doctrine of election, which will admit of as plain a solution as those above; but it being my purpose to collect what I shall find in the scriptures for it, and not to controvert the point; I proceed no further, but go on to the usefulness of the doctrine; only by the way let me premise a caution or two.

1. Let no man tax God with injustice or partiality because he takes not all; or because not those of highest esteem among men. Do not the princes of the world exercise dominion over men like themselves? Or is there a subject so mean, but will think himself wronged, if questioned for disposing of his own (which yet is his own but as borrowed?) And shall vain man presume to arraign his sovereign Lord! "Wo to him that striveth with his Maker," Isa. 45: 9. If you must be meddling, let it be with potsherds of earth like yourselves.

2. Let no man depreciate the doctrine of election because it takes in but a remnant. Why are they styled, "the little flock," but to heighten the mercy and privilege of it in their esteem? Noah did not contemn the grace of God to himself and his sons, because the world of ungodly were excluded the ark; nor the remnant that escaped the sword in Egypt, Jer. 44: 28. reckon their own deliverance the less mercy, because the rest of their countrymen had not a share in it. Men do not use to slight their own immunities for others not being interested in them; but rather to value themselves the more upon it.

And now, as a means to prevent or remove the evil surmises cautioned against; with those other sinister deductions which carnal reason may be apt to suggest; let us draw up a few of those many and worthy improvements this doctrine is capable of, above and beyond that of the contrary tenor; as also of those laws of duty which it lays upon us. And here I would see, first, what fruit may be gathered from the several branches of the proposition; and then, what from the gross or whole of it promiscuously.

1. Since there is an election of men to salvation, put you in for a part and interest in it: though their number be but small, cast in your lot, and make one among them. My meaning is, that though ever so few are the objects of election, you will make it your business to prove yourself of that few. If but two in the whole world, who knows but thou mayest be one of them? And do it the rather, for fewness' sake: it is our Saviour's argument, "They are but few that go in at the straight gate;" therefore strive. The Ninevites had not that ground to believe God would accept them that you have; for their ruin was pronounced in peremptory words, and no room expressly left for re-

pentance; and yet they humbled themselves, and turned from their evil ways, upon this only consideration, " Who can tell if God will turn away his fierce anger, that we perish not?" Jonah 3: 9, 10. It is a happiness worth your venturing for: for, 1. You can lose nothing by endeavoring. 2. You can hardly have a more solid evidence of your being elected, than to have your heart taken with electing love, and casting yourself upon it: and 3. Never did any perish who ventured on this bottom.

II. From the doctrine of election's absoluteness is evinced the exceeding riches of the grace of God, in that he hath not left this great concern to human contrivance, but hath laid it more sure and safe than men themselves would have done: for it is too evident, (by the reasonings that are used to make election dependant and conditional,) how it would have gone, if left to the wisdom of men. But I shall not doubt to affirm, that this doctrine of election's absoluteness is much beforehand with that which teacheth it to be conditional, both in point of encouragement, and otherwise; and that as well before believing as afterwards.

1. Before a man comes to believe; supposing him to be notionally instructed therein before. For being under conviction of the greatness and multitude of his sins, and finding the power of indwelling corruptions so insuperable, having also some sight of the holiness of God, and that he will by no means clear the guilty, it needs must prove a difficult matter, to believe that there is mercy and pardon for such a one as he; or that ever those domineering lusts should be made to submit: but then considering, 1. That electing love pitches on the chief of sinners. 2. That it flows not from, nor is founded upon, any condition to be performed by men. And, 3. That election has in it all that conduceth to life and godliness: these things (I say) considered, it cannot but have a far greater influence on the soul, to cleave unto God, and follow hard after him, than if his election were suspended upon his doing that which he finds in himself no power to perform: for he sees by woful (and yet, through grace, happy) experience, that as the law is made weak through the weakness of the flesh; so also, setting aside the absoluteness of electing love, all the means of grace, which are given in common among men, would be wholly ineffectual to salvation: which difficulties, electing love in its absoluteness will supersede, and set

him above them all; especially considering, that faith and holiness are as absolutely promised and provided for in election, as salvation itself, as the end of faith.

2. After a man comes to believe, this doctrine of absolute election is of singular use and benefit to him, both as tending to keep him on his feet, and to raise him when he is down. 1. It is a great preservative in time of temptation. The remembrance of that love which looked upon him when he was in his blood, and said he should live, and hath now also made good its word to him, must needs operate strongly with a gracious heart, against whatever might be unworthy of such love: let the bait be ever so aptly suited, he will turn from it in a holy disdain, as good Joseph did, "How can I do this great wickedness, and sin against God!" Gen. 39: 9. who hath dealt so bountifully with me! 2. Nothing more tends to recovery after a fall, than the consideration of the freeness of God's love at first, and his mighty power in quickening, when altogether dead; and that both these, namely, his love and his power, are engaged by an absolute covenant, to bring every one that takes hold thereof to glory; and therefore will receive him, not only after, upon return to his duty, but in the midst of his backslidings, he will come and heal him. The Lord's way of dealing with Ephraim is an instance pertinent to the case in hand: "For the iniquity of his covetousness was I wroth, and smote him: I hid me, and was wroth, and he went on frowardly in the way of his heart. I have seen his ways, and will heal him: I will lead him also, and restore comforts unto him, and to his mourners," Isa. 57: 17, 18. And in the 44th chapter, he doth, as it were, clench and fasten this nail in a sure place: "Remember, O Jacob, I have formed thee; thou shalt not be forgotten of me: I have blotted out thy sins; therefore return unto me." And Jer. 3: 14. "Return, O backsliding children, for I am married unto you," (to wit, by his covenant of election.)   To this purpose also is the edge of Samuel's argument applied in 1 Sam. 12: 20. 22. "Fear not; ye have done all this wickedness; yet turn not aside from following the Lord:" as if he had said, your wickedness indeed is great, ye have highly provoked the Lord, by your casting him off: yet, be not discouraged, as if the Lord would cast you off: "For the Lord will not forsake his people;" but why? "Because it hath pleased the Lord to make you his people."   And in

ver. 24. he further backs it with the remembrance of the great things God hath done for them afore-time: than which there is nothing of stronger tendency to a soul's recovery.

III. From the personality of election: and, IV. From the eternity of its original, I gather in general,

That since the scriptures have so highly renowned these two circumstantial parts of election, by so frequent a mentioning of them: and that on occasions of the solemnest import, we ought not to pass them by, as things of an indifferent notice; but as being diversely instructive, worthy to be kept, and soberly contended for. The Holy Ghost doth not use to inculcate matters of ordinary observance, or little import; but as noting to us some great importance in them: as taxing also our sloth, and aptness to neglect them; and to stir up our minds to make the more diligent search, what, and what manner of things they are, and how to be improved: in particular,

From the personality of election I infer:

Infer. 1. That it ought to be minded as matter of the highest honor to the parties concerned. The Lord illustrates Moses at no ordinary rate, when he tells him, "I know thee by name:" Exod. 33: 17. and, doubtless, intended that Moses himself should so account of it, and be highly satisfied therewith, though denied some other things he would fain have had. Thus also Paul signalizeth those eminent saints, who were his fellow laborers in the gospel; that "their names were in the book of life," Phil. 4: 3. And our Saviour propounds it to this disciples, as matter of the highest exaltation, that "their names were written in heaven," Luke 10: 20. That our poor insignificant names should be written in God's book, and laid up among his treasures in heaven, when the generality of names (even names of note,) are written in the dust, let it not seem a light matter to us: for this is that "everlasting name, which never shall be cut off," Isa. 56: 5.

Infer. 2. The knowledge of this, namely, that God has thus taken notice of our name, is a great privilege to them that know it. It enlarges the heart to higher expectations; it gives boldness, or freedom of speech towards God; as if nothing were too great for such a one to ask. See how Moses grows upon it; no sooner, says God, "I know thee by name," but Moses (as wrapt into the second, and fain would be in the third heaven) presently replies, " I beseech thee, shew me thy glory."

Infer. 3. As it is a matter of honor and privilege, so it will prove one of the best titles to your heavenly inheritance. It will signify something one day, (however by some too lightly esteemed now,) when it shall be the great distinguishing character between you and the world: whoever he be that derives not his genealogy from this register, will be put from the heavenly priesthood. Neh. 7: 64. The new Jerusalem admits none but those whose " names are written in the book of life," Rev. 21: 27. yea, every one that is not found written there, shall be cast into a lake of fire, chap. 20: 15. therefore " give all diligence to make your election sure."

Infer. 4. It also imports matter of duty from us. When princes confer titles of honor, lands, or immunities; they use to reserve some kind of rent or other service, to mind their subjects, though favorites, of whom they hold. You have no such way of owning your great benefactor, nor such means of being considerable in the world; as by bearing the badge and impress of him who gave you this name of honor. Let his name therefore be named upon you; carry his name in your bosom; bear it on your shoulders, and the " palms of your hands:" let the choicest of your affections, the chief of your strength, and the whole of your activity, be employed for his honor; let every thing you do, bear an impression of him whose name is holy.

Then from the antiquity of election.

Infer. 1. Let the ancientness of electing love, draw up our hearts to a very dear and honorable esteem of it. Pieces of antiquity (though of base metal, and otherwise of little use or value) how venerable are they with learned men? and ancient charters, how careful are men to preserve them; although they contain but temporary privileges, and sometimes but of trivial moment? how then should the great charter of heaven, so much older than the world, and containing matters of eternal weight and glory; which also hath been confirmed by so many promises; exemplified by multitudes of cases; with a seal affixed more precious than heaven itself, all which proclaim the eternal validity of it; how should this, I say, be had in everlasting remembrance, and the thoughts thereof be very precious to us; lying down, rising up, and all the day long accompanying us! and how careful should we be, not only to keep this charter uncancelled, but also to keep it clean from all sorts of dust and soil, by which the legibleness thereof might any way be obscured to ourselves or others!

Infer. 2. Let election's eternal origin be an argument for its eternal duration; and so, of the saints' invincible perseverance to glory. That which is from everlasting, shall be to everlasting; if the root be eternal, so are the branches. Surely, for this good end (among others,) it is twice recorded in the Revelation, that " their names were written in the book of life, from the foundation of the world," Rev. 13: 8. and 17: 8. namely, to signify and assure, that the elect shall be safely and surely kept from those dreadful apostasies, which the rest of the world shall fall into, and be overwhelmed with. And hence, perhaps, it is that we read of nothing done in eternity, but election, and things appendant, or peculiar thereto; as the promise of eternal life, the Lamb slain, the kingdom prepared, &c. Election is an eternal fountain, that never leaves running while a vessel is empty, or capable of holding more; and it stands open to all comers: therefore, come; and if you have not sufficient of your own, go and borrow vessels, empty vessels, not a few; " pay your debts out of it, and live on the rest" to eternity, 2 Kings 4: 7.

V. From the doctrine of choosing in Christ.

Infer. 1. It is an high demonstration of God's love to his chosen. We may say of it as Huram to Solomon, " Because the Lord loved his people, he set his Son over them," 2 Chron. 2: 11. It is also an eminent proof of his manifold wisdom, to contrive the blessedness of his people in such a manner, as should most certainly secure their obtainment of it; most signally illustrate his love to them; and so, most affectionately win upon their hearts, and to oblige them to himself for ever. We may hence also discern something of that immense greatness and holiness of God; that though he so loved his elect, as to make them " one in himself," John 17: 21. that union could not be admitted without a mediator equal with himself.

Infer. 2. Gather hence your stability and safety: whatever strait or difficulty you are entering upon, " drink of this brook in the way," and lift up your head. Whatever pertains to life and godliness, grace and glory, this life and that to come, is all laid up in Christ (as all sorts of food in the ark, for those who found grace in his sight,) all fulness dwells in him, Col. 2: 9. John 1: 16. and that for you. He is not only a root stable in himself, but establishing to you; communicating sap and spirit to all his branches: while there is life in him, you cannot die. This it is that makes the saints stand firm and secure in the midst of dangers; " the evil one toucheth them not," 1 John 5: 18. Let all the rebel-crew of adversaries (Satan, the world, and your own evil hearts) associate themselves, and take counsel together, it all comes to naught: let their assaults be renewed again and again, they are still beaten off: they gird themselves, and are broken in pieces; they gird again, and again they are broken in pieces: thus it is, and thus it shall be, to the end of our warfare; " for God is with us," Isa. 8: 9, 10. This was it made David fearless, even " in the valley and shadow of death; the Lord was with him," Psal. 23: 4. And those three noble confessors, they walked secure in the fiery furnace, because " the Son of God was among them," Dan. 3: 25. Therefore do all, suffer all, and expect all, as being in Christ, and not otherwise: but wo to him that is alone, who, when he falls, hath not Christ to help him up.

Infer. 3. Let this your relation to Christ be evidenced by your likeness to him: He that is joined " to the Lord, is one spirit," 1 Cor. 6: 17. " The holy oil that was poured on your head, runs down to the skirts of his garments;" that is, to the very meanest of his followers; and they carry along the pleasant scent with them wherever they go, or should do, as Paul did, 2 Cor. 2: 14. It is natural to these married unto Christ to bring forth fruit unto God, Rom. 7: 4. and see it be such as will abide the test, endure all sorts of weather, and be bettered by it.

Infer. 4. This doctrine illustrates that of justification; as shewing wherein the true matter of justifying righteousness doth consist, and how it comes to be ours. Our faith (or act of believing) cannot be the matter of it, for that it is an imperfect thing; and so cannot be reckoned in the place of perfect righteousness: for it must be a righteousness perfectly perfect that justifies, as it was a sin perfectly sinful that condemned. This righteousness also must be our own, in a way of right, as Adam's sin also was, though performed in the person of another. Christ and Adam being parallels in their head-ship, the imputation of one's guiltiness, and of the other's righteousness, are righteously applied to their respective seeds. And this was a main end of the Lord's putting those he would justify into Christ: that he " being made sin, and a curse for them, they might be made the righteousness of God in him; and so, God might be just in justifying them. Faith in this matter holds the place of an evidence or seal of that righteousness which belonged to us as being in Christ, before we believed (as Canaan did to Abraham's seed before they were born:) and is given us on account of our interest therein, Phil. 3: 12. that we might apprehend it, and enjoy the benefits of it, Phil. 1: 29. which is surely a far better ground to build our justification upon, than our weak and imperfect faith, which stands in need daily of righteousness of God for its own support. But let not faith lose of its due respect: it is a precious grace, and may not suffer disparagement. Though it doth not originate your title to justification, it is the best evidence ye can have for it; though it be not your peace-maker (primarily,) it is yet of that important usefulness, that your peace cannot be completed, nor can you know that your peace is made, without it. Your record is in heaven, and cannot be pleaded here (the court of conscience takes no notice of it,) until exemplified under the seal of faith. It is somewhat like the *instrumentum pacis*, where parties have been at variance; though the peace be made, and terms agreed, it has not its full effect until ratified on both sides, and exchanged. Therefore,

Infer. 5. Make it the main part of your care and business to get into Christ, and to abide in him.

VI. The founding of election upon grace, affords us divers useful instructions: as,

Infer. 1. To fall down and adore the great God, for this unspeakable discovery of his love to men. It is one of the richest mercies that he would not entrust us in our own keeping: that another (and he one that had not the least need of us) should be more provident for us than we would have been for ourselves: that our chiefest interest should have the highest security: that it should be founded upon grace; the attribute which our great King most delights to honor: and that he should do it, as it were, against our wills; for so it is, inasmuch as to graft our happiness on the will of another, is contrary to nature; of all bottoms, we should not have pitched it there; and yet, in truth, no other ground would hold us: his name may well be called Wonderful; " It is not after the manner of men, this is the Lord's doing, and let it be marvellous in our eyes," Psal. 118: 23.

Infer. 2. It shews what reason we have to discard and cashier for ever that groundless and blindfold opinion, which lays the stress of salvation on a thing of nought: for what else is the will of a frail and mutable man! to forsake a living fountain, and rest on a cistern, a broken cistern, what folly is it! to cast our eagle's wings, and trust to a foot out of joint; who would do it that is not void of understanding! surely Job was aware of it, when he professeth, " He would not value a life that depended on his own righteousness," Job 9: 15. 21.

The grace of God is little beholden to that doctrine which would give the glory of it to a graceless thing; and as little have the souls of men to thank it for: it feeds them with dreams and fancies; which, when they awake, will leave them " hardly bestead, and hungry: and it shall come to pass, that when they shall be hungry, they shall fret themselves, and curse their king and their God, and look upward," Isa. 8: 21. Therefore, sit not down under the shadow of that gourd; it hath a worm at the root; and they will not be held guiltless, nor kept from the scorching sun, whoever they be, that shelter themselves in the covert of it. It is a spark of men's own kindling, wherewith, though compassed round, they will lie down in sorrow, chap. 50: 11. Therefore let those who disrelish this doctrine, because it founds not salvation upon self, look well to their standing, and shift from it in time.

Infer. 3. Fall in practically with the doctrine of election, as founded upon grace. As it was grace which gave you your elect being, so let it be your spirit and utmost endeavor to improve this your being to the praise of that grace. 1. Give it the sole honor of election's original: suffer not free-will-grace, or any thing else, to pretend to a share in the parentage of it: let not your faith, whether foreseen or perfected, be reckoned the ground-work, or motive of your election: it is a branch of it; and the

branch, you know, " cannot bear the root," Rom. 11: 18.
Even faith itself must not (and if it be right faith, it will
not,) " gather where it hath not strewed." Own nothing,
therefore, that may detract from the honor that is due to
sovereign grace. 2. Bear yourself upon this grace, against
all your weakness and unworthiness: let not these discourage you, but rather plead them as occasions by which
grace will be manifested and magnified, and shew itself to
be what it is. Thus did David; " Pardon my sin; for it is
great," Psal. 25: 11. and Moses, when all the people's obedience could not furnish him with an argument for God's
continuing his presence with them, what is his plea? They
are an honest ingenuous people; tractable to thy commands;
pliant to thy will: they are worthy for whom thou shouldst
do this; for they love thy company, and have built thee a
tabernacle? No, there is none of this stuff in it: but, " Let
my Lord, I pray thee, go with us; for it is a stiff-necked
people; their neck is an iron sinew, and their brow brass,"
Exod. 34: 9. therefore go thou with us, to better us, to
soften us, and to pardon us: and by this shall the freeness
of thy grace appear to us: for, " how else shall it be known
that I and this people have found grace in thy sight?" Exod.
33: 46. but yet, withal, (1.) Look that ye make not a light
matter of your sins, or of your sinfulness: you cannot
think bad enough of yourself, or of them; nor be too much
humbled; only, be not cast down. (2.) Use the means
that grace hath appointed; " Watch, and be sober; watch
unto prayer; put on the whole armor of God," and keep it
close about you; your sword and shield be sure you forget
not: but still let your eyes be towards the hand of grace,
through Christ, for counsel, strength, agency, and every
good thing; and depend on it for conserving and actuating
the grace it hath wrought in you, as plants do on their
roots: the spouse, after married to Christ, prays to be
" drawn to him," Cant. 1: 4. (3.) Whatever befals you,
remember the good pleasure of God is in it; hold your
peace, as Aaron did, Lev. 10: 3. or if you must speak,
" let your speech be seasoned with salt: it is the Lord, let
him do as it seemeth him good," 1 Sam. 3: 18.

Other useful instructions from the doctrine of election in
general, and together.

I. It being a doctrine of so great importance, be not indifferent about it: put yourself on the trial touching your interest in it, and bring forth your evidences for it: observe what are the properties of God's elect, and see if they stand on your side.

1. As touching the great business of salvation, do you submit to mercy without indenting, and making terms with God? have you laid yourself at his feet, with " peradventure he will save me alive;" and if he say, I have no pleasure in thee; Lo, here I am, and here I will lie: if I must perish, I will perish here; I cannot die in a better place or posture. Thus did Job, when the Lord seemed to set himself against him, as resolved to destroy him, yet still he resolved to trust in him, and to hold fast his integrity, Job 13: 15. This is a love more noble, and of an higher extract, than those are acquainted with, who conclude, that upon their doing this and that (which they suppose every man hath power to do,) they shall be saved; for such kind of love is mercenary: he will not stir, nor look towards the vineyard, until he hath agreed for his penny; the other goes in, and falls to his work, and leaves it to his master to give him what is meet, Matth. 20: 2. 7. 11. which also he leaves to his master's judgment, and not his own: and truly he speeds not the worse for his so doing. But I would not be taken to intend a contentedness or willingness to be destroyed: this I hope is pleaded before, under the first general head.

2. Do you own God's sovereign commands, without disputing? Abraham did thus in the business of Isaac; although he could not see how the promise of God and the killing of his son could stand together; and so will Abraham's children do. They know that their Lord is a great King, hath absolute dominion, giveth account of none of his matters: what he is pleased to command, their duty is to obey, without asking a reason why? or, how will these things consist? such demands become not the lips of those who live upon grace.

3. Doth your love towards God hold the same course that his love hath done towards you? All that God hath done, or will do, for his chosen, is the product of electing love. Does all your obedience arise from love? and does this love of yours grow out of his? is his electing love the root of it? is all that you do towards God in a way of gratitude and duty, and with design to glorify his grace? and

when the Lord seems to go from you, do you follow the harder after him, as he for a long time followed you, waiting that he might be gracious unto you? this is truly a God-like love; the eminency whereof lies in this, that " he loved us when enemies to him;" and loved us into a likeness to himself; answerable whereto, we should love him, even while our fears may apprehend him to be our enemy; and, through the power of his love secretly working in our hearts, go on to love him, until the glory of the Lord be risen upon us. You could not thus love God, if he had not loved you first, 1 John 2: 19.

4. Do you rejoice in the thoughts of electing love, what it is, and whence it came? what it hath designed you for, and will bring you unto at last? is it your delight to converse with the book of life? and do you rejoice more that " your names are written in heaven, than if devils were subject to you;" when your flesh and your heart fail you, do you look to electing love as your strength and portion, and count it a goodly heritage? Psal. 16: 6. Do you aim at that which electing love designed you for; and because so designed, if by any means you may attain to it? and are you better satisfied to be at the good pleasure of God, than at your own? and bless his wisdom and grace for undertaking the disposure of your eternal interest? such fruit could not be, but from that seed of God.

Let me add a few tokens more of true love, according to its ordinary acceptation and conduct among men. 1. He that loves another, will delight in his presence, and seek occasions of conversing with him. 2. Being absent, he thinks much upon him, and gives welcome entertainment to whatever may be a remembrance of him. 3. He will seek the well-pleasedness of him who is the object of his love, by presenting things lovely to him; by avoiding whatever may disgust him: by a wary preventing, or a speedy removing, what might give the other occasion to be jealous of his love to him. 4. He will candidly interpret whatever might seem a declining of the other's love to him; and not be satisfied until it be recovered, or better understood.

II. If you be of this happy remnant of election, then look for ill-usage from the world. The men of the world have always hated God's elect, and will: why did Esau hate Jacob? because of the blessing, Gen. 27: 41. And our

Saviour expressly says to his disciples, " I have chosen you out of the world, therefore the world hates you," John 15: 19. While in nature, they love the world, and the world them: but when election breaks forth in its fruits, when once they are called according to purpose, then " a man's enemies will be those of his own house," Micah 7: 6. And hence it is, that the very doctrine of election is so disgustful to the world, and contended against; wherein I wish that some of the elect themselves were not (unwittingly) involved. Therefore think it not strange, but take it as an appendix of election, John 15: 17, 18, 19. as a part of that you were chosen unto; and as that by which, partly, you must be fitted for the main end: your Lord himself was made perfect through sufferings, Heb. 2: 10. and those foreknown, were predestinated to be conformed to their head, in suffering as well as glory, Rom. 8: 29. and 6: 5.

III. Having trusted electing love for eternal salvation, see you distrust it not for things of lesser moment. When the Lord ordained you to life! he ordained also to those various occurrences, windings and turnings, you should be exercised with in your way thither; and, it is sure, he does nothing in vain? There is need of all sorts of weather for the earth's good; all fair would destroy it. Know it therefore of a truth, that all your concerns were fore-determined of God; and that so well, that all your prudence and love to yourselves could not mend it: nor can all your care and solicitude alter any of them, either as to matter or form; no, not to change the color of a hair: " Take therefore no thought for the morrow: for the morrow shall take thought for the things of itself. Sufficient unto the day is the evil thereof," Matt. 6: 34.

But whence is it that believers, who have trusted God for their souls, should yet make a difficulty of trusting him for their outward man? and so cumber themselves with unprofitable burdens?

Earthly things are nearer our senses; and thence we are more sensible of the comfort of them, as also of their want: they also seem more within our line and compass; and so we reach more earnestly after them, and are answerably troubled when we fall short: whereas we should carry it for temporals as we do (or should do rather) for our souls and spiritual portion; that is, look to our present duty, be diligent in our place, and content with such things as we have, Heb. 13: 5. bearing ourselves as becomes the children of such a Father, so rich, wise, bountiful, tender, and faithful to us; who always gives the best supply; and that in the best proportion, manner, and time.

Have therefore your faith exercised, as about the greater, so also about the smallest and commonest matters; use grace, and have grace: it is want of use makes you lame of your right hand; and much using renders it more useful. Faith is the head of your spiritual senses; and if that be active, the rest cannot be idle, nor much at a loss. Faith also is a plain-dealer: it represents things as they are; shews them in their true dimensions, with their use and end. See therefore that you never hold a consultation unless faith be present, yea, and president too, else all will be in disorder at once: one act of faith shall sooner remove the mountain, than all the cattle on a thousand hills.

Lastly. You that have closed with this truth, and having made diligent search, do find in yourselves those marks of God's elect, sit down and take the comfort of it; let this joy of the Lord be your strength: " eat your bread, and drink your wine" (or water either) " with a merry heart, since God hath accepted you," Eccl. 9: 7. If David's heart was so taken with that temporal favor which chose him to be king before the house of Saul, 2 Sam. 6: 21. how should our souls be wrapped into the third heaven, that we (poor, unworthy, wretched we) should be taken into that peculiar favor, in which the generality of men have nothing to do? How should it affect our hearts, and raise up our spirits, both in all active obedience, as David, who danced before the ark with all his might, and also to all long-suffering, with joyfulness; as Paul, and other chosen vessels, who rejoiced in tribulation; because this " love of God was shed abroad in their hearts," Rom. 5: 3, 4.

Art thou of those who are wise and noble according to the flesh? Be filled with an holy amazement, and exultation together, rejoicing with trembling, that the great God (to whom thou wast no more than others, thy consorts that are left, and who commonly chooses the base and foolish, thereby to magnify his grace) should thus go out of his way to call in thee; and hath also made his call effectual to thee, even then when thou wast environed with a world of temptations to obstruct it. And if thou be a man of low degree, poor, weak, foolish, of no account among men, even as one that is not; and hath the Lord regarded thee in thy low state, and magnified thee, by setting his love upon thee? Hath he taken thee from the dunghill, to set thee among princes, even the princes of the world to come? This is that exaltation which the poor should always rejoice in. Were you the head instead of being the tail; were the necks of your enemies under your feet; yea, were the devils themselves made subject to you; it could not afford you the thousandth part of that cause of rejoicing, as that " your names are written in heaven."   Are other men prosperous in the world, and free from trouble, while you are reduced to a low estate, and chastened every morning? have, perhaps, but a handful of meal, and a little oil in a cruse, &c. yet think not your portion mean, or hardly dealt out: your good things are to come; they are growing in the other world; and at the time of harvest the Lord will send his angels for you: yea, your Lord himself will come and fetch you thither; and " you shall be for ever with him, in whose presence is fulness of joy, and at whose right hand are rivers of pleasures for evermore:" and then you will sing, " The lines are fallen to me in pleasant places;" at least say so now.   As Abraham dealt by his concubines' children, so doth God by the Ishmaels of the world, he gives them portions, and sends them away, Gen. 25: 6.   But the inheritance he reserves for his Isaacs; to them he gives all that he hath, yea, even himself; and what can we have more?

REDEMPTION

In this point we are equally concerned with that of Election, as the great comprehensive means of bringing about the greatest end, namely the glory of God in the salvation of his chosen. Redemption is not another foundation distinct from election; but the chief corner-stone that election hath laid of the world to come.

That our Lord Jesus Christ hath a body or church, to whom he is Head and Saviour, is not supposed a question: but, who they are that make up his body; whether the whole of mankind universally, or some particular persons? Whether he had in his death the same respect to all as to some? And whether any of those he died for, may miss of the benefit accruing by his death? are questions of great import, and worthy a serious deliberation: and the rather, because they are points too lightly discoursed of by many. To resolve which is the scope of the present discourse; which I cast into three branches:

    I. That the body, or church of Christ, consists of elect persons.
    II. That for these it was that he laid down his life.
    III. That the intent of his death cannot be frustrated.

I. That the body, or church of Christ consists of elect persons. By this body, or church, I understand the designed subjects of his spiritual kingdom or members of his mystical body, to whom he was appointed by the Father to be Head and Saviour, and they to stand related to him as their Prophet, Priest, and King: which three-fold office he bears peculiarly towards the elect, the church of the first born, and heirs of that world to come. And of these doth his body consist, that is, it is made up of these, exclusive to others; their number is certain and entire, and cannot be broken, either by addition or diminution: of this the tabernacle was a figure, 1. In respect of its symmetry or proportion of parts, which induced a singular beauty upon it; towards which nothing could be added, nor any thing abated. 2. In that all the parts and dimensions thereof were predetermined of God; and not left, in the least, to human arbitrement or contingency: and these are express-ly said to be "patterns of things in the heavens," Heb. 9: 23. that is, of the heavenly temple, or church of the first-born, which are written there, chap. 12: 23. and in the appointed time shall be gathered together to him, as the materials of Solomon's temple were to mount Moriah, 2. Chron. 3: 1.

That the body or church of Christ consists of elect per-sons, is drawn from such premises as these.

I. In that our Lord and Saviour so manifestly shews him-self concerned for the elect, as having some peculiar in-stance and propriety in them, and charge of them. With these his delights were from everlasting, Prov. 8: 31. (a manifest proof of Christ's divinity!) and as soon as they were actually in being, began his actual converses with them; and therein did even confine himself to the elect seed. With what unbelievable patience and goodness did he superintend the church, or elect nation, forty years togeth-er in the wilderness, Acts 7: 36, 38. bearing them as on eagle's wings, and tendering them as the apple of his eye! And when he dwelt upon earth, he went not beyond the bounds of the Holy Land; where also all his delight was among the saints, Psal. 16: 3. These he made his con-sorts, and men of his council: and when you find him with others, it was for the elect's sake that were among them. How frequently, and with what well-pleasedness doth he speak of these! professing his love to them, and that accor-ding to the highest pattern! even " as the Father loved him, " so he loved them!" John 15: 9. and how great things he would do for them! not to the halving of his kingdom, but the laying down of his life for them! chap. 10: 14, 16. and 6: 40. gathering them in, raising them up, and giving them to sit with him in his throne! Rev. 3: 21. But for the world he takes little notice of them, except with a kind of contempt and commination; " Let them alone," Matt. 15: 14. " Shake off the dust of your feet," chap. 10: 14. "Give not that which is holy unto dogs," &c. chap. 7: 6. " Yea, though they seek him, they shall not find him," John 7: 34.

But for his elect, he is found of them, even while they think not of him, Isa. 65: 1. The instances of Matthew, the woman of Samaria, the possessed Gadarene, his people at Corinth, are records of it. And all this, because these are "his portion, and the lot of his inheritance," Deut. 32: 9. "They are the men which the Father gave him out of the world," John 17: 6. for as Christ, our Head, is not of this world, chap. 18: 36. so neither is his kingdom, nor the subjects of it.

It is true, the Father hath given Christ to be Head over all: but his lordship over men in general, and his headship over the church, have a far different respect and consideration: he is God of the whole earth, but Jeshuron's God in a way peculiar to his chosen, Deut. 32: 26. Isa. 44: 2. A headship of dominion he hath over rebels, and service he hath from them, though they think not so, nor intend any thing less. Nebuchadnezzar was his hired days-man against Tyre, Ezek. 26: 18. and Cyrus against Babylon, Isa. 45. whose right hand he held, though he knew him not: so Moab was his wash pot, Psal. 60: 8. But for the elect, they are his natural subjects (though not naturally so;) they are his by another title, and to another end: and so intimate is the relation between him and them, that they are said to be "of his flesh, and of his bones," Eph. 5: 30. They both have one soul and spirit; he and they make one perfect man, Eph. 4: 13.

That the whole world is put in subjection to Christ, is for the elect's sake; the power he hath over others, is in order to their salvation; "He is Head over all things to the church," Eph. 1: 22. that is, to subject, dispose, and order all for the church's good: "He hath power over all flesh, that he might give eternal life (not to all he hath power over, but) to as many as the Father hath given him," John 17: 2. which giving imports election; as going before it: and therefore he says, "I have manifested thy name to the men which thou gavest me out of the world, thine they were, (that is, by election,) and thou gavest them me," John 17: 6. That in Heb. 10: 5. "A body hast thou prepared me;" though chiefly intended there of his human nature, holds true of his body mystical; "All the members of which were written in God's book (of election) when as yet there were none of them" actually existing, Psal. 139: 16. He therefore prays for these, as a party distinct from the world, and given to him for an higher end; as appears by comparing the 2d, 6th, 9th, 24th, and '26th verses of the 17th chapter of John.

II. We find, by scripture usages, that church, and elect, are but two several titles of the same persons, in a several respect; elect, as chosen of God to salvation; and so they are called the church of God, and said to be sanctified by God the Father, Jude, ver. 1. and the church of Christ, as given or committed to him by the Father, in order to that salvation, John 17:6. Of this church were those particular congregations, to whom the apostles inscribed their epistles; where we have them sometimes entitled, "beloved of God," Rom. 1: 7. sometimes, "the church of God," and "sanctified in Christ," 1 Cor. 1: 2. at other times, "saints and faithful brethren in Christ," Col. 1: 2. then "churches of the saints," 1 Cor. 14: 33. and "church of the first-born," Heb. 12: 23. and sometimes expressly, "elect," 1 Pet. 1: 2. By all which is signified, that the church of Christ consists of elect persons; that these various appellations are but so many terms indifferently used about the same subject, and all as notes of distinction from the world.

When Christ shall appear in his glory, then shall all his members be gathered to him: "The Lord my God shall come, and all the saints with thee," says Zecharias, Zech. 14: 5. And Paul, discoursing the same thing, says, "They that are Christ's at his coming," 1 Cor. 15: 23. which shows that they are Christ's so as others are not. And that it is meant of elect persons, appears by our Saviour's own words, when speaking of his coming, and of the same persons who are said to be his, and to come with him, he gives them expressly that denomination, "He shall send forth his angels, and they shall gather together his elect," Matth. 24: 31. " but as for the rest of the dead, they lived not again until a thousand years after," Rev. 20: 5. therefore these [rest] were no part of this body. It may also be noted, that those who did not rise with the saints, are specified here by the same word, or note of distinction, as those not elected are, in another place; "the election hath obtained, and the rest were blinded," Rom. 11:7. and that those who had part in the first resurrection, are the same persons that are "written in the Lamb's book of life," is evident, by comparing Rev. 20: 4. with chapter 13: 8.

III. It is necessary, that the body or church of Christ

should be composed of the elect seed; 1. Because none else were fit to be of this body, but such as should be like the Head. Carnal members would be as uncomely to a spiritual head, as one of the brutes to be Adam's companion: The king's daughter-elect, to make her a suitable match for his Son, must be " all glorious within:" not only of the same outward metal (for so were those other creatures with Adam) but made in the same mould, and endued with the same spirit and understanding: there must be a congruity in all the parts throughout: they must be copies of him; "each one resembling the children of a king," Judges 8: 18. If the head be heavenly, so must the members: they cannot walk together, if not thus agreed. 2. Because this likeness to Christ is proper to the elect: it is a royal privilege entailed upon them, and cannot descend or revert to any out of that line. That this likeness to Christ is requisite to all his members, and also peculiar to elect persons, are both attested in Rom. 8: 29. " Whom he did foreknow, he also did predestinate to be conformed to the image of his Son, that he might be the first-born among many brethren:" which implies, that the foreknown, or elect, only are predestinated thereto; and that, were it not for predestination, the first-born should have but a thin assembly to preside among; indeed, nothing but blanks for his great adventure, and long expectation. In Eph. 1: 3, 4, 5. He further appropriates those spiritual blessings, by which men are conformed to Christ, to the same persons; " Blessed be the God and Father of our Lord Jesus Christ, who hath blessed us with all spiritual blessings in heavenly things in Christ: according as he hath chosen us in him:— having predestinated us to the adoption of children," &c. By these two scriptures it appears, that God's children, and Christ's brethren are the same persons: and that they were so made by election. But, are Christ's brethren and his church the same persons? take your solution from Heb. 2: 12. " I will declare thy name unto my brethren; in the midst of the church will I sing praise unto thee." 3. This likeness to Christ is not attainable by any, without first being in him as their head: for which cause the elect were chosen in him, Eph. 1: 4. It is out of Christ's fulness that all grace is received: and in order to that reception, there must be union: the branch cannot bear fruit of itself, nor indeed be a branch, unless it grow out of the vine. For which cause and end, the designed members of his body were decretively separated from their wild olive root, and put into Christ by election: and in the fulness of time actually. And hereby they are made partakers of the fatness of that heavenly root; that is, of the Spirit of Christ, which is called the anointing, 1 John 2: 27. In this respect, the first and second Adams are set forth as parallels, touching headship to their respective bodies. As from Adam, their natural head, all mankind have derived their natural being; so from Christ, their spiritual head, do all the elect seed receive their spiritual being and nature: on which account he is styled "the everlasting Father," and they "his children," Isa. 9: 6. Heb. 2: 13. They were all in Christ from eternity as truly (but spiritually) as mankind in Adam when he fell; or Levi in Abraham's loins when Melchizedee met him. Eve's production, as to the manner of it, was a pattern of this: she was made of Adam's substance; but she came not out of his loins, but out of his side, Gen. 2: 21. 23. so is the new creature extracted out of Christ's: they are " bone of his bones, and flesh of his flesh," spiritually understood. And none can thus proceed from him, but such as were in him decretively before the world: men are blessed with these spiritual blessings, as being in Christ, and not otherwise, Eph. 1: 4. Tit. 3: 5, 6.

Inferences

Infer. I. Let no man pretend to this honorable relation of membership to Christ, without something to show, by which he may warrantably avouch it. The most current mark will be your conformity, not to men, or self, but to Christ Jesus your head: it is that must denominate you christians indeed. At the latter day Christ will know none but such as have made "their robes white in the blood of the Lamb." All hangby's and ivy-claspers will then be shaken off, and those only retained that have his substance in them. Many shall come, and plead their works, what they have been, and what they have done; and their old hypocrisy will be so immoveable and impudent, that they will even expostulate the matter with him; " Have we not prophesied in thy name, and in thy name cast out devils, and done many wonderful works!" Mat. 7: 22. of whom our Lord will profess, that he knows them not; " no, nor he never knew them." Ver. 23. His own he knows, by their likeness to him: he knows, and cannot but know, the members of his body: " my sheep I know, but who are ye?" will he then say to all that are but professing members of him; which will (indeed) be a doleful conclusion of their groundless (though specious) confidence: look to it therefore in time.

Infer. II. We gather hence the safe and honorable estate of the church.

First. Their state is honorable. If the woman's dignity rise in proportion with that of her lord; how highly dignified is the spouse of Christ, in having the Son of God for her head! that seed of Abraham, which the second person took on him was instantly ennobled with a glory becoming the Son of God, and the head of principalities and powers; and no more to be considered merely after the flesh: in like manner, having accepted those his church is composed of, he communicates to them of his own condition and nature; "the glory his Father had given him, he gives to them," John 17: 22. and notwithstanding their former and natural baseness, he reckons them now as one with himself; and according to what he will make them at last. A tincture thereof he gave them here in regeneration; which also he carries on from glory to glory, and at his appearing it shall be perfected: they " shall be like him" indeed, 1 John 3: 2. To say of the Church's Head, that he is the Son of GOD, is to give him all titles of state and honor: it is that which every knee must bow unto. His glory is so incomprehensibly glorious, that we shall sooner be lost in searching into it, than compass encomiums worthy of such a subject: I therefore say no more of it; nor can more be said, in so many words, to illustrate the church's glory, than that she is the spouse of CHRIST. Hence the glory of our religion, and of its real confessors. And, let it be noted, that it is not a bare titular or temporary dignity they are vested with; but that which is real, solid, and durable. Princes confer titles of honor, but cannot infuse dispositions worthy those titles, nor keep them from degenerating: CHRIST, as Head of the church, does both: he derives into his own, his own prince-like virtues; and that as really, and intelligibly too, to those that partake of them, 1 John 1: 1, 2, 3. as the vine its sap into its natural branches. What a labyrinth is it, both of honor and consolation, that the blood royal of heaven runs in their veins, and will never run out! but true as it is, how few do believe it? and of those few, who is it that lives up to the faith of it? Two ends, therefore, I mention it for:

[1.] To bear up your spirits against the world's frowns and calumnies, which the serious thoughts of your relation to such a Head, may well counterbalance and relieve you against. Princes in exile, (or, if in their own country, unknown and meanly attended,) are but coarsely used: and we marvel not at the matter, which yet the thoughts of their high birth, and confidence of restoration, do mightily support them under. Much more should the sons of God, (whose descent is not reckoned from the kings of the earth,) have still in their eye their divine extract, with that circumferent reward that is coming, and bear up their heads in a prince-like manner! and for "the joy that is set before them, both endure the cross, and despise the shame;" until they come to be exalted, not only above those nick-names the world imposes on them, but above the most honorable names, and most serene titles that are found under heaven! Then shall it be known "whose ye are;" your lustre shall be no longer hid: those that despise you now, shall "lick the dust of your feet," Isa. 49: 23. Psal. 72: 9. and then shall be accomplished that great word of your Saviour (and that as surely as if it were done already,) "The glory which thou gavest me, I have given them," John 17: 22. yea, you shall sit with your Lord in his throne, Rev. 3: 21. Besides, (which also shall add to that day's solemnity,) this thing shall not be done in a corner; but as ye have been openly reviled, so shall ye have a public vindication. "The great trumpet shall be blown in the land," Isa. 27: 13. the archangel, with the trumpet of God, 1 Thess. 4: 16. shall come, and that with so shrill a note, that heaven and earth shall ring again; and this shall be the tenor of his song, "Arise, shine, for thy light is come, and the glory of the Lord is risen upon thee," Isa. 60: 1. 20. and shall set no more, "thus shall it be done to Zion, whom no man (now) seeketh after." Jer. 30: 17.

[2.] To mind you that your honorable state obliges to an honorable deportment, both towards your Head, yourselves, and your fellow-members.

(1.) As touching your Head. 1. Own his supremacy,

giving him pre-eminence in all things; call no man on earth Master; that is, in point of faith: give unto Cæsar the things that belong to him; only respect Christ as supreme lawgiver. 2. Submit to his government; steer your course by his counsels, and follow his conduct; go after him wherever he shall lead you; let all your senses have their seat in your Head; let every thing be understood by you according to his sense and interpretation of it; and if there needs an argument to back the exhortation, that ordinance, " thy desire shall be unto thy husband, and he shall rule over thee," Gen. 3: 16. is as true and cogent concerning Christ and the church, Eph. 5: 24. 3. Expose yourself for him; stand between him and wrongs; preserve his honor and interest with the utmost hazard of yourself; let life and death be as things indifferent to you, so " Christ may be magnified in you," Phil. 1: 20. 4. Look to your Head for supply of all grace; from his fulness it is to be had, and no where else: hold to your Head, lest notions beguile you of your reward, Col. 2: 18, 19. Be also sure that you keep to your place and duty, lest you miss of the nourishment that belongs to you, John 14: 4, 5. a member out of its place, is, for the time, as a member cut off. 5. *Lastly.* Adorn your Head, by your daily aspiring to a nearer resemblance of him: show forth his virtues: be holy as he was: let all your fruits be such as are meet for such a root. God the Father is the Head of Christ, and he bore the express image of his person, Heb. 1: 3. in all that he did: He could do nothing but what he saw the Father do," John 5: 19. So do you by your Head Christ: make him your example; and, in order thereto, live upon him as your immediate root, and give him the honor of his own productions; remembering withal, that every slip of yours casts soil upon him.

(2.) There is a respect due to yourselves: (a superfluous item, one would think, though needful.) There is aptitude enough to honor ourselves, but, as belonging to such an Head, is too much unthought of. Things that well enough beseem the common rank, would be a disgrace to persons of honor: the king's daughter should be known by her outward garb; glorious within, and clothing of wrought gold, decypher the same person, and may not be separated. Ye have an " high calling," walk worthy of it, Phil. 3: 24. Col. 1: 10. and show your thankfulness, by an humble retribution: honor that which honors you, by comporting with its end: make not yourself cheap; stoop not beneath your degree: make Christ alone the object of your love, delight, dependance; to do otherwise is to debase yourself, Isa. 57: 9. The church is the glory of Christ; its members, therefore, should think themselves too good and too great, to be spent on the world; and the world too mean and empty, to afford them either satisfaction or adornment. A circumspect walking, soberness of mind, humility, self-denial, with a meek and quiet spirit, are jewels of price, and ornaments indeed: by these the invited guests should distinguish themselves from intruders; and real christians from merely nominal. In christianity, it is no badge of pride or ill husbandry, to wear your best every day; we should not be seen without it; much wearing will better it, and it cannot be damaged but by lying by. Your bodies too are worthy of consideration, and not a little: they are the figures of Christ's humanity, and temples of the Holy Ghost; therefore keep them unspotted, and profane them not, either by fashioning them to the world, or subjecting them to servile uses. But I would not cause any to err: these, though ornaments, are not your righteousness: when ye stand before God, ye must put over all the righteousness of our Lord and Mediator: (the priest's holy garments were to be sprinkled with blood, Exod. 20: 21.) This was that the speechless guest wanted, and was therefore cast out; though not discriminable by them that stood by: Abraham was justified by works before men; but before God, it was the righteousness of Christ wherein by faith he shrouded himself: faith justifies the person, and works justify his faith, both to himself and other men.

(3.) Then carry it towards brethren as members of the same body. 1. Usurp not upon them, as if more than fellow-member with them: judge not the strong; despise not the weak: who made thee a judge? There is none but hath need of forbearance from others; though, for the most part, they that need it most, are most backward to yield it: but this take for a rule, that the less you see your need, the more need you have of it. 2. Intrude not in another's place and office: each member hath its own, to which it is fitted: this it best becomes, and here it is most useful; elsewhere it would be both useless, and a deformity: as a finger transposed, and out of its own joint. 3.

Show your co-membership, by your love and tender regard towards others: have compassion upon the ignorant, and those out of the way, Heb. 5: 2. as your head towards you. If one be weak or wounded, let him that is strong and whole support and bind it up: if one foot stumble, let the other step in for its help: "Consider thyself, lest thou also be tempted," Gal. 6: 1. Members of the same natural body need no arguments to persuade to this duty; they do it by instinct. Our want of compassionateness towards others, though it shall not dry up, yet, may much restrain, at least in our apprehensions, the springs of Christ's pity towards ourselves. 4. *Lastly.* Let the good of the whole have preference before a particular part; and let that of a lower use deny itself for the safety and assistance of that which is more noble: this, in a degree is to lay down our life for " the brethren." He that in these things serveth CHRIST is acceptable to GOD, and approved of men and a good evidence it is of your membership to CHRIST.

Secondly. The church is safe. The Son of GOD being their Head and Saviour, bespeaks aloud their security. They are indeed compassed about with difficulties, dangers, and deaths, and yet they live; yea, they overcome, and shall in the end prove more than conquerors: the reason of all is, their Head is in heaven, whence all relief comes; and that avenue cannot be stopped. If ye speak of principalities and powers, which rule in the air; CHRIST has a power above them; "they are under his feet," Heb. 1: 13. and 2: 8. Their power of hurting lies much in their subtilty; but even in this they are still circumvented; he catches them in their own net: and hence it is, that the devil has from the beginning been a liar to himself. His first bait in tempting was, " ye shall be as gods," Gen. 3: 5. when his meaning was, to make us like himself; but the wisdom of God turns the temptation into a prophecy, and CHRIST will make it good, John 17: 21. as he also did that pernicious counsel of Caiaphas, chap. 11: 50. The serpent in bruising Christ's heel, got a bruise in his own head; that all his devices have still proved abortive, or turned on himself: he stirred up Judas to betray CHRIST, the Gentiles and Jews to condemn and crucify him; and what got he by it, but the loss of his empire? If ye speak of his seed, the same infatuation hath descended to them: this nothing makes plainer than their still making it their

interest to exterminate the church: with as much reason
they might think to unhinge the world, or unbottom the
rock of ages. But their projects have ever been defeated,
and shall; as men mistaking their measures, and made to
subserve the interest they design to crush. The Egyptians' dealings with Israel, and nominal Christians' with
those that are really such, are instances above contradiction. It is a consideration of no small importance to our
faith, that all things were made for CHRIST, and are at his
disposal: therefore, whatever the church's enemies have,
they have it from the Church's Head; who knowing his
own interest and intent, will give out no more than to
serve that turn; nor can they act what they have, but under his government. He is Prince of the kings of the
earth, he ruleth among the gods, sits at the helm invisibly,
steers the most secret and violent counsels, and carries the
casting voice. Among other observable things it is matter
of wonder, 1. That the divine prescience hath so interwoven the secular interest with that of his church, as
induceth a kind of necessity to protect the church for the
world's support. 2. That our Lord frequently compasseth his work by letting his enemies do their own, Exod.
1: 11, 12. And, 3. That in all their devices, he still
countermines them; and either takes out their powder, or
blows them up with their own train: "Then the king of
Syria warred against Israel, and took counsel with his servants, saying, In such and such a place shall be my camp.
And the man of God sent unto the king of Israel, saying,
Beware that thou pass not such a place; for thither the
Syrians are come down," 2 Kings 6: 8, 9. "The heathen
are sunk down in the pit that they made: in the net which
they hid is their own foot taken. The Lord is known by
the judgment which he executeth: the wicked is snared in
the work of his own hands," Psal. 9: 15, 16. 2 Chron. 20:
22, 23.

But suppose that hell be broke loose, and legions of
locusts, belched out of the bottomless pit, come up against
them, armed with strength, winged with fury, ambuscaded
with policy, edged with enmity, and headed by the red
dragon; and by these is besieged the camp of the saints
and the beloved city, and the church as unable to resist as
a woman that is ready to travail: and now say their enemies, what will become of their dreams? Take this for

your comfort: 1. There still hangs a cloud between the two camps, and its bright side is towards the church, Exod. 14: 20. 2. The enemy's camp is again surrounded by the church's succors, and kept in a pound, as by "chariots and horsemen of fire," 2 Kings 6: 17. And, 3. That "he who sits in the heavens, will have them in derision," Psal. 2: 4. Jerusalem will prove a burdensome stone to all that trouble themselves with it: and if other means fail, and to make a total end, "fire comes down from God out of heaven, and devours them," Rev. 20: 9.

But there is yet a more dreadful sort of enemies than these; the devil, in the head of original sin, is a beast not to be dealt with. The church itself, reflecting on self, and looking no higher, may cry out with amazement, "Who is able to make war with the beast?" Indeed the whole of your native militia, with all the troops of free-will auxiliaries, will not do it; they are but mercenaries; and if you trust them, they will turn against you in the battle; or, if they stand to it, according to their best skill, it shall not avail you; they are with this beast but as stubble to his bow; yet be not discouraged, but renounce them all, and depend on the triple league above, that omnipotent and inviolable confederation, of all whose forces the Lord is commander in chief. This lion of the tribe of Judah is able to deal with that beast, and to tear him in pieces; yea, he hath done it already; "On his cross he triumphed over them," Col. 2: 15. yea, and which is more, he followed the rout to the gates of hell; there he shut them in, and carries the key on his shoulder: they cannot wag but by license from him, nor tarry a moment beyond his prescript. To be short, the only dreadful thing is sin; the devil, death, and hell, are but subordinate attendants, as effects on their causes, and therefore that taken away, the rest are unstung, they have lost their power of hurting: so that the church still remains invincible; and the reason of all is, "It is founded upon a rock," Matt. 16: 18. "and that rock is Christ," 1 Cor. 10: 4. All which being true, not only of the church in gross, but of members in particular. Therefore,

Infer. III. Let every one that is of this body be well pleased with his lot; be glad, and rejoice for ever in this your portion: this is the exaltation the brother of low degree should value himself by, James 1: 9. Be your rank and condition ever so mean in the world, care not for it; but rest contented with your place, and be thankful for it: desire not yourself to change it, but strive to fill it up, and be as useful in it as you can. Look also for troubles, and think them not strange, 1 Pet. 4: 12. the "Captain of your salvation was made perfect through suffering," Heb. 2: 10. " and the servant may not look to fare better than his Lord," Luke 23: 41.

Infer. IV. If Jesus Christ be your head, be confident, then, of all love, counsel, care, and protection from him; union with him entitles to all that is his. It is natural to the head to love and cherish the body, and every member of it; to contrive and cast about for its welfare and safety: " As a man cherisheth his own flesh, so doth Christ his church," Ephes. 5: 29. What though thou be, in thyself, an uncomely member? He will put the more comeliness upon thee, 1 Cor. 12: 23. he will clothe thee, and feed thee, and physic thee. " He will give grace and glory, and no good thing will he withhold from thee," Psal. 84:11. For he being the first-born, prince, and head of the family, all the younger brethren are to be maintained upon his inheritance.

Infer. V.   Rest also assured of safe-conduct to the promised land.   Adversaries and difficulties you will certainly meet with; remaining corruptions, like the mixed multitude, will be tumultuating and tempting within; the Amalekites, and people of his wrath, will stand in your way without, and be falling on your rear, to cut off the weak and feeble; and the serpent will yet be nibbling and bruising your heel; but higher than that he toucheth not: your heart and your head are out of his reach, therefore safe: if it come to the worst, ye can but die, and death itself shall not hurt you: nay, you conquer in dying: it shall but mend your pace heavenwards, and hasten you up to the throne of God.   Therefore quit you like men, and as men of nearest relation, by blood and spirits, to the man Christ Jesus: for, " God shall bruise Satan under your feet shortly," Rom. 16: 20.   Come (will your captain say to you, come,) " set your feet on the neck of this king of pride," Josh. 10: 24. and do by him as he hath done by others, and would have done also by you; give him double according to his works, Rev. 18: 6.   This is the time when ye shall judge angels, 1 Cor. 6: 3. and all under the conduct of this your head and captain, who will now " present you faultless, even before the presence of his glory, with exceeding joy," Jude, verse 24.

II. That our Lord Jesus Christ gave his life a ransom for the elect.

That the elect are Christ's peculiar portion is shewn before; and what engagements were upon him, on that account, for their redemption, will appear afterwards. By " giving himself a ransom," I understand the whole of his humiliation, whatever he did or suffered as Mediator, from his incarnation to his resurrection; all which are summarily expressed by " the blood of his cross;" as all the precious fruits of his death are by " forgiveness of sins, and reconciliation with God." That was the price wherewith he bought them that should be saved; and this the salvation he bought for them, and them for it. For although Satan (through their free-will-failings in Adam) had got a temporary mortgage upon the elect themselves, they are not his; the fee-simple, or right of inheritance, remains in Christ; and therefore, at the year of jubilee, they return to him, as the right heir; though not without both conquest and full price; which two together make redemption complete.

My scope here is to shew that " the body, or church of Christ, are especially concerned and interested in redemption:" and, in order thereto, I would consider two other of the divine works, both which respect the world universally, as redemption doth, and yet have a specialty in them, as redemption also hath, namely, creation and providence.

1. Creation: one God was the maker of all; but all were not made for the same use and end: he had a peculiar scope in the making of some, which was not common to the whole; yea, the whole was made for the sake of that some. As in the great house are many vessels (all of one master's providing, and all for his own service,) " some to honor, and some to dishonor;" so in the world, some God raised up to be monuments of his power and justice, Exod. 9: 16. Jude 4. Rom. 9: 22. 1 Pet. 2: 8. called therefore " vessels of wrath," Rom. 9: 22. Others are " vessels of mercy," whom he formed for himself, Isa. 43: 7. 21. and are therefore said to be " afore prepared unto glory," Rom. 9: 33.

2. Providence: this also extends to all, and to each individual: he hath power over all, and doth govern them in

their most ungoverned designs and actions: but as touching his church, the " people of his holiness," Isa. 63: 18. he holds a peculiar kind of government over them, and steerage of their concerns: and this so far exceeds the other, that, in comparison, it is said, " He never bore rule over them," ver. 19. and, which is still to be remarked, the others' concerns are made subservient to theirs; " He is head over all to the church," Eph. 1: 22. in like manner redemption may be said to be general, and yet to have a specialty in it: it is general, 1. In respect of persons. 2. In respect of things. Both which are true apart, though not conjunctly: it purchaseth some good things for all; and all good things for some. As it respects persons, it obtains a general reprieve, extensive to all the sons of Adam: the sin of the world was so far expiated, that vengeance was not presently executed; which must have been, had not the Son of God interposed himself: his being slain from the foundation of the world, was the foundation of the world's standing, and of all the good things which the world in general are partakers of. All that order and usefulness which yet survives among the creatures, with all the remains of our primitive state, was preserved, or rather restored, by redemption: Christ is " that light which lighteth every one that cometh into the world," John 1: 9. that is, the light and blessings which any man hath, he has them from Christ, as a Redeemer; " by him all things consist," Col. 1: 17. Thus far redemption was general as to persons; and in this sense Christ is the Saviour of all men. But let us not omit, that all this had a special respect to the church elect: for them it was that the world was made: they are the substance of it, Isa. 6: 13. and but for them it had been dissolved into a lake of fire. What the prophet speaks of Israel, was true of the universe, " Except the Lord of hosts had left us a remnant, we had been as Sodom," chap. 1: 9. as those days of tribulation were shortened for the elect's sake, Matt. 24: 22. (not yet in being) so for them it was, that when sin came in, destruction was warded off.

But temporary things, though ever so great and good, were of too low an alloy to be the purchase of divine blood; their line is too short to measure redemption by, and their bulk too narrow to fill up the height and depth of that great abyss: there must, by that glorious achievement, be some nobler obtainment than short-lived blessings; and an higher end than to bring men into a mere possibility of being saved. The life of the Son of God was infinitely too precious to be given for perishing things; nor would it be consistent with divine wisdom to venture it for an uncertainty. It had been a light thing for Christ, and not worthy his sufferings, to raise up the ruins made by Adam to such a degree of restoration as would only have set him in his former state, and that upon terms more unlikely to succeed: this had been to give a greater value for things of lesser moment; for it needs must be a happier state, to be made upright, without bias to evil, than to be moved with all manner of motives, while fettered by unbelief, and a natural bent to revolt further; for notwithstanding all those motives and means, not the majority only, but the universality of mankind might have perished, and gone to hell; which would in no wise have answered God's end in making the world, much less in redeeming it. It was therefore necessary redemption should have a further reach than to bring men into a mere salvable state, and that could not be less than a state of certain salvation. And, in order to this, redemption was general as to things, even all that pertaineth to life and godliness; eternal life, and whatever conduceth thereto, as will after be made evident. And this is that redemption we are treating of; and this is the sense of the present position, namely, that redemption, thus qualified, is peculiar to the church; and that election is the pattern by which redemption is to be measured: " the Son can do nothing but what he sees the Father do," John 5: 19.

To make redemption larger than electing love, is to overlay the foundation; which (all men know) is a very momentous error in building, especially of such a tower whose top must reach to heaven. It therefore behooves us to see that we separate not what God hath conjoined, either by stretching or straining the bounds he hath set. The Jews were of opinion that the promise of the Messiah belonged only to them, exclusive to the Gentiles: others since would extend it to all the sons of men universally, and alike; not considering the reason why the promise was made to the woman's seed, and not to Adam's: but the Messiah himself, who best knew the line of the promise, and end of his mission, exempted none; but extends it to " all nations" indifferently; yet so as that he restrains it to the elect among them, describing them still by such appellations as import a select party: they are called " his seed," and the " travail of his soul;" with respect to whom he should " make his soul an offering for sin," Isa. 53: 10, 11. these also he terms " his sheep," and himself " the good shepherd" (as he well might) " whose own the sheep are, and for whom he laid down his life," John 10: 15. and that he might not be taken to intend those only of the Jewish nation, he presently adds, " And other sheep I have, which are not of this fold: them also must I bring," ver. 16. The evangelist, expounding the high priest's prophecy, " that it was expedient one man should die for the people," delivers it thus: that " he should not die for that nation only, but also, that he should gather together in one the children of God that are scattered abroad," chap. 11: 52. in consequence whereof, they are said to be " made nigh by the blood of Christ," Eph. 2: 13. though before afar off: and that " he reconciled both (that is, Jews and Gentiles, or the elect scattered amongst both,) in one body by the cross," ver. 16. and this in pursuance of that blessed compact made with him, for restoring the preserved of Israel, as you find it recorded in Isa. 49: 6. It further appears by Isa. 53: 6. that they were " sheep whose iniquities were laid upon Christ:" and again, ver. 8. " For the transgression of my people was he stricken." And here let me note (for it is very remarkable,) that we read not of any party of men termed sheep, the people of God, and his children, in distinction from others, but with respect to some particular interest he hath in them above others; and what that interest may be, excepting election, doth not appear to us; for those other sheep were not yet called, and therefore not yet believers, and sheep on that account; but as they were of God's elect. For, though all men were lost, Christ was " sent but to the lost sheep of the house of Israel;" that is, those persons of the lost and perishing world, whom God hath chosen peculiarly, as he did the house of Israel from among the nations; and who, in that respect, were a special type of the spiritual election. And, on this account, the promises of the new covenant were made to the church under such names and titles as were proper to that people, as distinguished from other nations.

In Isa. 62, we find holy and redeemed applied to the same persons; whether it be meant of elective holiness, or actual, it comes to one; for both of them, together with redemption, do refer to the same subject: for as actual sanctification is the next fruit and consequent of redemption, so election is the root of them both; as ye have it in 1 Pet. 1: 2. " Elect unto obedience and sprinkling of the blood of Jesus Christ." 1 Pet. 1: 2. To be holy, is to be sacred, selected, and set apart for holy uses, by appointment of God; and they were actually sanctified by the " sprinkling of blood," Heb. 9: 19. in both which respects, the people of Israel, the tabernacle, temple, priests, altars, &c. are all said to be holy.

In Luke 1: 72. God's sending of Christ is said to be, " in performance of his holy covenant," which was first proclaimed in Paradise, as made with the woman's seed, Gen. 3: 15. and afterwards renewed with Abraham, Gen. 12: 3. and is therefore termed, " The mercy promised to Abraham, and to his seed:" And who are Abraham's seed? Not the world, but believers; that is, the elect: for these only obtain faith, Rom. 11: 7. and Gal. 3: 29. saith plain, " If ye be Christ's, then are ye Abraham's seed." We also read, that it was a peculiar people that Christ " gave himself for, and purchased," Tit. 2: 14. it denotes some special propriety he hath in them above others; and so, a special cause for his giving himself for them. It also seems that peculiar and purchased are so nearly allied, that one word is used to signify both, 1 Pet. 2: 9. According with this, is that in 1 Pet. 1: 20. where Christ is said to be " verily fore-ordained, and manifested," for those he writes that epistle to: that they were persons elected, is evident by the first and second verses; and elect unto the " sprinkling of his blood:" and as they were elected to it, so in John 17, he professes to make it good; " for their sakes (says Christ) I sanctify myself;" and twice in John 10, " that he laid down his life for the sheep," John 10: 11. 15. which is as exclusive of others, as where he saith, " My righteousness extends unto the saints; and he that believeth shall be saved;" that is, such, and none else.

It further appears from Acts 20: 28. that it was " the church of God he purchased with his own blood." Now, the church and the world are plainly distinct, as a garden enclosed is from the common fields. That the church consists of elect persons is proved before; and that it was the church he died for, is proved by this scripture; as also from

Eph. ch. 5, where husbands are required to love their wives, as "Christ loved the church, and gave himself for it," Eph. 5: 25. which shows, that as the husband's love to his wife is another kind of love, than that he bears to others of the same sex; so Christ's love to his church; and therefore his death, which was the special effect of that love, is peculiar to the church only. The elders about the throne sing a new song to the Lamb, because "he redeemed them to God by his blood," Rev. 5: 9. among other reasons for that style of elders, this may be one, that they "were chosen from the days of old, and their names written in his book of life from the foundation of the world," chap. 17: 8. They are also said to be "redeemed out of every kindred, and tongue, and people, and nation;" which rationally implies, that the bulk of those people and nations were not redeemed with them. We also read, that a certain number are said to be redeemed "from the earth, and from among men," chap. 14: 3, 4. If some from among others, it follows, of course, that those others were exempted. Here note, by the way, that these elders were now in heaven, above the clouds of misconception and prejudiced opinion; and therefore no reason to doubt their testimony. And further, these redeemed ones are there also styled, "The first-fruits unto God, and to the Lamb," Rev. 14: 4. which appellation insinuates, that they were separated from the rest, as the first-fruits under the law were by God himself, who took them for his own portion, Numb. 3: 13. and 8: 16. They are likewise said to have the "Father's name written in their foreheads," Rev. 14: 1. (election marked them out for Christ) and to be "written in the Lamb's book of life;" and that as a lamb slain; who on that account says to his Father, "Thine they were, and thou gavest them me," John 17: 6. Where also in his prayer to those whose sacrifice he was now to offer, he styles them, "the men whom the Father had given him out of the world;" and in ver. 10. "all mine are thine, and thine are mine:" that is, all that were Christ's in order to redemption, were first the Father's by election. It is as if he had said, All that I undertake for, are thine elect; and all thine elect I undertake for. He therefore reciprocates the terms of relation, turns them to and again, to show the sameness of the persons concerned in both. From all which it seems undeniably evident, that as a certain number were elected, so a certain number, and those the very same persons, were redeemed.

The ground and truth of this assertion, is further confirmed by such arguments as these:

Arg. I. The Levitical sacrifices were offered for the house of Israel, exemptive of other nations: and these being a type of the spiritual election, it follows, that this sacrifice of Christ (typified by theirs) was also peculiar to Jews in spirit, or spiritual Jews: "for he only is reckoned a Jew, that is such inwardly in the spirit," Rom. 2: 29. So Aaron's making atonement for his household, and bearing the names of the twelve tribes on his breast-plate, were typical of our great High Priest's bearing the names, and sustaining the persons of those for whom he offered himself on the cross: of all those legal shadows, Christ and the church of the first born are the body and substance

Arg. II. The right of redemption among the Jews (which shadowed this) was founded on brotherhood: hence I infer, that that relation, spiritually taken, was both the ground and limit of Christ's office as a Redeemer. The apostle's discourse in Heb. ch. 2, seems to point at this, where he says "they were brethren, children, and sons, whom Christ should deliver from bondage, make reconciliation for their sins, and bring to glory." But how came they to be God's children, and the brethren of Christ, above others? It was by predestination; and that it was it entitled them to redemption; as is evident by comparing the 5th and 7th verses of Eph. 1. "Having predestinated us to the adoption of children by Jesus Christ: in whom we have redemption through his blood." And it is worthy of your notice, that by the law of redemption, a stranger (one that was not of the brotherhood) might not be redeemed; but one that was, though not redeemed, must yet go free in the year of jubilee, Lev. 25: 46, 48. with 41: 54. which shews the peculiar respect the Lord has for his peculiar people.

Arg. III. The saving benefits of redemption do not redound to any but elect persons, whatever in one place is ascribed to redemption, as the special fruit and consequent thereof, is elsewhere ascribed to election, and to this as the first and original root: and, that redemption itself is the fruit of electing love, is evident by 1 Pet 1: 2. (quoted before) "Elect unto obedience, and sprinkling of the blood of Jesus Christ." They are also said to be " blessed with

all spiritual blessings in Christ, according as he had chosen them in him," Eph. 1: 3, 4. and if all spiritual blessings be dispensed by the law of election, then all the
saving benefits of redemption (which are the same with
those of election) must be dispensed by the same rule; and
so, to the same persons only. We also find that Christ's
actual distribution of the gifts he received for men, is
guided answerably: " he manifests the Father's name to
the men he had given him out of the world," John 17: 6. to
these he expounds that in private, which to others he spake
in parables: and thus he did, because " to them it was given
to know the mysteries of the kingdom of God; but to the
multitude it was not given," Matt. 13: 34. 36. and election
was that which gave it them, as it follows there, " for so
it seemed good in thy sight." In like manner, the apostle,
in Rom. 8, puts election and redemption together, as pertaining to the same persons, and justification, which is the
next effect of redemption, he makes also an unquestionable
consequent of election; " Who shall lay any thing to the
charge of God's elect? It is God that justifieth: who shall
condemn? It is Christ that died," Rom. 8: 33, 34. The
question being put concerning God's elect, and the answer
referring to those for whom Christ died; is a plain impli-
cation, that redemption and justification are commensurate
with election; that either of them concerneth only the
same persons; and that neither of them extends to any, but
whom the other also taketh in.

Arg. IV. The price of redemption was of that precious
and matchless value, that it could not be parted with, but
with respect to the certainty of the end for which it was
paid. Now, the end of redemption was the salvation of
men: below which there could not be an end worthy the
death of Christ; and this nothing could secure but election.
The elect always have obtained, and shall: this is a rule
affirmed in Rom. 11: 7. But for the rest, they are blinded;
that is, they are left to their own voluntary misunderstand-
ing; and being so left, not only they do not, but they cannot believe. And Christ knowing from the beginning
who they were that believed not, but would certainly
reject him, to what end should he make his soul an offering for them? Why for the world of the ungodly, whose
spirits were in prison some thousands of years before?
Whom the Lord intends to save alive, he appoints an

"atonement to be made for them," Numb. 16: 46, 47. but for those he intends to destroy (which is always done justly,) he will not accept an offering, judges 13: 23. and therefore not appoint it: as he did not under the law, for those crimes which men were to die for.

Arg. V. I confine redemption to elect persons, because intercession, which is of equal latitude with redemption. is limited to them, exclusive of others. The priests under the law were to pray for those whose sacrifice they offered; and what they did, was a pattern of our Saviour's priestly office; whom likewise we find to sacrifice and pray only for the same persons; he is an advocate for those for whose sin he is a propitiation, 1 John 2:1. whose transgressions he was smitten for, for them he makes intercession, Isa. 53: 8. 12. for their sakes he sanctified himself, and for them it was that he made that solemn prayer in the 17th of John. And he then prayed for them, as being just then upon offering their sacrifice: he also shuts out the world expressly from having any interest in it: "I pray not for the world, but for them which thou hast given me," John 17: 9. And he adds the reason, the foundation reason, why he would pray for these, "for they are thine;" that is, they were the Father's by election: for in all other respects, "the earth is the Lord's and the fulness thereof," Psal. 24: 1.

Arg. VI. Another argument for peculiar redemption, is founded on the merit of Christ's death, together with its efficacy. He was not cut off for himself, Dan. 9: 26. but those he undertook for: and it was to procure them a right to those glorious privileges which election ordained them to. Hence I argue, 1. That which Christ laid down his life for, that he merited; and, 2. What he merited, is due to those for whom it was merited. Now, the principal thing intended and merited by his death, was the justification of sinners; and "that God might be just in justifying of them," Rom. 3: 26. and, finally, that they might have "eternal life," John 17: 2. If, therefore, he merited this for all, then all must be justified and saved, Rom. 5: 8, 9, 10. and it cannot be justly denied to any: for it is their due, by virtue of a price: and that price well worthy of it; which also was paid to that very end, and this by the Creditor's own appointment; who cannot condemn any for whom Christ died, Rom. 8: 34. his justice shall not be liable to such a reflection. Whence it may rationally be concluded, that if all men are not justified, justification doth not belong to all; and, consequently, that Christ did not give himself for all. And, as for efficacy, Adam's transgression was efficacious on the will, and whole man, to deprave; why not then the righteousness of Christ to restore, since the pre-eminence, in that very thing, is given to him? " For if by one man's offence death reigned by one; much more they which receive abundance of grace, and of the gift of righteousness, shall reign in life by one, Jesus Christ," Rom. 5: 17.

Arg. VII. The doctrine of special and peculiar redemption is further confirmed by those perilous consequents which attend the doctrine of general redemption, as it is commonly held forth; for, 1. It seems to reflect on the wisdom of God; as imputing to him such a contrivance for men's salvation, as might be possibly frustrated; which is far from convincing the world that Christ crucified is the wisdom of God. 2. It also seems to tax God with injustice, as not discharging those whose transgressions are answered for by their Surety; or else, that the sufferings of Christ were not sufficient to make a discharge due to them. Or, 3. It insinuates a deficiency of power, or want of good will, to prosecute his design to perfection. 4. It makes men boasters; suspending the virtue and success of all that Christ hath done for them, upon something to be done by themselves, which he is not the doer of; and consequently, that men are principals in procuring their own salvation; and so Christ shall have but his thousands, in truth his nothing, while freedom of will shall have its ten thousands to cry up the praises of men. This is not " that the Lord alone should be exalted." 5. It would also follow, that those who are saved and gone to heaven, have nothing more of Christ's to glory in, and praise him for, than those who are perished and gone to hell. For, according to the principles of general redemption, he did and doeth for all alike; and no more for one than for another. 6. It makes men presumptuous, and carnally secure: how many have soothed up themselves in their impenitency and hardness of heart, and fenced themselves against the word, upon this very supposition, That Christ died for all; and why then should not they look to be saved as well as any other? and so they lean, pretendedly, on the Lord, and transgress; not considering, that those for whom Christ died, he purchased for them a freedom from sin, and not a liberty of sinning; nor impunity, but upon terms of faith and repentance. And that the tempter disturbs them not in their rest upon such a foundation, may be one reason why men so stiffly adhere to it; and that those of the general principle are so seldom troubled with terrors of conscience.

Lastly. There was yet another reason of Christ's dying peculiarly for the elect; they were his designed spouse; and that brought upon him peculiar engagements to die for them. 1. As being his spouse, he was chargeable with their debts: they being made under a law, and he assuming them into a spousal relation, made himself one with them, and answerable for them: it was, in the law's account, as well as his own intent, a making himself their Surety, Isa. 53: 8. 11. and, consequently, in case of forfeiture, his life must go for theirs. He is therefore said to be "made under the law," Gal. 4: 4, 5. as they were, and to be "made sin for them," 1 Cor. 5: 21. and being so, "it behooved him to suffer," Luke 24: 46. and it could not be avoided, Acts 17: 3. For the law being just and holy, its violation must be answered for, either by principals or surety: and here it was that mercy and truth, grace and justice met together; making that due temperament which answered the ends of both. Grace takes hold of him as a Surety, that the sinner might go free; and justice as of the most responsible party, for none else could answer the law's demands, and being apprehended, he readily yields to make satisfaction, and says to the law, as once to the Jews, when he was on the point of suffering for his spouse, "If ye seek me let these go their way," John 18: 8. 2. Another engagement was the love he bore to them; if possibly he might have been quit of that suretyship engagement, this of his love would have held him to it; he could not bear to see his beloved fast chained, like slaves, to the devil's galleys, and forced to serve against their natural Lord: and this bondage they could not be freed from, but by conquering him whose bond-slaves they were; nor could that be done, but by his own death, Heb. 2: 14. John 12: 31, 33. And this his love constrained him to, Eph. 5: 25. Rev. 1: 5. Gal. 2: 20. "for love (to be sure his love) is stronger than death," Cant. 8: 6. and accordingly we find that this is still made the ground and motive of his dying. 3. As the contract could not be dissolved, for he hates putting away;

nor his love taken off, for he changeth not; so neither, as
the case stood, could he and they cohabit and dwell together. Creatures defiled with sin, were not meet consorts
for the Lord of glory: nor could they be brought to a
meetness, but by being washed in his blood: as he says to
Peter, "If I wash thee not, thou hast no part with me,"
John 13: 8. The church must be "sanctified and cleansed,
without spot or wrinkle, or any such thing," Eph. 5: 26.
before they are fit for the presence of Christ in glory; and
this could not be effected, but by "his giving himself for
them:" to this, therefore, the spirits of just men made perfect, do ascribe their being in heaven: "And they sung a
new song, saying, Thou art worthy to take the book, and to
open the seals thereof: for thou wast slain, and hast redeemed us to God by thy blood, out of every kindred, and
tongue, and people, and nation," Rev. 5: 9.

Whether they might possibly have been saved some
other way, is to me a needless inquiry: but it seems the
import of our Saviour's own speech, that if he had not thus
done, he must have been in heaven without suitable company; where, speaking of himself, he says, "Except a corn
of wheat fall into the ground and die, it abideth alone,"
John 12: 24. But it was not good that the man should be
alone; no, not "the man Christ Jesus." It was therefore
ordained, that he should have a seed to serve him; a church
to preside over; in the midst of whom he should sing
praise to his Father, Heb. 2: 12. who are also called his
fellows, Heb. 1: 9. but his blood must be the seed of that
church, Isa. 53: 10. the price of their redemption, Rev. 5:
9. the laver of their regeneration, Eph. 5: 26. And so
dear is the church to Christ, that he thinks himself not
complete without them, Eph. 1: 23. It was one of the last
requests before he died, that they might be with him, John
17: 24. And if the body must be with its Head, the holiest
of holies must be their mansion: but such is that place's
holiness, as not to admit them, without a perfect purity; nor
could they, if not so purified, bear the holiness of the place.
All which considered together, shew such a reason of Christ's
dying for the elect, as was not predicable of other men.

For the rest of the world, they were given as hand-maids
to his spouse: by virtue of which donation, they also are
his; "He is head over all to the church," Eph. 1: 22. They
are his, but not as his spouse; as Sodom's daughters and

Samaria's were to Jerusalem; "but not by her covenant," Ezek. 16: 61. His relation to them was not such as to make him responsible for their defaults, or to oblige him for their recovery: yet, the price wherewith he ransomed his spouse, took in her handmaids also; as Abraham's rescuing his brother Lot, brought back the Sodomites with him. All the benefits the world have by redemption, they may thank the church for, next unto Christ himself; for they have it upon her account, as the Sodomites theirs from Lot's. And, to speak freely, the spouse of Christ could not well have been without her handmaids: we little think what service the world does for the church; although, because they intend not so, they are not rewardable for it, Isa. 10: 5—12. I shall only add our Saviour's own assertion in the 17th of John, where speaking of those his Father had given him, that he might give them eternal life, he saith expressly, that for "their sakes he sanctified himself," John 17:19. Which was to say, in effect, that had it not been for them, he had not stirred out of heaven for the rest.

I should now come to the inferences: but finding this doctrine as much opposed as that of election; observing also a great proneness in men to embrace the notion of general and conditional redemption (which proceeds, partly, from nature's inability to discern a reason, why one should be redeemed, and not another; partly, for that it is grateful to lapsed creatures, to fancy themselves active in their own recovery; partly also, from an aptness to catch at any thing that but seems to give quiet under convictions,) I hope it shall not be time lost to weigh their exceptions and our reply together: in doing which, I shall not answer every text that is made to serve in that cause; the sense they give of some, being refuted, may serve for many.

Object. In Rom. 5: 18. the restoration by Christ is made as large and as extensive as Adam's sin.

Answ. The comparison there stated is not put extensively, as respecting the objects of sin and grace; but intensively, as respecting the different efficacy of the several means by which those contrary effects were produced: the apostle, therefore, to obviate such objections, restrains it in verse 15. " But not as the offence, so also is the free gift:" *q. d.* The free gift of righteousness and life doth not extend to mankind universally and efficaciously, as sin and death did; and he adds a reason to it; " For if through the offence of one many be dead, much more the grace of God, and the gift by grace hath abounded unto many," Rom. 5: 15. which is as if he had said, if the free gift had taken in all, as the offence did, then all should have been saved; for that grace hath abounded more than the offence: which super-abounding of grace, must be meant of the prevalent efficacy of grace (for, as to the objects of it, it could not take in more than all;) and therefore, those towards whom it hath so abounded, shall surely partake of the benefits of it. And further, that the word *all* might not be taken universally, he presently varies the term of comprehension, and renders that *all* by *many:* "As by one man's disobedience many were made sinners, so by the obedience of one shall many be made righteous," Rom. 5: 19. "As all in Adam died, so all in Christ shall be made alive," 1 Cor. 15: 22.

Object. But redemption is often set forth in terms importing universality, namely, "That Christ gave himself a ransom for all; that he takes away the sin of the world; and is the propitiation for the sins of the whole world," 1 Tim. 2: 6. John 1: 29. 1 John 2: 2. which we cannot but take in a literal sense.

Answ. Both sacred writ and common discourse do frequently speak in general terms, when nothing is less intended by it than universality. John 4: 20. "Come, see a man that told me all things that ever I did!" when it was but how many husbands she had had, and that her present man was not one. 1 Cor. 10: 23. Paul is said to please all men in all things; whereas, in fact, he pleased but few in any thing, and in all things next to none. Col. 1: 6. the gospel is said "to be come into all the world, and to bring forth fruit as it did in them;" when yet, it was but a corner of the world, and but few, very few, in whom it brought forth as in them: examples are endless. It is therefore to be noted, that where those general, or rather indefinite, terms are used about redemption, it is mostly to shew, that the church of God, which Christ was to gather in, was not confined to the offspring of any particular head, nor consisted of any separate sort or rank of persons, exclusive of others; but some of every kindred and nation under heaven, classes and degrees among men: the church of God takes in of all, and so doth redemption; however different in other respects, they are "all one in Christ," Gal. 3: 28. And where this is not the scope, there the persons concerned are described by a narrower list; as that he gave his life a ransom for many, Matt. 20: 28. and 26: 28. and that he was once offered to bear the sins of many, Heb. 9. 28. that he laid down his life for the sheep, John 10: 15. that they are redeemed " from the earth, and from among men," Rev. 14: 3, 4. " and out of every kindred, tongue, people, and nation," chap. 5: 9. That in Timothy, " who gave himself a ransom for all," gives the objection no support; for *all* in the 6th verse must intend the same as *all* in the 1st verse, which the text itself expounds to be " kings, and men in authority." As for the *world*, it hath many and various acceptations in scripture: it is not always meant of men; and of men, it seldom intends the universality; yea, it is often meant of very few, in comparison of the whole: it would, therefore, be unanswerable rashness to limit so indefinite a term to any particular construction, as, in part, is seen by the following instances: it sometimes intends the place of men's habitation here on earth, Neh. 1: 5. the time and state of things, after the dissolution of the present frame, Luke 20: 35. the extent and compass of the Roman empire, chap. 2: 1. the religion and manners of the world, Acts 17: 6. the troubles which in this world do attend the disciples of Christ, John 16: 33. the splendor, wealth, honor, or whatever else is taking with the hearts of men, Gal. 6: 14. to set forth the greatness of something that cannot be well expressed, John 21: 25. for the Gentiles, in distinction from the Jews, Rom. 11: 12. for the numerous increase of some particular party, John 12: 19. More might be cited, but these may suffice to shew how much it behooves us to consider well the scope and context of scripture, and not to be led by the vocal sounds of words.

There are yet two interpretations, which come nearer the matter in hand: one is that which takes in the whole party of wicked men alone, and by themselves; as where it is said, " That saints shall judge the world," 1 Cor. 6: 2. it must be meant of the world of ungodly, for the saints shall not judge one another: so, " All the world wondered after the beast, and worshipped the dragon," Rev. 13: 3, 4. This also must intend the herd of idolaters, exemptive of those who followed the Lamb, Rev. 14: 4. It is also said, that " the whole world lieth in wickedness," 1 John 5: 19. here ye have the very words, and alike connected, as in the place objected; which therefore may as well be supposed

of the same comprehension; and yet it may not be understood of mankind universally, but such of them as are
under the power and conduct of Satan, which the saints
are not, and therefore are no part of the world, or whole
world there intended.   The other interpretation of the
word seems couched in the places objected, where Christ
is said to " take away the sins of the world, and to be a
propitiation for the sins of the whole world:" for, why may
not the world be taken in a restricted and limited sense
here, as in the places quoted? If by world is sometimes meant the world of ungodly, as separated from the
saints; by like reason, at other times, it may be meant of
the world of saints, as separated from the wicked, especially when nothing in the scope or context contradicts it.
And what then shall hinder, but that world, in the places
objected, may be intended of the elect, exclusive to
others; as the world that lies in wickedness, is of those
others exclusive of the elect?   To be sure there can be no
peril in so understanding it; for we know that Christ is the
propitiation for their sins: but to affirm it of the bulk of
mankind, hath many unruly and unworthy consequences
attending it, some of which are shown before.   But what
world was it that Christ would not pray for?   It could not
be that for which he died, for the priest was bound to pray
for those he offered for?   It must then be another; and then
it will follow that there are two: 1. A lesser, which consists of a select party, and was taken out of the world universal, as the Israelitish nation was out of the Egyptian,
Deut. 4: 34. or as the christian church, at first, was out of
the Jewish, Acts 2: 44—47.   These our Saviour styles
" the men which his Father gave him out of the world,"
John 17: 6.   For these it was that he sanctified himself,
that is, set himself apart to suffer for them, and for these
he prayed: and of these is made up that world whose sin
he taketh away, and for whose sins, even of the whole of
them, he is the propitiation.   These are the men that shall
be counted worthy of the world to come, Luke 20: 35. and
they are as properly termed a world, as that blessed state
and place of glory they shall be taken into; or as the dwellers
upon earth are denominated a world, from the place of their
habitation, Rom. 13: 3, 4. 8.   2. There is also a world of
ungodly, from among whom that lesser world was taken
and rated, John 15: 19. 17: 6. of whom it is said, " the

devil is their god," 2 Cor. 4: 4. and that " their names are not in the Lamb's book of life," Rev. 13: 8. but, " the whole of it lieth in wickedness," 1 John 5: 19. And this is that world for whom Christ professedly says, " He did not pray;" surely, then, he " would not make his soul an offering for their sins."

But because so great a stress is laid on the literal sense of the word, let us scan a little further this world whose sin is taken away. I think it cannot intend the universality of mankind, because, though the world in general be concerned in redemption, those general concerns are too light to balance the weight of the text; temporary things could in no wise answer the end and worth of eternal redemption; which being the most tremendous act that ever the sun had seen, or shall, the effects thereof must be answerably great and glorious; and, consequently, it must peculiarly respect the elect, for it suits adequately to none else. To make out this, let us inquire what the sin of the world is, and what the import of taking it away, Psal. 103: 12. For the first: it is either some one grand transgression, or the whole body of sins together: if a particular sin, it must be unbelief; for that was the first, and parent to all the rest; and it is thus marked out, *the* or *that* sin of the world; 1. Because it was the sin of the whole, both Jews and Gentiles. 2. It gave entrance to all other sins; they sprang from it as their root. And, 3. It is the condemning sin; no man perisheth but for unbelief; where the gospel is not, they perish for not believing in God; and where it is, for not believing in Christ. Or if it be meant of all sins universally, then the text considers them as put together; and taken away at once, as if but one. But be it unbelief singly and specially, or the whole body of sins conjunct, it comes to one; for unbelief is a member of that body, and a capital one; and so that be taken away, it matters not, this world is safe: the reason is, that Christ, in saving from unbelief, saves from all: for as faith is a complex of grace, so is unbelief of sins; take away this, and the gulph is shut, all other sins disappear; there is an end of them, both as to guilt and prevalency; " he that believes shall be saved." For the second, touching the import of taking away; 1. The putting of it in the present tense, implies a constant and continued act, still pursuing the same end; it also imports a perfect act, not a partial taking away, or frustrable endeavor, but complete and certain, as a man takes away any thing until it all be gone. 2. That Christ alone, and by himself, performs this work. 3. That he takes away sin, as a lamb slain; not for himself (for he was without spot,) but for those whose surety he was. And, 4. As the Lamb of God; a lamb of God's own providing, to save the lives of his Isaacs. This taking away is no less than a total removing of sin, a setting it at the utmost distance, and placing it in the "land of forgetfulness," Jer. 31: 34. And further, to assure us of its utter abolition, this taking away is termed destruction, the crucifying of the old man; slaying the enmity, and destroying the body of sin, Eph. 2: 16. Rom. 6: 6. this was the work of the devil, which the Son of God came to destroy; and destroy it he hath, by "nailing it to his cross," Col. 2: 14. The blood of the Lamb hath so overcome, that there needs no more sacrifice for sin; nor any thing exterior to itself, to make its redemption eternal. And to have sin thus taken away, cannot be said of the world universally: the reason is plain, because sin being gone, nothing remains to charge the world with. But nothing is more evident, than that the generality of men lie plunged in sin, and are bond-slaves of corruption to the last: it must therefore be another world, or tribe, to whom this great blessing must be assigned, and of whom verified: and since there is but one more (who are called God's elect,) I conclude that they are the men, and the world intended in the text: for we know that they "are of God; and that the whole world besides lies in wickedness," 1 John 5: 19.

Object. But if some only are redeemed, and those but few in comparison, then all ground of believing is taken away from the most of men.

Answ. 1. That Christ did not die for all, hinders none from believing, any more than that many of those he died for are not saved: or that because only one can win the prize, hinders others from running. Nay, to teach (as they do) that Christ died for all, and that yet the generality of men shall die in their sins, and perish for ever, is a greater impediment to believing, than that he died only for some; and that every one of that some shall certainly be saved. 2. If we judge of trees by their fruit, we shall find, that the generality of men (such as reckon the matters of religion worth speaking of,) hold stiff for the general point;

which shews, that that notion has no great influence towards the working of faith: if it had, the number of converts would not be so thin. It is also found, that the generality of carnal men, and such as hate to be reformed, are the greatest despisers of peculiar redemption, as well as of election. 3. To make faith an evidence of a man's interest in redemption, puts by the claim of unbelievers, as much as if it were a condition. 4. He that will know his own particular redemption before he will believe, begins at the wrong end of his work, and is very unlikely to come that way to the knowledge of it. The first act of faith is not, that Christ died for all, or for you in particular: the one is not true; the other not certain to you, nor can, until after you have believed. He that would live, must submit to mercy, with " peradventure he will save me alive." 5. Any man that owns himself a sinner, hath as fair a ground for his faith, as any in the world that hath not yet believed; yea, as any believer had before he believed: nor may any person, upon any account, exclude himself from redemption; unless, by his obstinate and resolved continuance in unbelief, he hath marked out himself.

There are reasons enough, and of greatest weight, to induce men to believe, without laying general redemption for the ground of their faith: as, (1.) That " faithful saying, and worthy of all acceptation, that Jesus Christ came into the world to save sinners," 2 Tim. 1:15. and such are you. (2.) That he gave his life a ransom for many, Matth. 20: 28. and you may be of that number, as well as any other. (3.) That those he died for, shall be justified upon their believing, Rom. 5: 9. and shall have faith also, upon their seeking for it, as a part of his purchase, and given on his behalf, Phil. 1: 29. (4.) That to believe on his Son, is the will and commandment of the everlasting God, Rom. 16: 26. 1 John 3: 23. whom we ought to obey though so it were that salvation were not concerned in it. (5.) Those many faithful promises, assuring salvation to them that believe, John 3: 16. 36. and chap. 6: 47. *Lastly.* The remediless danger of unbelief, Mark 16: 16. John 8: 24. And if such considerations as these will not prevail with you to believe; the notions of general redemption, together with the general failure of success of it, will never do it.

Object. The extending of redemption to the whole race

of mankind, tends to magnify the grace of Christ; but confining it to a remnant, is a lessening of it.

Answ. It no more disparages the grace of Christ, to die peculiarly for that remnant, than his choosing a single nation, and fewest in number of the universe, and giving them laws that tended to life; while he suffered all besides to run wild in the broad way, which inevitably leads to destruction. And as for redemption made general, with conditions annexed; it is so far from magnifying the grace of Christ, that it plainly contradicts it; for if he knew from the beginning who they were that believed not, nor would ever believe; it would rather have argued a degree of grace and favor, not to die for them, than that their sin and condemnation should be thereby so greatly aggravated; as it had been better for some, they had never known the way of righteousness, than to depart from it, 2 Pet. 2: 21.

Object. This leaves the most of men without remedy.

Answ. The fallen angels were higher than we, yet have no cause to complain, that no Mediator was appointed for them, and if they be left remediless, the fault is their own. For, if freedom of will, as now it is, empowers men to make a remedy, (viz. by acceptance and application,) much more, as it was, it might have kept them, if they would, from needing a remedy. You will say, perhaps, as some do, why were men left to this freedom of will, if foreseen thus to use it? Nay, rather, why do men, after so woful an experiment, choose to be so left? They have their option, let them look to it.

And so I leave their objections; for I heartily wish, both for the truth's sake, and for peace, to see these contests buried, rather than agitated, lest they eat out the life of religion. (They breathe in a healthless air, who make them their element.) And I verily think, that if the controverted texts were duly weighed,—that is, if spiritual things were compared with spiritual, and fleshly consultations laid aside,—the present differences would be quickly composed, being mostly fomented by a loose and luxuriant way of philosophizing in divinity; and by holding to words of an indefinite signification, more than to the scope and context.

Inferences

Infer. I. Upon what has been said of the work and ends of redemption, I would turn, a while, to those of the general point; I mean not such as are men professing godliness, (too many of whom are yet leavened with it,) but those very sordid and disingenuous spirits, who pretend to general ransom, (covering themselves with the shadow of it,) and yet study nothing less than to answer its end: who dream of redemption from hell; but for redemption from sin, it comes not into their mind; they contend, that Christ died for all; and yet carry it as if he died for none: at least, not for them: for they have no mark or tincture of such a redemption upon them; but remain evidently bond-slaves of corruption. Can you think that the Son of God died for you, while you despise living to him, hate them that love him, oppose whatever is dear to him, and persecute to the death (if your line would reach it) those that have any special mark of redemption upon them? Did he make his soul an offering for sin, to procure men a liberty of sinning? or, was Christ crucified, that the body of sin might remain unmortified; yea, get ground, and be the more rampant upon it? Is this your kindness to your friend, to be so in love with his enemies (the spear and the nails that pierced him,) that you will spend and be spent for the service of your lusts? He died, that those he died for might live: live to whom? Not to themselves, but to him that died for them: and did you really believe that he died for you, you could not but so judge; his love would constrain you. Redeemed ones are the Lord's free-men; and you are free to nothing but the devil and sin. Is this the badge of your freedom? the cognizance by which the subjects of Christ are known from rebels? No; it is the rebel's brand, and you will find it at last. This is what will aggravate your condemnation, and make it a condemnation to purpose, thus to deny the Lord that bought you: you are haters of God, and he will make you to feel it: wrath will come upon you to the uttermost. If God spared not his own Son, who had no sin (but by imputation) how shall he spare you, that are nothing else but sin? "He that despised Moses' law, died without mercy: of how much sorer punishment shall he be thought worthy, who hath trodden under foot the Son of God; and counted that blood (which you pretend to believe was shed for your redemption) an unholy thing?" Heb. 10: 28, 29. The wrath of the Lamb is dreadful; he will tear you in pieces, and none shall deliver you. Bethink yourself, therefore, in time; consider how you shall bear that weight of wrath which the Son of God sunk under! There is yet hope concerning this thing: and if ye have any mind to escape, delay it not: "If ye will inquire, inquire to purpose; return, and come." Isa. 21: 12.

Infer. II. The doctrine of peculiar redemption may not be taken to discourage or weaken the hopes of any in their coming to Christ for salvation; any more than that "many shall seek, and shall not be able to enter," should keep men from striving: but, on the contrary, which also was Christ's intent in telling us so, it should quicken our diligence and speed in going to him, lest the door should be shut; which is certainly open while he calls. Suppose the worst: suppose, I say, that your interest in redemption were only as it is, general, that is, for temporal mercies, even that deserves all you can do, and more. What criminal is it, that lying at his prince's mercy, would not think himself obliged to spend the time of his reprievement in his prince's service; especially considering, that even that service shall have its reward? But why will you shut out yourself? no man is namely exempted; and for any to exclude himself, is to sin against his own soul; and to be a second time guilty of destroying himself. Put it upon the trial: you can lose nothing by venturing: but all without. Who can tell, but your name may be written on the High Priest's breastplate; as well as Reuben's or Judah's? besides, you have no way to prove it, but by going to see; which never any, in good earnest did, but they found it so.

Infer. III. From what hath been said of redemption, as peculiar to the elect, with the plausible shows brought against it; I infer, the important necessity of "trying the spirits and the doctrines they bring, whether they be of God." A plausible outside, and fair show in the flesh, are no arguments of truth in the bottom: agreeableness with nature, should render things suspicious to us, rather than approved. Our best rule of judgment in this case, is that of our Saviour, "The tree is known by its fruits." And if by this we measure the general point, it will be found wanting in what it pretends to, and not a little reproveable: for, 1. Instead of magnifying the grace of Christ, and merit of his sufferings, it does, in effect, nullify both: it makes redemption general, as to persons, but not as to things; it redeems the whole of mankind from part of their bondage, but no part of them from the whole; or upon such a condition as no man in nature is able to perform: which is too defective to be the device of sovereign wisdom and grace. That cannot be called a catholicon, or general remedy, that suffers itself to be generally worsted by the disease: nor that a perfect redemption, which leaves still under bondage. I doubt not at all, that the blood of the Son of God in our nature, is of infinite merit; but withal, that it is of like infinite virtue and efficacy, and will for ever operate accordingly. But, if the success and saving effects thereof should depend upon something to be done by men, which redemption itself doth not invest them with; then will men come in for a share with Christ, in the glory of their salvation: yea, in this case, any addition of human ability annihilates the grace of Christ, Gal. 5: 2. whereas, to depend upon Christ for sanctification, as well as righteousness; to expect from him a power to repent and believe, as well as acceptance upon your believing, gives him his true honor, as entitling him to the whole of your salvation; which is indeed his proper due, and due to him alone. And this may be a main reason, why men professing the name of Christ, are so generally strangers to faith and holiness: they do not seek it at the hands of Christ, John 5: 10. as a part of his purchase; but rely on their own ability. 2. Instead of laying a foundation for faith, and a help to believing: the general doctrine muzzles the soul in its unbelief, upon a presumption of power in himself to believe, when he will. We little think how much presumption and carnal security derive from this root; whereas peculiar redemption, in the vigor and latitude of it, namely, as procuring for us a right to faith and holiness, with the Spirit of Christ to work them effectually in us, is far greater encouragement to apply ourselves to Christ for them as a part of his purchase, Phil. 1: 29. and that without which we cannot partake of the other benefits of his death. And I cannot but think, that any man in his right mind, Luke 8: 35. upon due inquiry, and a thorough consideration of the matter, would rather depend upon such a redemption as redeems from all iniquity, though the persons concerned in that redemption be but few, than on that which is supposed to redeem all universally, upon condition of faith and repentance, but does not redeem from impenitency and unbelief. In that redemption let my part be, that saves from sin, that slays the enmity, that reconciles to God effectually, that makes an end of sin, and brings in everlasting righteousness; that does not only bring into a salvable state conditionally, but works also and maintains those conditions and qualifications that have salvation at the end of them.

Infer. IV. If Christ gave himself a ransom for the elect, then is redemption also of grace, and free as election itself; which bespeaks both our thankful remembrance, and all self-denial. There is a great aptness to forget our original; to pay tribute where it is not due, and to withhold it where it is. It was needful counsel of old, and no less at this day, " Ye that follow after righteousness, look to the rock whence ye were hewn," Isa. 51:1. Your Redeemer first brought you out of nothing; and when you had sold your-selves for nought, he himself became your ransom, though he needed you not; see therefore that ye ascribe all to his love. It was not any excellence of yours that gave you preference in redemption, nor was it your ingenuous com-pliance that made redemption effectual to you, (these are slight pretences.) Had not your Redeemer bought you from yourself, released you from your imaginary freedom, and saved you from unbelief, you had never known what this redemption had meant, nor what it is to be free in-deed. No, it was purely your Redeemer's love: he valued you as being his Father's gift; and as given to be one with himself; " He therefore loved you, and gave himself for you." When you were in your blood, and no eye pitied you, no, not your own; then was the time of his love; even then he accepted the motion made by his Father and yours, and signed the contract. He knew both your weight and your worth; your natural unfitness for him, and aversion to the match: he also knew what it must cost him to make you both meet and willing; and that it was so stupendous a work, that all the hosts of heaven would have broken under. He further knew, that after all he should do and suffer for you, you could not advantage him in the least; only he should have the satisfaction to have made you hap-py against your unrenewed will; and yet he declined it not: he came " leaping upon the mountains, and skipping over the hills" of death and difficulties, as longing for, and de-lighting to be in that work: he was straitened until it was accomplished; such was the intenseness of his love to you! And a great deal ado he had with your wills, before you were made willing. And for all this he only expects you will carry it worthy of so great a lover, and such manner of love: which is, in effect, but to accept of, and to continue in his love, and be willing he should save you freely; and own this love of his, as the immediate fountain whence your happiness is derived.

Infer. V. Since your propriety in redemption is founded in electing love, " give all diligence to make your election sure:" spare not for pains; its fruit will be worth all the labor and cost you can lay out upon it; if clear in this point, the whole body will be full of light. And among other evidences of election, review the marks specified before under that head. Make out also your interest in redemption, by walking worthy of redeeming love; which cannot be, but by doing and being something more than others; some singular thing must warrant your claim to that singular privilege: hold forth, therefore, in your life, the effects of your union with Christ in his death: let the scope of redemption be the scope of your conversation. You have no such way, if I may so speak, to gratify your Redeemer, as by letting him see the travail of his soul: a thorough newness of life, with a total devoting yourself to God, will illustrate redemption not a little, and proclaim convincingly both its merit and efficacy. It will also be a good office done to yourselves, as an evidence of your special concern in redemption; and much more vindicate your Christianity, than formal professions, or eager contests. And in order to this, 1. Determine to " know nothing but Jesus Christ, and him crucified;" count all things else not worth your knowing; for, in truth, all knowledge else will come to nothing. Let all, therefore, be " loss and dung, for the excellency of the knowledge of Christ Jesus our Lord," Phil. 3: 8. And study the doctrine of his cross; that ye may not stand by and hear him defamed, and not have a word to say for him: so also observe him, that when the world and he part, you may know your own Master, and be known by him: 2. Let nothing be so dear to you, as not to part with it for your Redeemer when called for; and rise early to do it: take up your cross, and inure yourself to the bearing of it, before it be laid on: the Lord parted with his delight for you from eternity; there is nothing more reasonable, nothing more natural to a heart rightly postured, than to love and live to him who died for you: and whoever hath known the grace of God, and the love of Christ in truth, cannot but so judge. 3. Deal with sin according to its kind; the dreadful nature whereof nothing discovers, nor can, but hell itself, and the sufferings of Christ, and mostly these: let it die no other death but that of the cross, and the more it cries out to be spared, do you cry out the more urgently that it may be crucified. 4. Let not Christ be divided: his offices are requisitely conjoined, and cannot be separated with our security; nay, not without our certain ruin. Know him, therefore, for your Prophet and Lord, as well as your Redeemer; and for your wisdom and sanctification, as well as your righteousness; one and all. Take orders from him as your Captain-general; recieve your law from his mouth; whatever he bids you do, do it: follow him wherever he goes, and carry it as becomes his attendants: the armies in heaven follow him upon white horses, and arrayed in white: be not your own director in any thing, nor over-hasty; stir not up your beloved until he please, but await his counsel and conduct, as preferring his knowledge of times and seasons, with the manner and method of his working and prescribing, before your own. 5. Let nothing divide you from Christ: Let nothing but death, yea, let not death itself separate between you and him. Nothing, you see, could separate him from you, nay, had it not been for you, and such as you are, he had not died: "We are not our own, we are bought with a price," 1 Cor. 6: 20. which is the highest engagement in every state and duty, whether living or dying, to be the Lord's, Rom. 14: 8.

Infer. VI. Christ's giving himself a ransom for you, warrants your largest expectation of good things from him: what sins too great to be pardoned? or iniquities so stubborn as not to be subdued? Heb. 9:14. or graces so precious as not to be obtained? The Lord delights in nothing more than mercy; the only bar was sin; which being dissolved by the blood of Christ, grace and glory run freely. The making us kings and priests unto God, yea, "one in the Father and himself," John 17: 21. being the thing he died for, no inferior good thing can be withholden from us. Faith and holiness are great things indeed, and highly to be valued: yet, let me say, that even these, and all other good things laid together, will be but a very little heap, to that grace which put us into Christ; the honor and privilege of union with him; and the price he hath paid for our ransom: "Herein is love, "That God sent his Son to be the propitiation for our sins!" 1 John 4: 10. The purchase is paid, releases are sealed, and he in possession; all things are ready: it is now but his giving forth the revenue that lies by him, which also he delights to do.

Other notes of use this doctrine affords, which I can but touch, as Jonathan the honey: 1. It shews the high esteem that God has for his chosen; whom " he went himself to redeem, and purchased with his own blood," 2 Sam. 7: 23. Acts 20: 28. 2. That by this standard those favorites of heaven should value themselves; not weighing the world's contempt, nor clouding those marks of worth redemption has put upon them. 3. It shews the contagious nature of sin; the deadly venom whereof nothing but the precious blood of the holy One could possibly subdue, nor withstand the torrent of that fiery lake; as also its dreadfulness, in that the Son of God died in the conflict. 4. It argues the greatness and preciousness of the soul; the redemption whereof had ceased for ever, if Christ, the Son of God, had not made his own soul an offering for it. 5. That the world is not a little beholden to God's people for all the good things they possess; for they have them on their account, and should therefore afford them better quarter. 6. That God will not lightly pass by the wrongs done to his people: redemption hath made them kings, Rev. 5: 10. against whom even hard speeches are criminal: how severely then will he make inquisition for blood! Psal. 9: 12. 7. It argues the absoluteness of election, for that an infinite price was irrevocably decreed and paid to confirm its title. 8. It also evinceth the absolute freeness and independency of electing love, since creatures could not possibly deserve or be worthy of so great a ransom. 9. It infers the exceeding weightiness of that glory, which required so vast a price, and could not be had for less. *Lastly*, It further yields a chief corner-stone for the saints' perseverance: for, 1. They are not now at their own disposal; redemption has transferred their title to another, who loves them better than to leave them exposed to a second peril, from which there is no recovering. 2. Redemption being a valuable consideration, and so accepted, even the righteousness of God is engaged to save them; and must there-

fore prevent, remove, or over-rule whatever would hinder
that salvation. On all which accounts (and others) redemption should be much the subject of our discourse and contemplation: it was the first-born promise after the fall; by
the repetitions whereof, and further explanations, the Lord
hath perfumed the breath of all his holy prophets which
have been since the world began. Our Lord and Saviour
himself was frequently speaking of it; which shews that
his mind was much upon it, and that the same mind should
be in us. It is a theme that glorified saints take pleasure
to dilate upon; witness Moses and Elias on the holy mount,
Luke 9: 31. and John, wrapped into heaven on the Lord's
day, found them at this service before the throne of God,
Rev. 1: 10. chap. 5: 9. 12, 13. where I cannot but make, by
the way, three observations. 1. That the saints in heaven
were celebrating the work of creation, and that of redemption, both in one day; and it was the Lord's day: a good argument for our Lord's day sabbath! 2. That they ascribe the
same glory and honor unto the Lamb that was slain, as to
him that sits on the throne; an evident proof of Christ's
divinity! And, 3. That the ground of their triumph and
exultation was not the general point (no speech of that in
heaven,) but peculiar redemption: a good confirmation of
the present truth. And further, our Lord and Saviour still
bears about him the marks of his crucifixion; he appears
" as a Lamb that had been slain," Rev. 5: 6. and he glories in it. " I am he that was dead," Rev. 2: 8. and 1: 18.
and with these marks he will appear when he cometh to
judge the world, Zech. 12: 10. Till when, the Lord's day,
and its most solemn ordinance, are for an unchangeable
remembrance of him, 1 Cor. 12: 26. Whatever therefore
befalls us, should remind us of this glorious transaction: if
it be evil, that redemption hath saved from the evil of it;
if good, redemption hath purchased it for us; whether good
or bad in itself, redemption will sanctify it to us. But
when ye think of heaven, and the heaven of heavens, as
your portion, with all that heavenly viaticum (angels food,
and better) that attends you at every stage, " until ye appear before God in Zion," Psal. 84: 7. especially when ye
are admiring, for what it is ye cannot think, I say, when
ye are admiring that transcendent glory which shall arise
from that ineffable oneness, to be then completed between
the Father and Christ, and his saints, say with that heaven-

born psalmist, " What shall I render unto the Lord for all
his benefits?" And answer yourself with him; " I will
take (not this or that single benefit, but) the cup of salvation (glorious redemption, which that cup signifieth,) and
call on the name of the Lord." All the divine attributes
centre in redemption, as light and heat in the sun, and are
thence savingly reflected upon men redeemed: and this is
the most compendious way of beholding the glory of God,
and of celebrating our dear-bought happiness. Something,
perhaps, like this may that " fruit of the vine" be, though
unspeakably beyond it, which Christ and his disciples
" shall drink new in his Father's kingdom," Matt. 26: 29.
" when he that sowed, and we that reap, shall rejoice together," John 4: 36. Therefore, " unto him that loved
us, and washed us from our sins in his own blood, be glory
and dominion for ever. Amen." Rev. 1: 5, 6.

III. That the purpose or intent of Christ's death cannot
be frustrated; that is, those for whom Christ died shall
certainly obtain all the benefits accruing by his death.

All the counsels of God from eternity; all his promises
and declarations holding forth those counsels; and all his
dispensations in order to their accomplishment; have a
special relation to Christ as dying for his people, and their
actual salvation thereby, as the end thereof. Now the end
of a thing, is that for which the thing itself is; and but
for which, it had not been; it is that the chief agent principally purposeth, and aims at; and if he be wise, he will
certainly use and appoint such means, and order them in
such manner, that the thing designed shall not miscarry.
Men indeed may miss of their end; they aim at this, and
that is produced, as in building the tower of Babel: but
this is still from some imperfection in themselves; either
the thing itself is not feasible, or the way to it imprudently
contrived, or the means unduly applied; their minds alter,
or they are made to desist by a power above them, &c.
But with the only wise and almighty God it is not so, none
of those things which impede the designs of men can happen to his; there can be no other event of them but what
he intended; the least of his purposes shall not suffer
disappointment, much less that great design of men's salvation by the death of his Son. That the thing itself is
feasible, is attested by that innumerable company already

in heaven on his account. It was so wisely contrived, that all interests concerned are secured and satisfied: God is just in justifying; the sinner saved, while vengeance is taken on his sin; and Christ well pleased with a seed to serve him. The way of obtainment is such as will certainly compass the end; the divine power is engaged in it; which rests not in the least on the concourse or compliance of any mutable agent, or frustrable instrument. His heart cannot be taken off from it; it is that his blessed thoughts have run upon from eternity; and those thoughts of his stand fast to all generations. And *lastly*, no higher power can supersede his decree; he is sovereign Lord, and controlleth all.

To confirm the point, take the following arguments.

Arg. I. Is from redemption itself; wherein, 1. The greatness of the price; 2. The kind or manner of payment; and, 3. The scriptural import of the word, are not a little considerable.

1. For the price: it was the life of the Son of God; whose personal dignity was such as put a transcendency of merit upon his death, which therefore could not be parted with for a doubtful or uncertain purchase; nor could any obtainment, inferior to salvation, compensate the price. In this lies the stress of the apostle's argument; who, to set forth the happy state of God's elect, and to prove them out of danger, brings in the price of their redemption; " Who shall condemn? It is Christ that died," Rom. 8: 33. The eminency of the person, and the sufferings he submitted unto, as they greatly illustrate his love to men; so they strongly affirm and ensure the event of his death: " For, if reconciled to God, by the death of his Son, much more shall we be saved by his life," chap. 5: 10.

2. The kind or manner of payment; it was by suffering. Had the ransom been of the nature of depositable things (namely, to secure satisfaction, in case the treaty took effect, and to be resumed, in case it succeeded not,) it had much altered the matter; there had no great damage accrued to the depositor; he might have received his own again, though not with advantage: but sufferings once undergone cannot be recalled: they are as water spilt upon the ground; they cannot be gathered up again, unless in their fruits, namely, in the accomplishment of the end they were designed for; which, duly weighed, will not allow redemp-

tion to be conditional, nor its intended effects to depend upon things contingent. Besides, that which is infinite, will not admit of addition; nor can that which hath all worth entirely within it, find any thing of worth without itself to depend upon. But this, methinks, should not need arguing, since it is so apparent.

3. From the scriptural usage and import of the word: which shews, that redemption hath made eternal life our due; and that all supposable conditions, all manner of graces, means, and helps, which must come between our natural state and glory, with glory itself, were all intentionally in the design of it, purchased by it, and contained in it; as the stalk which the flower must grow upon, is virtually in the same seed with the flower itself. Redemption doth not only allow men their book, and save them in case they can read (that is a heartless notion,) but enables them to read, and that in point of will, as well as knowledge. Faith is to salvation, as livery and seizin are to possession; they are no part of the price, nor condition of your right, but a legal and notifying introduction to your actual enjoyment; yea, the purchase-money entitles you to them, as well as to the inheritance. As we can ask nothing of God, either warrantably or successfully, but as entitled thereto by redemption, so, on redemption's account, ye may ask any thing that hath a tendency to its end; ye may claim faith in order to salvation, as well as salvation as the end of your faith.

And now, that redemption doth not barely make men releaseable, or capable of being saved, but doth, by its own proper virtue, prosecute its end to perfection, that the actual complete salvation of redeemed ones is bound up in it, and whatever might hinder it taken out of the way, I shall clear by a short induction of particulars. 1. Redemption imports satisfaction. Without this the world had not been reconciled; nor could it be said, "The pleasure of the Lord hath prospered in his hand;" but both these are affirmed, Isa. 53: 10. "It pleased the Lord to bruise him." It does not intend only, that it was the pleasure or will of God that the thing should be done, but that he was well pleased by the doing of it; that is, he was again pacified towards us, in whose stead he suffered; his justice being thereby atoned. And this very reason ye have annexed in Isa. 42: 21. "The Lord is well pleased for his righteousness' sake; he shall magnify the law, and make it honorable;" that is, by levying satisfaction upon Christ: which also accords with and explicates that in Rom. 3: 31. " Do we then make void the law through faith? God forbid; yea, we establish the law." It is further confirmed by 2 Cor. 5: 19. " God was in Christ reconciling the world to himself:" this must be reciprocally understood, for else the breach had continued: but, surely, the Lord would not be at such cost to have his work but half done; for what is reconciliation, but the renewal of friendship on both sides? and that this is Christ's own sense upon the word, is evident by Matt. 5. 23, 24. " If thy brother hath aught against thee, go and be reconciled to thy brother." It must, therefore, take in God's reconcilement to us, as well as our's to him; which could not be without satisfaction; his justice would not permit it; he will by no means clear the guilty. And, to put it beyond dispute, our grand creditor proclaims himself satisfied, by his sending from heaven to release our surety, Matt. 28: 2. It was to say, in effect, that he had no further demands upon us. 2. Redemption also imports justification, or freedom from guilt, Ephes. 1: 7. " In whom we have redemption through his blood, the forgiveness of sins," Rom. 3: 24. " Being justified freely by his grace, through the redemption that is in Jesus Christ," Rom. 5: 9. Gal. 3: 13. " Christ hath redeemed us from the curse of the law, being made a curse for us: he blotted out the hand-writing that was against us, nailing it to his cross," Col. 2: 14. 3. It imports the eviction, vanquishing, or binding of the strong man, who would not else have let go the prey, nor have left his possession; " By death he destroyed him who had the power of death; that is, the devil," Heb. 2: 14. " By the blood of his cross, he spoiled principalities and powers, and triumphed over them," Col. 2: 15. 4. It imports freedom from the power of sin, Rom. 6: 6. " Our old man was crucified with Christ, that the body of sin might be destroyed; that henceforth we should not serve sin:" upon which it follows, " He that is dead, namely, with Christ, is freed from sin," verse 7. And " sin shall not have dominion over you," verse 14. 5. It imports inherent holiness, or sanctification, Col. 1: 21. " You, who were sometimes enemies in your minds, now hath he reconciled, in the body of his flesh, through death, to present you holy," verse 22. Heb. 10: 10. " We are

sanctified through the offering of the body of Jesus Christ,"
Rom. 6: 18.   " Being then made free from sin, ye became
the servants of righteousness."   And that it was by virtue
of Christ's death, appears by verse 8. " For if we be dead
with Christ, we shall also live with him."   It is his blood
which " purges the conscience from dead works, to serve
the living God," Heb. 9: 14.   6. It likewise imports resurrection, John 6: 54, 55. " I will raise him up at the last
day; for my flesh is meat indeed," (that is, as crucified.)
Christ dying, was the death of death, Hos. 13: 14. " In
Christ shall all be made alive," 2 Cor. 15: 22.   7. It further extends to the actual possession of redeemed ones with
blessedness and glory, Rom. 8: 30, " Whom he justified,
them he glorified."   Liberty of entering into the holiest,
is by the blood of Jesus, Heb. 10: 19. " Thou hast redeemed us to God by thy blood," Rev: 5: 9, 10.   It is the
voice of those in heaven.   Now, that all these are in redemption, is evident; and as evident it is, that redemption,
thus qualified, is not, cannot be, liable to frustration, for
it brings us to heaven; and then we are sure beyond the
reach of danger.   And for this it was that Paul cared not
(he need not care) " to know any thing, in comparison,
but Jesus Christ, and him crucified," 1 Cor. 2: 2.   It is
true, the resurrection of Christ, his ascension, sitting at
God's right hand, and intercession, have their respective
influence into all these glorious privileges and parts of eternal glory; but they all spring from his crucifixion; if he
had not died, he had not been a priest for ever, as he is.

Arg. II. The end of redemption cannot be frustrate, because the righteousness of Christ is, at least, as prevalent
and effectual to his seed, as Adam's transgression was to
his.   All his posterity, indeed, were involved in the curse;
yet, so that there still remained, through the intervention
of grace, a possibility of release; but the righteousness of
Christ hath so perfectly recovered and established his seed,
that their justified state can never be lost: and the reason
is, because grace hath outdone sin, and gone beyond it;
" grace hath abounded much more," Rom. 5: 20.   Which
super-abounding of grace cannot refer to the subjects of
grace, as if they were more in number than the subjects of
sin; for sin came upon all, and grace cannot come upon
more than all: but it is meant of the prevalent efficacy of
grace, and the permanency of its effects towards all that

are the subjects of it: and thence it is, that grace is said
to reign through righteousness, and that to eternal life,
Rom. 5: 21.

Arg. III. If the end of Christ's death might possibly be
frustrate, as possibly might the main end of God's making
the world suffer disappointment. All things were made
for himself; and by this scale they ascend to him; the
world for the elect, and the elect for Christ; and Christ
for God. All his works praise him; but above all that of
redemption, as of highest note and eminency. Most con-
spicuously doth the glory of God shine forth in the face of
Christ as dying, and as dying for such an end, namely, the
salvation of his people. It is the chief of the ways of God,
the very meridian and height of his glory, (not essential,
but manifestive,) both in this world, and that to come.
Redemption was designed to glorify all the divine attributes; it therefore behooved so to be laid, that of all his
designs, this might be sure to succeed: for do but subtract
the certainty of its effect, and leave his redeemed in a
perishable condition, and it draws a blemish, instead of
beauty, upon all the divine attributes. For, 1. The end
of God's setting forth Christ as a propitiation, was to declare his righteousness in the "remission of sins," Rom. 3:
25. which it does doubly, 1. That without satisfaction,
sin would not be justly remitted. 2. That satisfaction being
given, it could not justly be imputed, chap. 8: 34. But if
those for whom satisfaction has been given, should not be
justified and saved, divine justice would be as liable to im-
peachment, as if they had been saved without: and so the
thing designed for the honor of his righteousness, would turn
to its disparagement. 2. It would not accord with the love
and goodness of God towards his elect, that that which was
meant for their recovery, and was also a price well worthy
their ransom, should possibly turn to their deeper condemnation; for so it must if they be not effectually saved, John
3: 19. This could not be that pleasure of the Lord, which
should prosper in the hands of Christ. 3. It would not be
according to the faithfulness and truth of God, that Christ
should fail of that he was promised, and earnestly looked for,
as the fruit of his suffering; which was a "seed to serve him,"
Isa. 53: 10. The thoughts of which were matter of com-
placency to him from everlasting, Prov. 8: 11. But if
those he died for, should not only abide in the same con-

demnation he came to deliver them from, but under a much sorer vengeance than if he had not undertaken for them: how grievous would it be to him, and contradictory to the faithfulness of God: 4. Another end of redemption was, that the manifold wisdom of God might shine forth in the sight of angels and men. "Christ crucified is the wisdom of God," 1 Cor. 1: 24. But if it were so contrived, that the thing chiefly designed might possibly miscarry, it would be no illustration of wisdom. Will one of common prudence part with his jewels and choicest treasure, and leave his purchase knowingly under hazard? Men, indeed, may possibly waste their estates in trials and essays that come to nothing; but did they foresee the event they would not so expose their prudence to reproach. 5. The greatness and power of God would suffer an eclipse if it were in the power of creatures to defeat his most wise and holy designs; and hinder the accomplishment of his greatest work. What would the Egyptians say, but that he destroyed them, because not able to go through with that he undertook? *Lastly.* If the end of Christ's death might possibly be frustrated, then that blessed project for glorifying the grace of God might possibly be disannulled and come to nothing; for none but saved ones do, or can, glorify that grace.

Arg. IV. Another argument for the sure effects of Christ's death, is that he hath the management of the whole work committed to himself; as well the application of redemption, as the procurement of it. He is the repository, root, and treasury, wherein all the benefits of redemption are laid up; and the great Almoner by whose hand they are dispensed. Adam was no more a public person after his fall: the new stock was not entrusted with him, but put into the hands of Christ, who will give a better account of it.

Arg. V. There is nothing wanting to our Lord and Redeemer, which might any way conduce to the final completion of his work. There are five things mainly requisite to make a great undertaking successful, namely, authority, strength, understanding, courage, and faithfulness: all which the Captain of our salvation is eminently invested with: "The Father loveth the Son, and hath given all things into his hands," John 3: 35.

1. Authority: he was appointed to his office, for, as Mediator, the Father is greater than he: "He came not of himself, but the Father sent him," John 9: 42. He was

" called of God," Heb. 5: 4, 5. It was laid on him, and
undertaken by him, in the way of covenant, Isa. 42: 6. and
confirmed by an oath, Heb. 7: 21. never to be reversed;
which also may partly be the meaning of God the Father's
sealing him, John 6: 27. " The government is laid upon
his shoulder," Isa. 9: 6. He hath the key of David committed to him, Rev. 3: 7. which shows the absoluteness of
his authority: without him, no man can lift up his hand, or
his foot, in all the earth.

2. Strength, or power: these cannot be wanting to him,
if all in heaven and earth be sufficient for it: for this he
hath, Matth. 28: 18. and he hath it to this end, that he
might give eternal life to as many as he undertook for,
John 17: 2. which if they should miss of, it would be said
that all his power was not able to save them. He that
made the world, is surely well able to govern it, and to
over-rule whatever comes into it: he would never have suffered sin, the only enemy, to invade it, if he could not have
quelled it at pleasure; their " Redeemer is strong: the
Lord of hosts is his name; he shall thoroughly plead their
cause," Jer. 50: 14. He must " reign until he shall have
put all enemies both under his own feet and ours,"
1 Cor. 15: 25.

3. Understanding, or knowledge: this cannot be wanting to him, who is the wisdom of the Father: the Lord hath
given him the " tongue of the learned, that he might
speak words in season to him that is weary," Isa. 50: 4.
He knows his work; what it is; how to effect it; and who
they be that are concerned in it. 1. He knows what his
work is; it was, in short, " to seek and to save that which
was lost:" not to bring them into a salvable condition, as
some speak, but to save them, and that from their sins,
Matt. 1: 21. He came to open the blind eyes; and to
bore the deaf ears; to restore the withered limbs; to cleanse
the lepers; to heal the sick; to raise the dead; to cast out
devils; to preach the gospel; and to cause those it belongs
unto to hear and receive it: he knows they are dead, and
he knows as well that he is to quicken them; and thence
we have it in John 5: 25. the " dead shall hear and live;"
and chap. 10: 16. " Other sheep I have; them also must I
bring, and they shall hear my voice." He is also to keep
them, and to look to them, so as not one be lost, John 17:12.
22. chap. 6:39. and, finally, to raise them up at the last day:

and to take them to heaven with him: all which he is perfectly acquainted with; his work is before him, Isa. 40: 10. 2. As he knows his work, what it is, so the best season and method for its performance. He came in the fulness of time; when things were ripe for his coming: He came then when there was most need of him; the devil's kingdom at the highest; his oracles in greatest credit; the world overwhelmed by the Roman power; and the true religion almost totally depraved among the Jews. It argues a dexterous undertaking, to take an enemy in his rough, at his highest pitch of strength and confidence, and throw him on his back; to succor a distressed friend or ally, when brought under foot, and set him on his high places. This the scripture calls, " a strengthening of the spoiled against the strong," Amos 5: 9. and thus doth our Lord Jesus Christ, who is partly, therefore, said to be of quick understanding, Isa. 11: 3. In all his undertakings he deals prudently, chap. 52: 13. And to this it is that Hannah ascribed success: "The Lord is a God of knowledge, and by him actions are weighed," 1 Sam. 2: 3. He knows who they are for whom he is to do it. The fruits of his death are not to be given in common; they fall not indifferently upon men, as rain upon all sorts of ground: he knows whom he came to redeem; not their number only, but their persons; they were all written in his book: and so well is he versed in it, that " he calleth them all by their names," John 10: 3. he does not omit any, nor call one for another: he knows whom the Father hath chosen and given to him, chap. 17: 2. 6. he can neither forget them, nor mistake them; they are written in his breast, and on the palms of his hands, Isa. 49: 16.

4. To a great undertaking is required courage or greatness of spirit, to confront opposition, and cut through difficulties: and if this be wanting, all other endowments will signify little as to success. And how was our Lord and Redeemer qualified as to this! When he was entering into his passion, against which he prayed, " If it were possible that this cup might pass from him;" he then needed courage in the abstract, and we find that he had it answerably. In the 50th of Isaiah, the prophet brings him in as putting on his armor of proof; " therefore have I set my face as a flint, and I know that I shall not be confounded," Isa. 50: 7. In the greatness of this his strength did he travel

through all those contradictions of sinners, temptations, reproaches, blasphemies, &c. And when his hour was come, he did not recoil, nor hide himself from them; no, nor stay till they came where he was, but goes to meet them, John 18: 4. And though he might have had more than twelve legions of angels for asking, he waives their assistance, and his own single person undertakes both this world and the powers of darkness, yea, and the wrath of his Father too, which was much more grievous, and of far greater terror than all the rest: and in all this he was alone, there was none with him; and that an angel appeared to him from heaven strengthening him, Luke 22: 43. it was rather a token and part of his deep humiliation (that the mighty God should seem to want, and so admit the proffered service of his creature), than a lessening of his sufferings. Now all this was for the procurement of redemption; and can he then be wanting to the effectual application of it? He cannot shrink at the sight of straggling parties, that hath won the pitched battle, and remains absolute master of the field; for this also, we have a sure word of prophecy, "He shall not fail nor be discouraged, until he have set judgment in the earth," Isa. 42: 4.

5. Faithfulness; this also is a grand and necessary qualification for a high undertaking; and for this our Redeemer is also signally eminent. To do the Father's will, was that he came about from heaven: and this was his will, "That of all he had given him he should lose nothing; but should raise it up at the last day," John 6: 38, 39. that is, that he should give them eternal life, chap. 17: 2. And we find him professing, that he had done it accordingly, verse 12. and that he will do it, ver. 26. according to his promise so often repeated in the 39th, 40th, 44th, 45th verses of the 6th of John. And he keeps them in faithfulness to his trust, namely, "That the Scripture might be fulfilled," John 17: 12. Judas was let go, to fall by his own transgression; whom doubtless he could and would have kept as he did the rest, had he been, as they were, committed to his charge: for he gives to every one according as he received for them, as is seen by comparing Psalm 68:18. with Eph. 4: 8. In the one place it is said, he received gifts for men; and in the other (which is a quotation of the former) he gave gifts to men: those, therefore, for whom he received eternal life, cannot fail of it, unless he should fail of his

trust; which, indeed, he cannot do; for, he is faithful in all his house, Heb. 3: 5, 6, and that as a Son; and joint interest, you know, is a natural and prevalent obligation to faithfulness. If any should offer to dispossess him, he would answer as Naboth did Ahab; "God forbid that I should part with the inheritance of my fathers," 1 Kings 21: 3. And this faithfulness further appears, in that he makes it a main part of his business, now in heaven, to have this work perfected; "he ever liveth to make intercession for them," Heb. 7: 25. There is great weight put upon this, in Rom. 8: 34. "Who is he that condemneth? It is Christ that died; yea, rather, that is risen again—who also maketh intercession for us;" and the sum of his prayer is, that those given to him might be kept from evil; that they might be one in the Father and himself; and that they may be where he is, to behold his glory," John 17: 24. 21. 15. Now, then, if the salvation of those he died for was the end of his death: and the price that he paid well worthy the purchase: if it be the Father's will that they should be saved: if also this salvation be the thing for which he prays, and whatsoever he asketh of God, he will give it, John 11: 22. It needs must follow, "that the intent of his death cannot be frustrated."

Yet does not this truth go unopposed; not for any fault of its own, but that it will not give place to another, which unduly affects the pre-eminence. Denied in terms it is not; none will say directly, that Christ's intent in dying may be frustrated: but, that intent of his is so narrowed by some, and clogged with conditions, as would bring it to nothing. The rise whereof, or its use, I understand not; but suppose that necessity drove to it, for want of a better, to shore up the general point. I thought, at first, of no objection here; but, having since found this in the way, I would put it in the sacred balance, and try its weight. The sum alleged is this,

Object. That the intent of Christ's death was only to bring men into a salvable state; with such means and helps as will bring them to salvation, if they will use them; and that any are not saved, is from their unbelief.

Answ. 1. That unbelief is the condemning sin, needs no proof; but men's not believing in Christ is not the only, or first procuring cause of their condemnation; but their apostacy and rebellion against God: although the condemnation of those who believe not, is greatly aggravated by rejecting the remedy; as one condemned for treason, refusing his pardon, that refusal is, indeed, the next and immediate cause of his execution, and perhaps shall heighten the rigor of it; but his treasonable practice was the first procuring cause of his death; which also he should have suffered for, if no such pardon had been offered. There will need no accusation from Christ to justify the condemnation of sinners. Moses, whose law they have broken, shall witness against the Jews; and the law of nature against the Gentiles. That faith is the one thing necessary on our part, in order to being saved, is a foundation truth, and most necessary to be known; and as true it is, that faith adds nothing of merit or virtue to the cross of Christ. Where men are said to be justified or saved by faith, it is meant of the object of faith, and not of the act, though not without it. For as bread must be eaten, and taken in, before it can nourish; so must the righteousness of Christ be apprehended by faith, before we can be justified by it. But as the action of eating or chewing is not the matter or substance of our nourishment, but the bread we eat; so neither is our act of believing, but the righteousness of Christ alone, apprehended by faith, the matter of our justification. But,

2. Why should redemption depend on a sovereign power to bring about its end? Why should so great a thing be left in the hands of a human arbitrement, to succeed, or be defeated, at the pleasure of a perverse will? That Christ should die, ought rather to have been conditional, and not the salvation of those he should die for; and so, in prudence, should have been deferred until the end of the world, to see if any fruit would come of it; and if not, then not to die at all; for why should he die in vain? But that Christ should die, and that at the very time when he did, was fore-determined of God, and confirmed with an oath; whereby it was made necessary, and impossible to be reversed. It could not, then, stand with the wisdom or truth of God, that the end of his death should possibly miscarry, or be frustrable: which it must be obnoxious to, if dependant on the human will; a thing so fickle and uncertain, that it knows not this moment what it will do, or pitch upon the next; besides a natural antipathy to the thing itself: but evident it is, that the end has the same insurance as the means, namely, decree, promises, and

oath. And now, shall so great solemnity, and expectation upon it evaporate into contingency? Christ was promised a seed to serve him, and such a sight of the travail of his soul, as should satisfy him: That he "should divide the spoil with the strong," Isa. 53: 10, 11. "That the heathen should be his inheritance, Psal. 2: 8. "That kings should see and arise; princes also should worship," Psal. 49: 7. "and his enemies become his footstool," &c. Psal. 110: 1. And this, as a reward of his sufferings; and he sits in heaven, expecting until it be done, Heb. 10: 13. And now, shall lapsed creatures usurp a negative vote to their sovereign's will? Shall it be at their pleasure, whether he who is heir of all things, shall possess his patrimony? Shall sinful dust so arrogate to itself as to say, My Creator's will shall be done, so mine may be the standard of it? Shall those statutes of heaven, in favor of the conditional doctrine, run thus? The strong man armed shall be spoiled and cast out, if he will: The heathen, whose god is the devil, shall renounce him, and turn tenants to Christ, if he will consent to it, and they also think it their interest: Kings and princes shall arise and worship him, if their own grandeur will bear it; and enemies become his footstool, in case they be free to submit to it, &c. Who would not tremble to hear such indignities put upon Christ?

3. There was no reason why Christ, the Son of God, should die for so small a purchase, as to make men but conditionally salvable: that the greatest thing in the world should be hung on so weak a pin as would not bear the weight of an apple. I call it a small purchase, because they had more than this in Adam: they had then a pure freedom of will, without bias to evil. But now, say you, they are helped by motives and arguments from the danger they are in, and the benefits attainable by changing their course: but what are these as the case stands? What motives will move, while insensible of that danger, and ignorant of the benefits proposed? Such motives also they had before, and more amply than now; inasmuch as the present sense of a happy condition was more attractive and prevalent to keep it, than the mere proposal of a distant and unknown privilege can be to attain it (for of things unknown, men are not desirous;) especially when things that are more suitable to present sense are theirs in possession; and to leave these for those they understood not, is contrary to their reason:

they see neither danger nor privilege, and therefore despise both. Or if they have skin-deep convictions at times, the present content they dream to have in their lusts, carries them headlong, as wind and tide.

4. If rational motives and argumentations were of that weight and efficacy for the working of faith, as some have pretended; then those of the largest endowments of nature should be the most capable subjects, and most likely to be wrought upon. But do any of the Pharisees believe on him? Do not the princes of worldly wisdom account the preaching of the cross foolishness? Do we see men of renown for human sapience, highly pretending to moral sanctity, and the highest flown in their free-will principles, nevertheless to despise the ways of holiness; yea, despoiling Christ himself of his deity, and the christian religion of its chiefest glory? Nothing more plain to common observance! Surely, then, it could not be reasonable, that this glorious redemption shall lie at the mercy of a perverse will; since that is the thing which hath hindered, and will hinder, until it be taken out of the way. Christ was but once delivered to the wills of men, and then they crucified him, Luke 23: 24. and ever since they crucify his cross. "Had they known him they would not have crucified the Lord of glory," 1 Cor. 2: 8. but so it is in the wisdom of God, that "the world by wisdom knew not God," chap. 1: 21. The wisdom of men never was the author of faith, either to themselves or others, chap. 2: 5. the preaching of the cross is to the Jewish legalists a stumbling-block, chapter 1: 23. and foolishness to the rational philosopher, and those at Athens, Acts 17: 11.

5. Conditionality will not consort with the scope of Christ's redemption, nor yet with the nature of the bondage it refers unto: it is summarily termed, the bondage of corruption: in parcels, it bears the name of blindness, darkness, death, hardness, unbelief, enmity, &c. And that, deliverance from these was the very scope and end of redemption, might be made out particularly: I shall instance only two or three generals: "For this purpose the Son of God was manifested, that he might destroy the works of the devil," 1 John 3: 8. "Our old man was crucified with Christ, that the body of sin might be destroyed," Rom. 6: 6. "God sent his own Son, in the likeness of sinful flesh, and for sin, condemned sin in the flesh," chapter 8: 3. Which text,

lest they might seem defective for want of universality, that also is supplied in Tit. 2:14. "Who gave himself for us, that he might redeem us from all iniquity," Ephes. 5: 25, 26, 27. Christ gave himself for the church, that he might sanctify and cleanse it, "and present it to himself a glorious church, not having spot or wrinkle, or any such thing." But was it not a thing in design only, and liable to frustration? No, it was determined and fixed; for, "he shall redeem Israel from all his iniquities," Psal. 130: 8. and the blood of Jesus Christ his Son "cleanseth us from all sin," 1 John 1: 7. it is spoken of in the present tense, as a thing still and always in doing. And this *all* here must be taken universally; because, if not saved from all, it would be, in the end, as if saved from none: one mite left on the score, binds over to wrath; especially unbelief, John 3: 18. Why then should they of all the rest be exempted or disputed? is it, that we think faith so easy a matter, that we need not trouble our master about it? Few believers have found it so: or do we think ourselves better able to deal with our own hearts, or truer to our interest than he? Is it our hearts' deceitfulness that makes us think so: or shall we impose upon Christ something of ours to increase his merits, or to make them effectual? He abhors it; for "if ye be circumcised, Christ shall profit you nothing," Gal. 5: 2. or do we aspire to sit on his right hand in the glory of redemption; I know not what it is; but am sure, that something not right lies in the bottom, though unseen. For since the honor of redemption lies in saving from sin, he that saves from unbelief, which is the capital, shares deepest in that honor: unbelief is the lock of our chain and bondage; and till that be unshot, there is no getting loose. Christ's redemption is not like those laws of men, who hold the small, but let the great ones break through: no, redemption aims at the head, and it was so designed from the first, Gen. 3: 15. But how are men saved from unbelief? is it their own act, or another's? if their own, then it is of works: which will not consort with grace, Rom, 4: 4. and chap. 11: 6. if another's that other does it either absolutely, or conditionally: if absolutely, the objection ceases: if conditionally, what was the condition of it? It could be nothing in us before we believed; for "whatsoever is not of faith, is sin," Rom.14:23. It must then be for another cause, and without condition, and that can be only redemption itself, for nothing else can pretend to it; and the pretensions of that are good, for Christ is expressly said to be the author of our faith, Heb. 12: 2. and the evangelist John affirms all grace to be out of his fulness, John 1: 16. Paul also shows, that Christ apprehends us, not because we do, but that we might apprehend him, Phil. 3: 12. And further, " the Holy Ghost, who is the immediate operator of all grace, is shed upon us, through Jesus Christ our Saviour," Tit. 3: 6. That faith which is not from Christ entirely, as its author and root, will never lead the soul to Christ as its object and centre. But methinks the doctrine of conditional redemption should be for ever silenced, by that one declaration of our Saviour himself, " I am found of them that sought me not," Isa. 65: 1.

Now shall this truth be yielded, namely, that Christ's redemption made an end of sin? or shall we say that our old man was crucified all but his vital parts? that all the works of the devil are destroyed, except his master-piece? that Israel is redeemed from all his iniquities, save only the worst and most condemning? Does the scripture speak fallaciously? or does vain man deal deceitfully in his covenant? I would ask (with great seriousness, for the matter requires it,) what good shall redemption do us, if it saves only from some sins, and not from all? or if from all excepting unbelief? this would too much resemble a pardon for petty trespasses (petty in comparison) while the guilt of our treason lies still upon us: to purchase salvation upon terms of believing, without purchasing faith also, is too like an undertaking to cure a man of his phrensy, upon condition he will be sober: what will they do, who content themselves with such a redemption as this?

Lastly. Consider redemption in its type: the people's sins, under the law, had not been expiated by the sacrifice, without sprinkling the blood; and it was not themselves that sprinkled it, but the priest; and can we then think, that Christ shed his blood for those on whom he will not sprinkle it? that he will not give a little faith to those he died for, when without that, all that he doeth besides will not profit them? hath he wrought so great a deliverance for his servants, and now shall they die for thirst? Judges 15: 18. It is impossible that his love should be so cooled (since his going to heaven,) as to be indifferent touching the travail of his soul: shall he perish for whom Christ died,

for want of a good word? especially when that word can be
spoken effectually by nobody else: if any say, he would,
but they will not; I answer, this will-not is their unbelief,
and the great thing they are to be saved from; he that is
saved from that, is saved every whit; and this Christ is to
do by making them willing: a will to believe, is believing;
and in the day of his power they find it. And for any to
say, that a will to believe is not purchased by Christ, and
effectually applied by him, but depends on something to be
done by men, is a great derogation from the merit of his sufferings; it is, in effect, to steal a jewel from our sovereign's
crown, and to wreath it on a fool's cap.

Inferences

Infer. I. The impossibility of frustrating the end of
Christ's death, is a manifest proof and argument of peculiar redemption. For if the salvation of those he died for
was the end of his dying, and the intent of his death cannot be frustrate, then he had not in his eye and design the
salvation of those that are not saved.

Infer. II. Take heed what you hear, and how. Beware
of those doctrines which tend to enervate the covenant of
grace, reducing it to a covenant of works, or somewhat
more difficult: a principal one is, that which makes redemption conditional, and dependant upon something to be
done by men, which Christ is not the doer of: of its evil
consequences I shall mention two.

1. It bereaves us of that solid ground of comfort (for the
joy of the Lord is our strength) which the absoluteness of
redemption intends and offers to us, exposing our naked
skin to every blast of temptation. Who can promise the
standing of that fabric which rests on a doubtful foundation? To build hay and stubble on the rock, has not half
that danger in it as gold and silver on the sand. The one
shall be saved, though with difficulty; the other loses both
his work and himself: for let redemption be ever so firm
and solid in itself, if yet its standing and efficacy depend
upon that which is fleeting and unfixed, the ground of our
confidence is gone: it is like those pumps that have water
within, but yield you none, unless you first put in some of
your own, which yet ye have not: like Jacob's well, but
nothing to draw with. But for men to annex conditions, is
to offer a bar to their own pardon; and, instead of amend-

ment, to add a destructive proviso to the bill of free grace: that paradox of the preacher seems pertinent here: " Be not righteous over much, neither make thyself over wise: why shouldst thou destroy thyself ?" Eccles. 7: 16.

2. To make redemption dependant on our faith, attributes to created grace and honor what is due only to Christ, which redeemed ones should be very tender of. Was he alone in the obtainment of redemption, and shall we think he needs a coadjutor in its application? Shall we impute to that glorious achievement a need of our help to make it successful? No; whatever graces ye have, you must thank redemption for them, and not them for your being redeemed. The whole constellation shines by a borrowed light; they have none of their own, but what the sun of righteousness communicates to them. Hast thou faith? Have it to thyself, and know it for thy good; take it as an effect and evidence, but not as the cause of your interest in redemption. Each grace is of use in its place, and beautiful; as each star hath an orb of its own; and to move out of that, is to break the harmony of the spheres: even gospel graces legalized, lose their excellency. I must say to faith in this case, Friend, sit down lower; this place belongs to your author; you are redemption's creature; from that you had your birth; and in that you live and move: ye are welcome as a guest, yea, as a chief ruler of the feast, though not as the bridegroom's compeer. But true faith, and unclouded, is more ingenuous than to incur such a rebuke.

Infer. III. If all merit and grace be virtually in redemption, and thence dispensed by the hand of our Redeemer himself, this yields both a friendly reproof and direction together: reproof to expectancy any where else; and direction to poor thirsting souls, where and how to be satisfied. Undone you are in yourselves, that ye find; and would gladly put this ruin under the hand of Christ, Isa. 3: 6. as one that is able to repair it. Thus far ye are right: but something you seek in yourself that may strengthen your hope, and induce his favor to you. Away with such pretences, and flee to your Redeemer as you are; for " from him alone is that fruit to be found," Hos. 14: 8. Be as sensible of your deformity and unworthiness as you can, and walk humbly under the sense of it; but let it not slacken your pace, nor abate your hope. If any thing may render you worthy, that is, a suitable object of mercy, it

is your coming boldly to the throne of grace with all your
unworthiness about you. It is a disgustful modesty to be
shy in accepting from those above us: it looks as if we
would not be thought to need their kindness; or else, as if
we thought they needed our requital; or, at least, as if we
were unwilling to be obliged by them: much more unbe-
coming it is, to be backward in accepting the offers of
grace from so great a person as our Lord and Redeemer.
O, the unnaturalness of our natural hearts, even to our
own good! We are pitiful objects of charity: all fulness
is in Christ, and may be had for going for; and yet, as if
he wanted clients, he is fain to make proclamation; " Ho!
every one that thirsteth, come ye to the waters; and he that
hath no money;" Isa. 55: 1. and, " if any man thirst, let
him come to me, and drink," John 7: 37. Great things are
proffered; and what is the price? Nothing: it is but come
and take; and yet this nothing will be found to be something; yea, a thing both of the greatest moment and difficulty: it is one of the hardest under the sun to become nothing (nothing in ourselves,) and to fly directly to Christ,
that we may be something: but go to him even for this.
Had the prodigal deferred his return till he had better
clothes on his back, and a visage more like the son of such
a father, rags must still have been his clothing, and husks
his entertainment. Do but consider how it is: Jesus Christ
calls you, because you are blind, to come to him for eye-
salve; and you will not go until you can see better: you are
naked, and he calls you to come and receive change of
raiment; and you will not go until better arrayed: he offers
you gold, for he knows your poverty, and you will not take
it until you have something of your own to give for it, &c.
Look over it again, and see if this be handsome dealing
either with yourselves or him. It is free grace in redemption that is to be glorified; but something of your own
would lessen your need of Christ, and lower your esteem
of his grace; nay, it would be a means to keep you from
him, as farms and oxen did the invited guests from the
wedding supper. Consider further; no man was ever accepted of Christ for what he brought to him: they are best
welcome that bring nothing, and yet expect all things.
What did you give to Christ, or what did you for him, or
even can, that might move him to die for you? Yea, to be
made sin, and a curse for you? Did he go into hell to fetch

you hence, and pawn his soul (his precious soul) for your
ransom? And can you think that he will stick at petty
matters? Deservedly may you and I be upbraided with,
" O fools, and slow of heart to believe!" He knows we
have nothing, and would have us know it; and withal that
he hath all things for us; and, for our invincible encouragement, that all things are ours in a way of right; his purchase hath made them so: we are his invited guests, and
shall not need to bring our seat and provision with us. I
shall add but one consideration more; namely, whether
your keeping off from Christ, until fit for his presence (as
ye term it,) be the way to better your state: search, and
see, if something like pride be not at the bottom: something you would have, ere you come, that might render you
acceptable; and that you can only have from him; and you
cannot have it, but by coming without it. Redemption
hath in it infinite treasures of what we want; our Redeemer
is infinitely more pleased to give them forth, than we to
receive them. Think, therefore, you are always hearing
that joyful sound, " Come unto me, all ye that labor, and
are heavy laden, and I will give you rest," Matth. 11: 28.
" and he that cometh unto me I will in no wise cast out,"
John 6: 37.

Infer. IV. This gives to believers the highest encouragement in their spiritual conflict. " For if our old man was
crucified with Christ, that the body of sin might be destroyed," and the intent of his death cannot be frustrate,
then, " sin shall not have dominion over you," Rom. 6: 6,
12, 22. than which there is nothing more fortifies our faith
in fighting against sin; nothing more comforts the soul
" concerning the work and toil of his hands," Gen. 5: 29.
For, to take away sin being the end of redemption; to
make the work sure, Christ himself was made sin, impu-
tatively, not inherently: all the sins of those he died for
met on him; he and they were so incorporated, as not to
be separated by death; sin could not die, unless Christ died;
Christ could not die without being made sin; nor could he
die, but sin must die with him: whole Christ, both head
and members universally, were all crucified together, and
they all rose together; all, excepting sin, and that he left
in his grave; and let us remember it is there. So that now
we have nothing to do, in comparison, but to take the prey;
for the enemy is beaten to our hands: Eleazer slew, and the

people returned after him only to spoil, 2 Sam. 23: 10. and so it is here: and herein is the saying verified, " One soweth, and another reapeth," John 4: 37. Our business now is to display our general's trophies; to tell of his victories; and prepare ourselves for his triumph, that we may be suitable attendants on him at that glorious and longed-for day.

There are straggling parties, indeed, who watch for our halting, and seldom, else, can they have advantage against us: but their heart is broke; and if followed in our Captain's victorious name, they will still be recoiling; nothing daunts them more than to see you stand to it. Your adversary would make you a bridge of gold, or any thing, even to the half of his kingdom, so you would sound a retreat, or speak no more in that name, " Gird up, therefore, the loins of your mind;" let an holy magnanimity possess you; as knowing your conflict shall end in your being crowned. You run not for an uncertainty, therefore fight not as they that beat the air: for it is nevertheless true that your enemy is stubborn; and your constant pursuit will make him desperate; since he may not have quarter, he will do all he can not to die alone; he will stand on his stumps when his legs are off, or lie on his back and fight, for his malice is im placable: he will never give over until quite out of breath: which yet he will not be without, while we have any: we expire together. But here lies the odds, that we, in the conflict, shall rise again with marks of honor, and our laurel hold green to eternity; yea, we shall sit with our glorious Captain in his triumphal chariot, Rev. 3: 21. But our enemy lies in eternal silence, and his name forgot; or remembered only to heighten our exultation and glory: only, as before, be sure and stand to it; set your face as a flint, as your Lord and master did; and know, that as he was not confounded, so neither shall you: all that he had, you have on your side, and the merit of his improvement added to it; what power the Father gave to him, he delegates to you; even a " power over all the power of the enemy:" as it were an antidote supersedeas, to invalidate all that comes against you. Wherefore then should you doubt: though they come about you like bees, " in the name of the Lord you shall destroy them," Psal. 118: 12. Remember the advantages you have; besides the bruising of your enemy's head, and that incurably, your own Head is in heaven; and he is there as on a mount, to behold both yours and your enemy's posture, and to send in relief, which he never fails to do at a dead lift, Isa. 41: 17. chap. 25: 4. And " he makes intercession for you," Heb. 7: 25. While you are fighting, his hands are up, and never weary, and therefore you may be confident of success. It was by virtue of his prayer that Peter's faith did not fail, when there was but a hair's breadth between him and death; the devil winnowed, but Christ stood by, and " held the wind in his fist," Prov. 30: 4. Jer. 31: 11. But,

Lastly. Suppose you be foiled; things go not with you as they were wont, as you expected; and that casts you back in your faith; makes you cry out, " If it be so, why am I thus?" Gen. 25: 22. Here the Lord says to you (as once to his servant Joshua,) " Get thee up; wherefore liest thou thus discouraged upon thy face," Josh. 7: 10. There is something to be done; find out the troubler of thy peace, and give it no quarter; and if it be too hard for thee, as certainly it will, call in the mercy promised in Psal. 12. " For the oppression of the poor, for the sighing of the needy, now will I arise, saith the Lord, and set him in safety from him that puffeth at him," verse 5. And then go on with your work: let nothing stop you of your boasting in this region, this upper region of grace that is in Christ Jesus; in that let your strength be renewed, the journey else will be too great for you, 1 Kings 19: 7, 8. and in that strength soar aloft; take the wings of that eagle, and mount towards heaven; above all the smoke and dust both of self-ability and self-weakness. Make your " boast of God all the day long: in the Lord have I righteousness and strength:" Of myself I can do nothing; but through Christ (the strength I have from his redemption) nothing shall be too hard for me. " O death, where is thy sting? O hell, where is thy victory? The strength of death is sin, and the strength of sin is the law: but thanks be unto God, who giveth us the victory, through our Lord Jesus Christ. Amen," 1 Cor. 15: 55, 56, 57.

EFFECTUAL CALLING

THE doctrine of Calling, (which I term Effectual, to distinguish it from that which is outward only, and prevails not) respects the means whereby, and the manner how, God's elect are actually prepared for that salvation he hath chosen them to: it is God's revealing his Son in them; and he doeth it by the Holy Ghost, whose office is to sanctify whom the Father hath elected, and Christ redeemed, 1 Pet. 1: 2. Jude, ver. 1. These three acts of grace are peculiar to the three persons of the sacred Trinity, respectively, and are all predicated of the same subjects; and that as a party select, and distinguished from others: they are "chosen out of the world," John 15: 19. "redeemed from among men," Rev. 14: 4. and taken "from among the Gentiles," Acts 15: 14.

Next to the glory of his grace, and the honor of his Son, the Lord hath placed the blessedness of his chosen as the principal scope and end of all he hath done in the world, or will do. It could not, therefore, stand with his holy wisdom, to leave those he was pleased to choose unto salvation, to the conduct of their own understanding and will, with such means and helps as they have in common with other men, and thereon to suspend the whole of his great design; for by such a course it would not only be liable to frustration, but be certainly defeated. For prevention whereof, and that the purpose of his grace might stand, he hath made it of the substance of predestination, to prepare and apply the means, as well as to appoint the end; which in sacred language is termed a "giving of all things pertaining to life and godliness." 2 Pet. 1: 3.

The sum of what I intend on the present subject is comprised of the following proposition; namely,

Prop. That whatever things are requisite to salvation, are given of God freely to all the elect; and wrought in them effectually, by the divine power in order to that salvation to which he hath appointed them.

By salvation here, I understand the saints' perfect settlement in blessedness and glory: and, by things requisite thereto, all those gifts, graces, and operations, that are any where necessary to their actual obtainment of that state. The divine power, is that ability of working which God hath reserved to himself; and is not moved or governed by the creature's act, but by the good pleasure of his own will.

That divers things are requisite to salvation, needs no proof: my business therefore is to show,

I. What these requisites to salvation are.
II. What root it is they proceed from.
III. Whom they do belong unto, and by what right.
IV. The way and manner of God's dispensing them.

I. What these requisites to salvation are.

They are three sorts; some to be done for us; some upon us, or in us; and others by us; yet so as not without the special aid and assistance of the first agent, that good Spirit who began the work, and worketh all in all. The great thing to be done for us (next after election,) is redemption from sin: this was a work of infinite moment, and as far above the undertaking of creatures; for, 1. The justice of God that must be satisfied, by bearing the curse due to transgressors: by this we are saved from wrath; and without this, divine justice will not open the house of his prisoners. 2. All righteousness must be fulfilled by an absolute perfect subjection to the law: by this, we are interested in eternal life; and without this, there is no entering into rest. 3. The devil, who had the power of death, must be destroyed, and his works of darkness (by which he leads captive at his will) dissolved; that life and immortality might be brought to light, and the prey delivered. None of which works could ever have been effected, but by one of the same nature with the parties peccant or aggressing, and yet equal in power and dignity with the majesty offended; for which cause and end, " God sent forth his Son, made of a woman, and made under the law," &c. Gal. 4: 4, 5. that what the law could not do, because of its weakness through the flesh, the Son of God, in the likeness of sinful flesh, might perform; and so condemn sin in that flesh which gave it entrance, Rom. 8: 3. This was the proper subject of the former head, namely redemption: the end of which, partly, was, to bring in the next sort of things requisite to salvation, that is, such as are to be done upon and in the elect, namely, their reconcilement to God, and receiving the adoption of sons. This is the actual performance of what was intentionally in election, and virtually in the death of Christ, as the necessary way and means to their ultimate end. The sum of these requisites consists in faith and sanctification, 2 Thess. 2: 13. the one imports our right, the other our capacity; faith entitles, and holiness meetens: both which, though expressed as two, go always together, as if but one; and are as inseparable as light from the sun: and, without these, our little world would still be in darkness, notwithstanding all the light that shines about us, or within us; neither knowing our danger, nor how to escape it.

1. Faith. This, in general, is that spiritual light in which we see ourselves by nature children of wrath, and wholly unable to change our state, and withal, do apprehend "God justifying freely by his grace, through the redemption that is in Jesus Christ," Rom. 3: 24. and to that end, do roll ourselves upon him, and give up ourselves to his law and government. It is of the essence of faith, to empty the soul of self-ability. And, 1. Of its own understanding. It is a beam of divine light, which evidenceth all a man's natural knowledge to be ignorance and darkness, as to spiritual things. The apostle speaks of it as of a faculty newly given, 1 John 5: 20. and the nature of its new objects requires it; for the natural man cannot discern the things of God, 1 Cor. 2: 14. They that have the best eyes now, were sometimes darkness. Faith empties the soul. Faith empties the soul of its own righteousness, 1. By discovering the uncleanness of it, Isa. 64:'6. 2. By showing the necessity of a better, Rom. 3: 20. 3. In whom this better righteousness is to be found, chap. 10: 4. 4. That it may be attained and had, chap. 3: 21. 5. That being attained, the soul is safe, and may triumph over all, chap. 8: 34. and chap. 7: 25. 6. That this better righteousness and its own cannot stand together, Gal. 5: 2. Rom. 10: 3. And then, 3. The next work of faith is, to empty the soul of its own strength; that is, of all confidence in himself, as to the obtainment of that better righteousness. He makes it, indeed, his business to get rid of his own,

and most gladly would he be invested with the righteousness of God; but finds it a matter of transcendent difficulty. Now he is convinced it is no easy matter to be saved; since to believe, and to keep the whole law, are things of an equal facility; that is, they are both alike impossible to him; but nothing, he knows, is too hard for God, and therefore takes hold of his strength, Isa. 27: 5. to work this faith in him; and so, by a faith unseen, believes to a faith that is visible, Rom. 1: 17.   It is faith that is at work all this while, though the soul knows it not till afterwards.

2. The other grand requisite to salvation, is sanctification, or personal inherent holiness.   Justification is by a righteousness imputed; sanctification infused; the former is first in order of nature; they commence together in point of time; even as light in the air at the sun's approach; or as the reversing an outlawry instantly re-instates the party in his former privileges; or as the cancelling a bill of attainder restores the blood.   Sanctification is the divine nature communicated; by which the whole man is expelled, with his deeds, or rather subdued and brought under; for they are not totally nulled in this life; only proud flesh is put down from its seat, and that is a great matter, its dominion is taken away, and the seed of God enthroned in its stead: and so we are said to be translated out of Satan's kingdom, or government, into Christ's, Col. 1: 13.   It is sometimes called regeneration, or a being born again, John 3: 3. the separating a man from his wild stock, and grafting him in the true, Rom. 11: 17. the forming of Christ in us, and the law written in the heart, Heb. 8: 10. that is, dispositions according to God, or a heart after his own.   It is also termed, the passing away of old things, and a becoming new of all, 2 Cor. 5: 17. there is a change of principles, scope, and end of man's life.   Not that the old faculties are blotted out or destroyed, but reduced or renewed, according to the "image of him that createth it," Col. 3: 10. Rom. 8: 29.   As the body, when it is regenerated, or raised again, shall be the same that was sown; but so changed, and dignified in its qualities, as if it were another; so, in the soul's regeneration, the same understanding, will, and affections do remain, but quite otherwise disposed and qualified, according to the new objects they are to converse with.   And this is so main a requisite to salvation, that we are not capable of heaven without it.

Even the local heaven would not be a place of happiness to a soul unsanctified; no communion there without concord; and that is the reason why spiritual notions are so disgustful to carnal men; and if they cannot endure the shadow, how should they bear the substance and thing itself? In this work the soul is passive; but being thus quickened by the Spirit of life from God, and set upon their feet, they are capacitated for action. And now (say they, as Daniel, now) "let my Lord speak, for thou hast strengthened me," Dan. 10: 19. And thenceforth their work and business is, " to walk worthy of the Lord;" to glorify that grace which hath saved them; to walk before God in the daily exercise of those graces he hath given them; and to press after perfection, that is, a ripeness of grace, or meetness for that state of glory which all these are preparatory to; to show forth his praises; the virtues of him that hath called them; making his law their rule, and his glory their end above all; and all in a way of dutiful gratitude. For though ye may, and ought to have respect to your own salvation, peace, and comfort; yet so, as to substitute all to the glory of the grace of God. And take this by the way, to encourage you in your duty, that the glory of God, and his peoples' blessedness are so interwoven, as never to be divided: while ye keep that most directly in your eye and scope, your own concerns are most currently going on; they fall in together, and keep in the same channel.

II. Whence these requisites to salvation do proceed.

That men might know themselves to be creatures, it was needful to know the world had a beginning, by whom, and how: and no less needful to know the original of the world renewed. The not minding of which, may have been the occasion of men's ascribing the new creation to the concourse of free-will atoms: which seems at least, as irrational as the contingent coming together of the visible frame.

Our present inquiry therefore is, touching the author of faith and holiness: what root they spring from; who, or what is the efficient cause of regeneration; what power it is by which the new creature is formed, and brought forth. Our assertion is, that the new creature is God's workmanship, entirely and alone. This the scripture seems evi-

dent for, and delivers in positive terms in James 1: 17.
"Every good gift, and every perfect gift, is from above,
and cometh down from the Father of lights:" which is so
full an answer to the question, as one would think admits
of no reply.   But being a truth unacceptable to nature, and
such striving among men to entitle the human power and
will to the fatherhood of this new creation, it must be argued: and our argument for it is this; that the new creature
must be wrought, either by a divine power, or by a natural
power, or a concurrence of both together.   But,

First. It cannot be wrought by a natural power, and
that for such reasons as these:

Arg. I. Because it is a creature; and, of all creatures,
the noblest and most excellent.   All the virtuosi in the
world are not able to make an atom: they may refine and
sublimate things that are, but cannot give being to the
least thing that is not.   How then should the natural man
give being to the new creation!   To suppose such a thing
would be a degrading to the divine nature; a setting the
image of the heavenly below that of the earthly: for he
that builds, is worthy of more honor than the thing that is
built by him, Heb. 3: 3.

Arg. II. Nothing can afford what it hath not in itself.
Now, every soul, in nature, is darkness, and possessed
with a habitual aversion from God: but light is not brought
out of darkness, nor friendship out of enmity: no man will
expect grapes from thorns; the product will be according
to that of which it is produced; every seed will have its
own body, 1 Cor. 15: 38. an evil tree cannot bring forth
good fruit, Matt. 7: 18. that which is born of the flesh is
flesh, John 3: 6. and will never be better: therefore the
new creature, being a divine thing, cannot be educed of
natural principles.

Arg. III. The natural man is not only void of all virtue and property that tends to regeneration; but is opposite thereto.   To be grafted into the true olive tree, is
contrary to nature, Rom. 11:24. "the carnal mind is enmity against God," Rom. 8: 7. and enmity being a principle
uncapable of reconciliation, it cannot be supposed it will
help to destroy itself: "they will not so much as seek
after God, nor take him into their thoughts," Psal. 10: 4.
Satan they follow with natural motion, John 8: 44. but as
for the word of the Lord, they profess stoutly, they "will

not hearken unto it," Jer. 49: 6. "they have loved strangers, and after them they will go," chap. 2: 25. So desperately wicked are the hearts of men, chap. 17: 9. they are even made up of fleshly lusts, which war against the soul, and whatever hath respect to his happy restoration. And this enmity is maintained and animated, (1.) By the darkness that is in them; which all men in nature are filled with; or with false lights, which are equally pernicious and obstructive to this work: by reason whereof; the most glorious objects, though just before them, are hid from their eyes; they do not, nor they cannot discern the things which are of God, 1 Cor. 2: 14. they have false conceptions of every thing; call good evil: and evil good; put light for darkness, and darkness for light; and the most excellent things are commonly farther off their approbation. It is a known experiment, that the more spiritual any truth is, the more will carnal reason object against it: "how can these things be?" John 3: 9. and "how can this man give us his flesh to eat?" chap. 6: 52. By all the understanding that men have before conversion, they are but more strongly prejudiced against the truth, Acts 17: 18. 1 Cor. 1: 19, 23. (2.) This enmity is further confirmed and fixed by the naturalness of it. If it were an adventitious quality it might possibly be separated; but now it cannot by any human power. And that it is natural, appears, in that the universality of men are infected with it: it is not here and there one, but all and every one, Jews and Gentiles, are all under sin; "none that understandeth; none that seeketh after God; none that doeth good, no, not one," Rom. 3: 9—18. "all flesh had corrupted his ways," Gen. 6: 12. "every imagination of their heart is only evil, and that continually," chap. 8: 21. "every man is brutish and altogether filthy," Jer. 10: 14. "and this is their root; conceived in sin," Psal. 51: 5. "they go astray from the womb," Psal. 58: 3. It also grows up with them; and the longer it lives, the worse it is, and the more impregnable, Jer. 13: 23. "it is not subject to the law of God, neither indeed can be," Rom. 8: 7. And though, at times, they look another way, like bullets of stone or lead, which, actuated by a foreign power, are mounted into the air, their upward motion quickly ceaseth, because it was not natural; they come again to their centre, of their own accord, and there they live and die: as was verified in Saul, Ahab, Agrippa, and others.

Arg. IV. The new creature cannot be the product of natural power, because every thing is received and improved according to the nature of that which receives it. Plants, and other creatures, turn all their nourishment into their own species and property. A vine and a thistle, both planted in one soil, have the same sun, dew, air, and other influences common to both, yet each one converts the whole of that it receives into its own substance and kind. You may plant and prune, dig and dung an evil tree, bestow what pains you will upon it, it does all but enable the more pregnant production of evil fruit: just so doth the natural man, even turn the grace of God into lasciviousness, Jude ver. 4. as to the pure all things are pure; so to the impure all things are defiled, Tit. 1: 15. "David, by his afflictions, learned to keep God's laws," Psal. 119: 6, 7. but Ahaz trespassed yet more, 2 Chron. 28: 22. Good Josiah's heart melts at reading the law, he humbles himself, and falls to reforming, chap. 34: 27. 31. but wicked Johoiakim, he cuts the roll in pieces, and burns it, Jer. 36: 23. thus sin, that is, corrupt nature, works death by that which is good, Rom. 7: 8. 10.

Secondly. That the new creature is not wrought by the concurrence of divine and natural power together, the following arguments shew.

Arg. I. The Holy Ghost needs no assistance in his work: who and where is he that stood up for his help when he moved on the waters, and brought forth this world into form? Gen. 1: 2. Job 38: 4. when he weighed the mountains in scales, and the hills in a balance? Isa. 40: 12. 14. He that made all things of nothing, cannot be supposed to need the aid of any. As man had nothing to do in the conception of Christ's human nature, but the power of the Most High was alone in that work; so also it is in forming Christ within us. Why should he call in the aid of another, unless deficient in himself? and he must be greatly put to it, that takes in the help of an enemy.

Arg. II. If the Holy Ghost had need of help, the flesh affords not the least help, nor can. For, (1.) The natural man is "without strength," Rom. 5: 6. The best natured man in the world (until regenerate) is but flesh; and "all flesh is grass, and the glory of it as the flower of grass," 1 Pet. 1: 24. which fades in a moment; it is an arm that has no strength, Job 26: 2. makes a show, but can do nothing.

And it is not only weak in itself, but it renders weak and impotent whatever relies upon it, or may be used by it, for any spiritual end: a straw in the hand of a giant will make no deeper impression than if in the hand of a stripling: the law itself, " which was ordained to life, is made weak through the flesh," Rom. 7: 10. with chap. 8: 3. The flesh is on an opposite principle, at perfect enmity against the holy seed; as you see before: it answers, as Pharaoh, " Who is the Lord, that I should obey him?" Exod. 5: 2. its whole business is to crush the workings of the spirit; and the conflict ceaseth not, but in the total overthrow of the one party. The flesh and the spirit always have been, are, and will be two; yea, even where the enmity hath lost its dominion, it will maintain a conflict to the last; and if the one fights against the other after the new creature is formed, it will doubtless oppose the first formation of it. (3.) If we should suppose the flesh able, in any respect, to give assistance in this work, the Holy Ghost would none of it: " what concord hath Christ with Belial?" 2 Cor. 6: 2. Such mixtures are an abomination to him: he would not permit his people to yoke an ox and an ass together in ploughing, Deut. 22: 10. nor to sow their land with divers seeds, verse 9. and if in building an altar their tools were lifted up upon it, the Lord reckons it defiled, Exod. 20: 25. (4.) Suppose a possibility of conjunction: what would be the issue of it? " when the sons of God went in to the daughters of men, giants were born to them," Gen. 6: 4. If creatures of several kinds should couple together, what could be produced but a monster in nature? such monsters in spirituals are hypocrites and temporary believers: in whom there is something begotten on their wills, by the common strivings and enlightenings of the Spirit, which attains to a kind of formality, but proves, in the end, a lump of dead flesh: it never comes to be a new creature: as you see in Herod and Agrippa. An owl's egg, though hatched by a dove or eagle, will prove but a night-bird: the seed of the bond-woman will be carnal, though Abraham himself be the father of it.

To illustrate this a little farther, I would briefly recount what most probably should influence the hearts of men, and lead them to repentance; with their common, if not constant effect, when left to their free-will improvements. I reduce them to five: a prosperous condition; afflictions;

the word of God; the strivings of the Spirit; and miracles.

1. Prosperity: this, we find, hath not done it. How many have been the worse, and how few, if any, the better for it? even "Jeshurun waxed fat and kicked," Deut. 32: 15. In the time of the Judges, whenever they had respite from trouble, they presently fell to idolatry: "when Uzziah was strong his heart was lifted up to destruction," 2 Chron. 26:16. Some there be that are not in trouble like other men; their eyes stand out with fatness; they have more than heart can wish, &c. But are they bettered by it? no; "pride compasseth them about like a chain, and they set their mouths against the heavens," Psal. 73: 3—9. so true is that maxim, "Let favor be shown to the wicked, yet will he not learn righteousness: in the land of uprightness will he deal unjustly," Isa. 26: 10.

2. Afflictions and judgments will not do it. It appears by Amos, that that people were loaded with a variety of judgments, "yet they turned not to him that smote them," Amos 4: 6—12. "the more they were stricken, the more they revolted," Isa. 1: 5. "The Lord was wroth with Ephraim, and smote him: he hid his face from him, and was wroth," (which, if any thing, should have moved him:) but what cares Ephraim? "he went on frowardly in the way of his heart," Isa. 57: 7. The Jews continue to this day in their unbelief, though "wrath be come upon them to the uttermost." The antichristian world, when vials of wrath were poured forth upon them, "they blasphemed God, and repented not," Rev. 16: 9—11. Hos. 7: 9, 10. thus "bray a fool in a mortar, yet his foolishness will not depart from him," Prov. 22: 27. it is natural to him, and therefore inseparable.

3. The word of God, and his ordinances.—Neither is it in these to turn the heart back again. Of this, the people of Israel are a pregnant example; "to them were committed the oracles of God," Rom. 3: 2. no nation had God so nigh them as they, Deut. 4: 7. and yet the most stubborn, stiffnecked people that ever the earth bore. "The Lord sends them his prophets, rising early and sending," 2 Chron. 36: 15, 16. and see how they are used! first, "they slight his messengers, and send them away empty," Jer. 25: 3, 4. they then fall to "beating and imprisoning of them," Jer. 37: 15. yea, they proceeded farther (for this enmity knows no bounds,) some they stoned, others they "slew with the

sword," Luke 20: 10—15. when was there one that escaped them? At last he sends them his Son; surely " they will reverence him!" No, this is the heir; come, let us kill him, Matt. 21: 38. and thus they went on, " until there was no remedy," 2 Chron. 36: 16.

4. The world of ungodly in Noah's time.—After warning of the flood, they had the " Spirit of God striving with them six-score years together," Gen. 6: 3. and yet, not a man in the whole universe prevailed upon. The people in the wilderness—how many ways did the Lord strive with them, by mighty deliverances, terrible appearances, merciful providences, dreadful judgments; and this forty years together! and yet, still they went on " rebelling against him, and vexing his Holy Spirit," Isa. 63: 10.

5. Miracles will not do it.—What a multitude of these, mingled with judgments, were shewn upon Pharaoh! all which did but further harden him, Exod. 7: 14—22. chap. 8: 19. chap. 9: 7, &c. Then the people of the wilderness: take but that one instance of Korah and his company; " the earth clave asunder, and swallowed up the chief of the mutineers, with all that they had: they went alive into the pit," Numb. 16: 32. two hundred and fifty more were consumed by fire from heaven, ver. 35. which one would think should cause them to fear the Lord, and do no more presumptuously; and yet the next thing we hear of them, on the very morrow, they are at it again; and that not a party of them, but the whole congregation, ver. 41. All which considered and laid together, it follows, with much evidence,

Thirdly, That the new creature is the product of divine power alone. A point of great concernment, if duly considered.

The evangelist John is clear on our side touching this original and pedigree of it, both whence it is not, and whence it is: " it is born, not of blood;" that is, it belongs not to, nor is brought forth in any, as they are men made of flesh and blood; nor as they are " Abraham's seed according to the flesh," Rom. 9: 7. nor is it born " of the will of the flesh;" the carnal and sensual affections have nothing to do in the spiritual birth: " nor of the will of man;" the rational faculties, by which men are set above the rank of other creatures, even these contribute nothing to our divine sonship: " but it is of God," John 1: 13. that is, it is his work alone; and the natural man has nothing to do in it: he is as perfectly unactive in it, as the dry bones in causing themselves to live, Ezek. 37: 5. 9. 14. or as Lazarus in reviving himself; of whom it is said, " He that was dead came forth bound hand and foot," John 11: 44. which was such a demonstration of divine power, that the Pharisees themselves acknowledge, " if they now let him alone, all men will believe in him," John 11: 48. (And if it were not so, the Lord alone should not be exalted.) And with this falls in the other beloved disciple, James; " Of his own will begat he us," James 1: 11. 2 Pet. 1: 8. that is, by his own divine power he forms and brings forth the new creation, without any assistance from the old, or co-operation of it: they contribute no more to it, than those who sleep in the dust to their own resurrection.   Peter also tells us, " It is born of incorruptible seed," 8 Pet. 1: 23. and John, again, " it is born of the Spirit," John 3: 8. which is plainly to be the offspring of God.   Of like tenor is that of the prophet, " Thou hast wrought all our works within us," Isa. 26: 12. and that of Paul, " We are his workmanship," Ephes. 2: 10. as also that of the Psalmist, " It is he that hath made us, and not we ourselves, his people," Psal. 100: 2.   We find it here, and in John, expressed both negatively and positively; as purposely and for ever to exclude whatever is in man from being so much as thought contributary to the new creation; and that the whole work might be fathered upon God only; which is, indeed, the natural result of all those scriptures which speak of it under the notion of a creature; which necessarily implies, that the whole of it, both matter and form, is from the Creator: for, in truth, a creature's foundation is nothing, besides the good pleasure of God.   It may further be noted, that in James, " the Father of lights" is said to beget it; and in the Galatians, " Jerusalem which is above" to be the mother of it; and in John, as before, that it is born of the Spirit.   Now, if father and mother, begetter and bringer forth, are both in heaven, what shall the man of earth found his pretensions upon, as to the parentage of the new creature?

And further, it is worthy of remark; 1. What sort of instruments were mostly used in this work. Not the learned, but illiterate men: and of these, such most eminently as had neither elegancy of speech, nor majestic presence, 2 Cor. 10: 10. and the end of this was, that it might appear, and men might be convinced, that " their faith stood not in (was neither made nor maintained by) the wisdom of men, but the power of God," 1 Cor. 2: 3, 4, 5.

The natural unaptness of the persons commonly wrought upon, to receive those high-born principles: not many of the wise and noble, but the poor, base, and foolish; that is, in comparison of others. And why these? Truly it was to make good the truth that is here asserted, namely, " That no flesh might glory in his presence," chap. 1: 26—29. And yet likewise take notice, that the wise and noble were not excluded; witness the wife of Herod's steward, Joseph, Nicodemus, and Sergius Paulus, a prudent man: which further illustrates the power of God, and that he did, by those weak and contemptible means, bring in also such as these.

3. The scripture is so emphatically ascribing this work unto God: which kind of ascription were very improper, if faith and holiness were things so common, and easily attained, and the natural man so able and virtuous an engine in that work, as most men imagine. Paul styles it, " The faith of the operation of God," Col. 2: 12. Isaiah makes it dependant on the " arm of the Lord revealed," Isa. 53: 1. that is, made bare, and put forth to the utmost. Our Saviour attributes it to God the Father, as Lord of heaven and earth, Matt. 11: 25. And Paul, again, to the " exceeding greatness of his mighty power, even the same by which he raised Jesus Christ from the dead," Col. 1: 12. even then, when the sins of all his people lay upon him; and all the malice, strength, and subtilty of the powers of darkness were up in arms against it: which was indeed the highest indication of divine power that ever was put forth, or shall be.

III. The next thing to be shown is, who those blessed ones are to whom these requisites to salvation do belong; and by what title.

The answer is, they all do belong to elect persons, and that in right of their election. Elect and believer are convertible terms: every believer is an elect person, and every elect person is a believer, or shall be in his time. This right, indeed, is nextly founded upon redemption; but being originally from election, I shall speak here only to that. To put effects in the place of causes, and causes of effects, is a great absurdity in natural things, and yet how prone are we to it in matters of divine concernment! which chiefly comes from the pride of our spirits, who fain would be somebody in procuring our own happiness; and do therefore ascribe it to any cause, rather than that which is proper to it.   This is a great evil; and the more perilous and catching, because espoused by some of no common profession, and that with great pretences of reason for it.   To refute which, your most rational course will be to search and consult the scriptures; whose testimony, and right reason, do always sort together: and if by this ascent you follow salvation, and all the conducements thereto, up to their head, you shall find them all to be entirely and absolutely of God, and contained in the same decree; and, consequently, that faith and holiness are the effects and certain consequences of election.

The genuine import of scripture-salvation is broad and comprehensive, extending to all manner of requisites which any way conduce to the perfect accomplishment of the thing itself.   Outward salvation, whatever belongs to the outward man's preservation; as water, bread, walls, bulwarks, &c. Isa. 26: 1.   " Salvation will appoint walls and bulwarks;" that is, the promise of salvation implies and carries in it all things pertaining to safety: so spiritual salvation, whatever pertains to blessedness and glory; as redemption from sin, faith, holiness, and holding out to the end: any of which being absent, would invalidate all the rest, as one round of a ladder plucked out, hinders your ascent to the top.   If one gives me a piece of land that is all around inclosed, the law gives me a way to it (though no express mention hereof in my deed,) so as to take the profits; his gift would otherwise little avail me.   Salvation is that the elect are endowed with; faith and holiness the necessary way to their actual possession; and, therefore, these they must be ordained unto, and are, as well as to salvation itself: for, being " predestinate to the adoption of sons," Eph. 1: 5. " and to be conformed to the image of Christ," Rom. 8: 28. (which is not perfectly accomplished until his appearing in glory) 1 John 3: 2. they must be predestinated also to all those intermediate dispensations and graces which are requisite thereto.   For, right to the end, gives right to the means; they are therefore said to be " chosen to salvation, through sanctification of the Spirit, and belief of the truth," 2 Thess. 2: 13. In order of intention, God wills the end first, and then the means: in order of execution, the means first, as directive to that end, Rom. 8: 30. The end is the cause of the means, Eph. 2: 4, 5. and election the cause of them both, chap. 2: 8. 10.

The promise of Canaan to Abraham's seed, did virtually contain whatever must come between the making of the promise, and the final performance of it: as, 1. To multiply his seed into a nation. 2. To keep Esau, Laban, and others, from hurting them. 3. To provide for them in time of famine. 4. To preserve and increase them in Egypt, notwithstanding the Egyptians' craft and cruelty to suppress them. 5. To bring them forth with an high hand, in contempt of Pharaoh's resolvedness against it, and his potency to withstand it. 6. To divide the sea before them, and provide them a table in the wilderness. 7. To cause their enemies' hearts to faint, and become as water. 8. To send the hornet before them, and to fight for them, &c. (For otherwise the Lord's giving them Canaan, had been but as the pope's giving England to the Spaniard, that is, if he could get it.) And, *lastly*, to pardon their manifold great and high provocations; by which they exposed themselves to wrath and extirpation daily. So is it in the case of election; it draws with it even all that is tendent to the saints' actual investiture with glory. The apostle, therefore, linketh eternity past with eternity to come: he makes election and glorification the two extreme points of the compass; calling and justification (which are parts intermediate) he founds upon the first, in order to the last; and gives you their set course. In Rom. 8. " Whom he did foreknow, them also he did predestinate (to what?) to be conformed to the image of his Son; and whom he did predestinate, them also he called," Rom. 8: 29. And what did he call them to? He called them to holiness, to glory and virtue, 2 Pet. 1: 3. and " whom he called, them also he justified and glorified," Rom. 8: 30. These all do belong to the same persons, and that by virtue of the decree, and no one of them did ever go alone.

The like succession of causes and effects ye have in the 16th of Ezekiel, 6—12. The Lord finds them in their blood, that is, in their natural lost condition: he enters into covenant with them, and makes them his own; there is their election: then he washes them, and that thoroughly;

there is their justification: and then adorns them; there is
their sanctification, which always is consummated in glory.
In the 17th of the Acts, ye have Paul preaching at Thes-
salonica, ver. 1—4. The same doctrine was propounded
to all indefinitely; and it must be so, for the minister knows
not the elect from other men: but the Holy Ghost, who
searcheth the deep things of God, and hath the management of this work committed to him, he knew the elect by
name, John 10: 3. and accordingly took them, " gathered
them one by one," Isa. 27: 12. (each one in his proper
time) " and opened their ears to discipline," Job. 26: 10.
making them what they were chosen to be. And the same
apostle, in his epistle to the Thessalonians, where he cele-
brates the effects of this sermon, brings in their election as
the cause of their conversion; " Knowing, brethren, beloved, your election of God; for our gospel came not to
you in word only (as it did to others,) but in power," 1
Thess. 4: 5. So in the Acts, " As many as were ordained
to eternal life, believed," Acts 13: 48. and " the Lord
added to the church daily (whom did he add?) such as should
be saved," chap. 2: 47. Effectual calling is a sure demonstration of election, and the first effect by which it can
be known.

   That precious faith through which we are saved, is obtained " through the righteousness of God, and our
Saviour Jesus Christ," 2. Pet. 1: 1. 1. It is given through
the righteousness of God the Father; and so, it either respects his ordaining us to eternal life; in which act he did
implicitly engage himself to give us faith, which may
therefore be " called the faith of God's elect," Tit. 1: 1.
or else it respects his promise made to Christ, " that making his soul an offering for sin, he should see his seed,"
Isa. 53: 10. Tit. 1: 2. with 2 Tim. 1: 9. or it may be intended of both. 2. The righteousness of Christ is concerned in it two ways: 1. As the meriting or procuring
cause thereof; and so this faith belongs of right to every
one he died for, Phil. 1: 29. Or, 2. As he is that faithful
servant, who gives to every one according as he hath received of the Father for them, Eph. 4: 7, 8. in all which respects it evidently flows from election. To confirm which,
Peter says expressly, in his former epistle, that they were
" elected unto obedience, and sprinkling of the blood of
Jesus Christ," 1 Pet. 1: 2. So the mystery of his will is

made known, according to his good pleasure, which he had purposed in himself, Eph. 1: 9. The same intention we have in the Corinthians; " the preaching of the gospel is to them that perish, foolishness: but to us who are saved, it is the power of God," 1 Cor. 1: 18. and in Timothy, " Who hath saved us, and called us with a holy calling," 2 Tim. 1: 9. in both places saving is put before calling, and then it must be before faith: and how men are saved before they believe, unless by election, or redemption, which is commensurate with election, doth not appear to us. To this purpose it is further observable, that in Rom. 8: 30. the apostle sets predestination before calling; as in Timothy and the Corinthians, he doth saving: and in Rom. 9: 23, 24. he puts calling in a tense subsequent to election, or preparing unto glory. The apostle Jude, in his sentence also accords with it: he directs his epistle " to them that are sanctified by God the Father, and preserved in Jesus Christ, and called," ver. 1. where, by sanctified he means elected, separated, or set apart: in this sense the word is used elsewhere, where it will not admit of any other, Exod. 3: 13. " I am the Lord that doth sanctify you:" and more plainly in Numb. 8: 17. " all the first-born of the children of Israel are mine: on the day that I smote every first-born in the land of Egypt, I sanctified them for myself:" here no other thing but choosing, selecting, or setting apart, can be intended: and I see no reason why it should not be so understood in that of Jude.

And it is termed a holy calling, not only as it calleth us to holiness; but as it is sacred, peculiar, set apart, and appropriated to a holy people, namely, those whom the Lord set apart for himself: whose eternal sanctifying them in his decree, was the original cause of their being sanctified actually; " he loved them with an everlasting love, and therefore with loving-kindness doth he draw them," Jer. 31: 3. and this their actual sanctification is so indubitable a consequent of the decretive, and so appropriate to the same persons, that the same word is used for both; as it is also for redemption: " for their sakes (says Christ) I sanctify myself," John 17: 19. A like instance of this we have in Eldad and Medad, who though they came not up to the tabernacle with their brethren, yet, being of them that were written, " the Spirit came upon them, and they prophesied in the camp," Numb. 9: 26. Election finds out men when they think not of it. So the Lord first determines Jeremy to his office; then puts forth his hand, and fits him for his work, Jer. 1: 9. Even Christ himself was first appointed to his mediatory office; and then the Spirit came upon him, because so appointed, Isa. 61: 1.

Quer. In the 1st of John, 16. it is said, that " to them which received him, he gave power to become the sons of God;" which seems to put their believing before their sonship.

Solut. Although faith goes before the manifestation of our sonship, yet not before our sonship itself; " the adoption of sons is that we were predestinated unto before the foundation of the world," Ephes. 1: 4, 5. That therefore in John, must be understood with that of Moses, when he pleads with God for his presence with his people; " so shall we be separated from all the people that are on the face of the earth," Exod. 33: 13. not that this separation was now to be made; it was done before, Lev. 20:24. but his meaning is, that by the Lord's going with them, this their separation should be manifested. This sense of the word ye have in Matth. 5: " Love your enemies; bless them that curse you; that ye may be (that is, that ye may appear to be) the children of your Father which is in heaven," Deut. 7: 6. Matt. 5: 44, 45. in like manner we become " the sons of God by faith," Gal. 3: 26.

The budding of Aaron's rod was not the cause of God's choosing him to the priesthood, Num. 17:5, 8. nor the falling of the lot upon Saul, and afterwards upon Matthias, the reason why God designed them, the one to the kingdom, and the other to the apostleship; they were both appointed before, and those events were but the effects of their fore-appointment, and evidences of it, 1 Sam. 9: 16. with chap. 10: 21. Acts 1: 24, 26. So the giving of the Spirit is that which follows election; " because sons, God hath sent the Spirit of his Son into your hearts," Gal. 4: 6. Although the manifestation of our adoption, and our actual enjoyment of its privileges, are in time; yet the thing itself we were predestinated to from everlasting, Eph. 1. 4, 5, 9, 11. Pursuant to this, our Saviour manifests the Father's name to the men he had given him out of the world; and these receive it, John 17: 6. 8. The sheep hear his voice, and follow him, chap. 10: 27. Of others he saith expressly, " ye believe not, because ye are not of my sheep," ver. 26. " He that is of God, heareth God's words; ye therefore hear them not, because you are not of God," chap. 8: 47. The same reason he gives for his different ministration towards his own and others: to the one it was given to know the mysteries of the kingdom of God; to the other it was not given, Matt. 13: 11. and, therefore, having ended his parables, he dismisses the multitude, as having no more for them; but to his disciples he expounded every thing in private, Mark 4: 34. and ye see he puts it upon election, as that which had invested them with this prerogative above the rest. " To you it is given;" that is, it belonged to them by God's donation and appointment. They are first saints by election, then saints by calling, Rom. 1: 7.

When Christ appeared to Paul going to Damascus, they that were with him were all in amaze; a voice they heard, but knew not what it spake. Why so, since they were as likely to yield as he? It was not intended for them, and therefore their ears were not bored, nor the speech directed to them, but to Paul, and to Paul by name. But why to Paul above the rest, since he was the ringleader and chief persecutor in the company? Paul was a chosen vessel; and this, in brief, was the reason of it, as you have it recorded in Acts 22: 14. " The God of our fathers hath chosen thee, that thou shouldest know his will." The Jews had many means of knowing the Messiah, and inducements to believe in him, which the Gentiles had not; and yet these embrace the gospel, while the Jews reject it. Those who sought after righteousness, fell short of it; when those who sought it not, attained it, Rom. 9: 30, 31. For the bottom reason of which different dispensation, we are referred to election; " The election hath obtained, and the rest were blinded," chap. 11: 7.

How variously are several men affected in hearing the same word? The sheep and the rest have both the same outward means; one neglects it, attends not at all, or regards not what he hears; a second quarrels at it; as the Jews often did; a third is persuaded almost, as Agrippa was, and those that would hear Paul again of that matter: a fourth is pricked in the heart, and persuaded altogether. It is a stumbling-block to some, foolishness to others, and

to some it is the power of God: and these some are such
as were elected; of those to whom the promise was made,
Acts 2: 39. and are therefore termed the called according
to his own purpose, Rom. 8: 28. and according to his own
purpose and grace, which was given them in Christ before
the world began, 2 Tim. 1: 9. they are first chosen, and
then caused to approach unto God, Psal. 65: 4.

There is almost no end of scriptures to this purpose: I
shall instance one more, and so close up this particular.
All the blessings which the saints are blessed with, in time,
are bestowed according to God's decree of election before time; as is manifest from Ephes. 1: 3, 4. 5.   Where I
observe, 1. That election goes before the actual donation
of spiritual blessings: for these are given in time, that was
before time; and that which comes after, cannot be the
cause of that which went before it: one effect may be the
cause of another; but not the cause of that which causeth
itself.   2. That the actual donation of spiritual blessings is
according to election; that is, election is the rule by which
the dispensation is guided; it is adequate with election, and
answerable thereto; even as the impression is to the printing
types; or as the fashion of David's body, to the platform
thereof in God's book; and the tabernacle, to the pattern
shown in the mount, according to which all things are made,
as well in respect of number, weight, and measure, as form
and figure.   Spiritual blessings are not given to one more
or fewer, or in other manner, but just as election had laid
it forth: which also is further confirmed by Rev. 21: 27.
where we find, that none are admitted into the holy city,
but such "whose names were written in the book of life;
and whoever was not found written in that book, was cast
into the lake of fire," Rev. 20: 15. which shows, that at
the latter day it will be taken for granted, that "as many as
were ordained to eternal life, believed;" and that all and
every one without the list of election, died in unbelief;
that "the election obtained," Acts 13: 48. "and the rest
were blinded," Rom. 11: 7. therefore faith and holiness are
not the cause, but the certain effects and consequents of
election.

Now if any should ask, by the way, wherein the special
love of God to elect persons discovers itself before their
conversion?   I cannot assign any plain or open discover-

ies of it, by which the elect may be known from other men, since all outward things fall alike to all: " the heir, while a child, differs nothing from a servant, although he be lord of all," by election, Gal. 4: 1. And yet there are divers gracious operations of that love towards them, even in common providences, although they are not perceived till afterwards: as,

1. In keeping alive the root or stem they were to grow from: this, perhaps, was not the least cause of adding fifteen years to Hezekiah's life; namely, for Josiah's sake, who was to come of his lineage; Manasseh, who was to be his grand-father, not being yet born: so those days of tribulation were shortened, and many of the Jews, by special providence, kept alive, for the elect's sake that should be of their progeny, perhaps two thousand years after.

2. In preserving the elect themselves from many a death they were obnoxious to before their conversion, as he also did Manasseh: and this was the cause, when Satan had them in his net, and had dragged them to the brink of hell, that "the Lord sent from heaven, and saved them," Psal. 57: 3. " Deliver him; I have found a ransom," Job 33: 24. q. d. He is mine, and I have designed him to another end.

3. In keeping them from the unpardonable sin. Thus Paul, being a chosen vessel, was kept without that knowledge of Christ which some of the Pharisees had; for otherwise his persecuting the church of God had been incapable of pardon, as appears from 1 Tim. 1: 3. " I obtained mercy, because I did it ignorantly."

4. In casting the lot of their habitation where he hath planted, or will plant, the means of grace; or bringing them, providentially, where some effectual word shall be spoken to them: the one is verified in those who dwelt at Corinth, where Paul must preach, and not hold his peace; for, says the Lord, "I have much people in this city," Acts 18: 9, 10. the other, in those who were come to Jerusalem at the feast of Pentecost, from all parts of the world; which gave them the opportunity of coming together, and of hearing Peter's sermon, by means whereof thousands were converted, chap. 2: 5. It is further exemplified by the story of the eunuch, chap. 8: 27. as also that of

Zaccheus, whose intent reached no higher than to see what manner of person Christ was, being so much talked of abroad; and being low of stature, he climbs into a tree, and there salvation meets both him and his house, Luke 19: 2—9.

IV. Our last inquiry is, Of the way and manner of God's dispensing spiritual blessings: and that is effectually and freely.

First. Effectually. The soul is not turned to God by a twine-thread; nor doth the Lord content himself with wishing and hoping that it might be so, after the manner of men, who either are somewhat indifferent about the thing, or have not wherewith to effect their desires: nor merely by propounding, moving and striving, by moral suasions, instructions, threatenings, and the like (which are of little avail with a dark understanding, and fixed enmity, which every natural man is actuated by;) but by the putting forth of a power invincible: a power that will not be said nay; but what it wills, that it will do; what it undertakes, it goes through with. To do a thing effectually, is to do it perfectly, thoroughly, successfully: so to use and apply the means, that the end designed is surely brought to pass; and this, notwithstanding all the weakness, averseness, and repugnancy of the carnal mind against it.

I might produce instances not a few, touching God's effectual working to bring about things of lesser moment. How unwilling was Moses to be his messenger to Pharaoh! Exod. 3 and 4: so opposite to it, that when he had no farther plea nor excuse to make, he carries it perversely towards the Lord; " Send by the hand of him whom thou wilt send," says he, chap. 4: 13. but God having designed him for the work, leaves him not until he had won him to it, verse 18. So Pharaoh resolved he would not let the people go: but " I will stretch out my hand, says God, and he shall let you go." Much more will he make his arm bare for the salvation of his chosen, whom he loved from everlasting: and it must be so done.

Arg. I. Because, otherwise, the elect should be in no better condition than other men; for, until conversion, Satan hath as fast hold of them as of the rest. Adam's fall was the devil's master-piece: to bring men into his own condemnation, is the trophy he glories in; and being a prince, both proud, subtil, and imperious, you may not think he will be baffled or complimented out of his hold: entreaties, menaces, and force of arguments, are of no weight with him; he laughs at your strong reasons, and counts them but rotten wood; Jesus I know, and his Spirit I know, Acts 19: 15. but what are these? No; this kind goes not forth by consent; nothing will move him, but that power which heaven and earth do bow under: he that made him (and he only) can cause his sword to approach unto him, and take the prey from this terrible one. And for this it was, that our Saviour tells the apostles (when he sends them to "turn men from Satan unto God,") that "all power in heaven and earth was committed to him," Matt. 28: 18. and that in this power "he will be with them to the end of the world," Matt. 28: 20. Luke 9: 1. which was indeed but needful; for they had surely gone on a sleeveless errand (a weak and fruitless design,) if Christ himself thus empowered had not gone with them. And for the elect themselves, they are of themselves, no better disposed to this work than those that never shall be wrought upon: they are enemies in their minds, darkness, dead in sin, and children of wrath, even as others: and this they are by nature: their state, therefore could not be changed, if a power invincible, and invincibly resolved in what he undertakes, were not engaged in it. Ephraim, though an elect vessel, yet while in nature, was of so bad a nature, that all moral endeavors were lost upon him. Let messengers be sent to him early and late, he pulls away the shoulder: the Lord was wroth with him, smote him, hid his face from him; he still went on frowardly: show him his sickness; so that he cannot but see it; and he sends to king Jareb, takes any course rather than turn to him that smote him, Hos. 5: 13. take off the yoke from his jaw, give him the scope of his will, and the first thing he takes to shall be the forbidden fruit: lay meat to his mouth, that which is meat indeed, and he will rather starve than eat; men left to their own will, will rather go to hell, than be beholden to free grace for salvation. But, says God, "Is Ephraim my dear son?" one whom I bought with a price? "Is he a pleasant child?" Jer. 31: 20. whom I loved from everlasting; and shall I so lose him? shall it be said, that I raised up a creature whom I cannot rule and bring to my bent? or, that I made him for such an end, as that any thing conducible thereto may not be done for him? shall my will be forced rather than his? mine to destroy him, rather than his to be saved? No; I have not done all this to lose him at last; nor have I suffered those unworthy repulses, for want of power to prevent them, but that Ephraim might see what would become of him if left to the conduct of his own will; (free indeed to nothing but his own ruin!) and now I will heal him: and the first effect of this healing was, Ephraim's applying himself to God; "Turn thou me, and I shall be turned," chap. 31: 18. Those cords of love, by which the Lord draws men to himself, are not love and kindness merely propounded, with frustrable motives to persuade acceptance, but "divine love shed abroad in the heart," Rom. 5: 5. not written with ink (a thing of human composition) but by the Spirit and power of God. And hence it is that we find those imperial terms, "I will, and ye shall," so much in use about this matter. Thus the Lord began with the serpent (which was a leading case to all that follows, " It shall bruise thine head;" in which compendious word, the destruction of Satan and sin is effectually provided for: and elsewhere he speaks as much for quickening the soul, " A new heart also will I give you, and I will put my spirit within you, and cause you to walk in my statutes; ye shall be my people, and I will be your God," Ezek. 36: 26, 27, 28. "They shall return to me with their whole heart," Jer. 24: 7. with many others. The Lord still utters himself in terms of omnipotency, as putting forth an almightiness of power; which, as it needs not, so it will not (yea, it cannot with a salvo to his honor) admit the least dependance upon created power to make it successful: " his word shall not return unto him void; it shall accomplish that which he pleaseth, and prosper in the thing whereunto he sends it," Isa. 55: 11. " He that was dead, comes forth at his word, though bound hand and foot," John. 11: 44.

Arg. II. Conversion is a creation-work; which, though done by degrees, must be gone through with, and that by him who laid the foundation; or all the foregoing parts (as conviction, &c.) will moulder and come to nothing. As, when Adam was to be made, the Lord first prepares the earth, then moulds it in such a form, and then " breathes

EFFECTUAL CALLING 201

into him the breath of life;" else that lump had never been a living soul. So, in the new creation, the Lord works, and goes on to work, and leaves it not, until he hath set it going. He doth not only cause the light to shine into darkness, but gives, withal, a suitable understanding, 1 John 5: 20. a faculty connatural with the object, as without which the darkness would never comprehend it, John 1: 5. Ezekiel might have prophesied till doom's day, ere those dry bones would have lived, if the Lord himself had not caused breath to enter into them; and, probably, he is called " the Father of lights," James 1: 17. (plural) to denote, that as well the light comprehending (or capacitating our comprehension) is from God, as that to be comprehended, 2 Cor. 4: 6. " In his light we see light," Psal. 36: 9.

Arg. III. God's effectual working in this matter, and the necessity of his so working, may also be argued from the common sense of those already wrought upon, and brought in; by whose prayers and confessions it is evident, that they still needed a powerful and effectual influence to carry on the work already begun: " Turn thou me, and I shall be turned," Jer. 31: 18. " Quicken us, and we will call upon thee," Psal. 80: 18. " Draw me, we will run after thee," Cant. 1: 4. " Not that we are sufficient of ourselves to think any thing, but our sufficiency is of God," 2 Cor. 3: 5. " I live, yet not I, but Christ liveth in me," &c. Gal. 2: 20. Hence it readily follows, that if those already turned, and made partakers of the divine nature, whose hearts are fixed in the good ways of God, and who desire nothing more than to walk in them, cannot yet keep themselves going, without a continued efficacious influx and spring from above; much less can the natural man, without the like supernatural and divine efficacy, effectually bend himself to a compliance with them: for, " It is an abomination to fools to depart from evil," Prov. 13: 19.

Arg. IV. If the Lord did not work effectually, he should lose the honor of his work. If the efficacy of grace should depend on the human will (that is, if grace should be rendered effectual by some motion or act of the will, which grace is not the author of,) then will nature assume the priority; works will glory over grace, and free-will will be said to be better than free grace; for, that the less is blessed of the better, is without contradiction, Heb. 7: 7. and

that that which sanctifies, is greater than that which is sanctified by it, is so obvious, that Christ appeals it to the reason of fools and blind, Matth. 23: 19. If, therefore, you
will grant, that grace is better than nature; follow it must,
that the will is blessed and sanctified by grace, namely, by
its powerful and effectual operation upon it. And here,
indeed, lies the honor and efficacy of grace; not in a vin-
cible moving, exciting, persuading, or threatening the will
to a compliance; but in taking off its natural bias, and
placing it, as it were, on the other side; working the heart
into a kindly agreeableness with the divine will, which before was so contrary to it: and thus the Lord doeth, and
thus he will do, wheresoever he will be gracious; though
ever so much against the present mind and natural propensity of the subject: and yet there is no such thing as
forcing the will, as ye will see afterwards.

Arg. V. The doctrine of effectual calling is further confirmed, from the office of Christ as a Redeemer; which was
not only to purchase, but to put us in actual possession of
the good things he purchased for us. Redemption, forgiveness of sin, and reconciliation, are relatives, commensurate, and inseparable, Eph. 1: 7. chap. 2: 13. 16. Heb 2:
17. It is not only a reconcilable state that redemption puts
us into, but a state of actual reconcilement, Rom. 5: 8, 9,
10. Col. 1: 20, 21, 22. it " abolishes the enmity," Ephes.
2: 15. " makes an end of sin, and brings in everlasting
righteousness," Dan. 9: 24. On this account our Saviour
bears that glorious title, " Thou shalt call his name Jesus;
for he shall save his people from their sins," Matth. 1: 21.
and for " this cause was the Son of God manifested, that
he might destroy the works of the devil," 1 John 3: 8.
Now, of those works, blindness of mind is the first-born,
and foster-mother to all the rest, 2 Cor. 4: 4. it is that keeps
the soul in unbelief, as under locks and bars; and therefore must of necessity be dispelled; which can only be
done by causing the true light to shine effectually; as he
did the light of this world in the first creation, which the
scripture resembles it to, ver. 6. Hence those frequent
mentions of his being sent " to open the blind eyes," Isa.
43: 7. to give light to them that sit in darkness, Luke 1:
79. and to bring forth the prisoners from the prison-house,
Isa. 49: 9. which may not be valued as things in design, yet

liable to obstruction; but to be as certainly performed as
that Christ should die. In the 107th Psalm it is spoken
of as done already; " He brought them out of darkness and
the shadow of death, and brake their bands in sunder,"
Psalm 107: 14. and that he speaks it of redeemed ones, appears by ver. 2. First, take them as in darkness, and he
is so to give them light, as to " guide their feet into the
way of peace," Luke 1: 79. The story of the blind man
in Mark, is a pertinent shadow of it; Christ spits on his
eyes, and puts his hand upon him; as yet he saw but darkly,
" men as trees walking;" but he puts his hands on him
again; and dismisses him not until he hath made him see
clearly, Mark 8: 23, 24, 25. Then take them as prisoners,
and prisoners in the pit, Zech. 9: 11. and he that will deliver them must not only open the gate, but disarm their
guard, knock off their shackles, and bring them forth as
the angel did Peter, even " while the keepers stood before
the door," Acts 12: 6, 7. He so calleth his sheep, that
he " leadeth them out," John 10: 3. and this he doth by
the blood of his covenant; it is that makes those in the pit
to be prisoners of hope, Zech. 9: 11, 12. And these effects as duly flow from redemption, as light from the sun;
it is therefore expressly said, that " the blood of Jesus
Christ cleanseth from all sin," 1 John 1: 7. and that " we
are sanctified through the offering of his body once for all,"
Heb. 10: 10. This gave the apostle to argue so positively
in Rom 6. that " if planted together in his death, we shall
be also in his resurrection," Rom. 6: 5. and to put that emphasis upon it, that " if reconciled to God by the death of
his Son, much more shall we be saved by his life," Rom.
5: 9, 10. That saying of Christ is much to our purpose;
and " other sheep I have, them also must I bring, and they
shall hear my voice," John 10: 16. This *must*, imports a
duty not to be dispensed with; he had " received a commandment for it from the Father," ver. 18. and this *shall*,
that effectual working, " whereby he subdues all things to
himself;" and whereby they are *made* to believe, Eph. 1:
19. The sheep, of themselves, lie as cross to this work as
other men: " What have I to do with thee?" cries the possessed Gadarene, Mark 5: 7. but being his sheep, he must
make them willing, Psal. 110: 3. But suppose they stop
their ears; then he is to bore them; for " he received gifts

for the rebellious," Psal. 68: 18. Men's averseness does not lose Christ his right; nor shall it render his work ineffectual. For this very end God raised him up, namely, " to bless his people, in turning them from their iniquities," Acts 3: 26. and to give them repentance, and that such as hath forgiveness of sins annexed to it, chap. 5: 31. which also he doth as a prince; that is, as one invested with power to remove whatever might hinder the effect of his purpose; to him are committed " the keys of hell and of death," Rev. 1: 18. From these premises I safely conclude, that what Christ, as a Redeemer, came to do, that he doeth, and will do; and that none of his work shall fall to the ground. What he saith in the 17th of John, is prophetical of what he will say at the latter day: " I have finished the work which thou gavest me to do; of all that thou hast given me, I have lost nothing; I have manifested thy name unto the men which thou gavest me out of the world; I have given them the words which thou gavest me, and they have received them," John 17: 4. 6. 8. More might be added; but by these I hope it is evident, that Jesus Christ was not only a Redeemer to pay our ransom, but the officer appointed of God to set us at liberty, even that glorious liberty of the sons of God: and this is that pleasure of the Lord which should prosper in his hands, Isa. 49: 10. as it hath done, and doth, and for ever shall: and it is matter of great consolation to them that take hold of his covenant.

Secondly. All that God doeth for men, or gives to them, in order to their salvation, is given and done freely. Now, a thing is then said to be thus given or done, when it proceeds from the mere good will and favor of him that worketh, or giveth; without respect to any thing done or deserved by the receiver: it is a voluntary act supposing no obligation in him that gives; nor any attractive or obliging virtue in him that receives; nor yet expectation of recompense from him. Much need not be said to prove the free giving of the things we are speaking of, did we duly consider, 1. The sovereign greatness of him that gives: it is the " Most High God, possessor of heaven and earth;" who is infinitely and independently blessed in himself, and therefore cannot be added unto, nor receive from any creature. Who can give to him, that gives to all their life and breath? 2. The super-excellent, unspeakable worth of the things that are given: the first and chief is our Lord Jesus Christ; whose dignity was such, that heaven and earth were too low a price to set them at, especially to be given as he was; and in him righteousness and strength, adoption and reconciliation, grace and glory. 3. The vanity and wretchedness of those on whom they are bestowed: both scripture and experience speak nothing of them in their natural state, but what bespeaks a condition every way deplorable, and incapable of yielding motives for such a gift; as is shown before. But being so greatly in love with ourselves, and fond of our own improvements, and stiffly bent to a covenant of works, to help us off those dangerous shelves, let us dwell a while on the following arguments.

Arg. I. Is taken from the nature and import of the covenant of grace. This covenant is that which all professing Christians profess to be saved by, however they differ about the import and latitude of it. But if we receive the scriptural notion (which needs must be the right,) we shall find, that it is of the very nature and substance of this covenant, to give freely and absolutely; without conditioning for any thing to be done by men, as the ground or motive thereof. All that God doeth for those he will save, is for his name's sake; which name is recorded in Exod. 34: 5, 6. "The Lord God, gracious and merciful," &c. To be gracious, is to do well to one that deserves ill; and if otherwise, it would be but after the covenant of works, or first covenant; which yet was not faulty or defective in itself, for it gave a sufficiency to obtain the benefits proposed by it; which if they had used and improved as they might, there would not have needed a second. But the Lord foreknowing the creature's mutability, and, consequently, what need there would be of another kind of power and grace than that Adam was created with, did therefore determine of a second; which in scripture is called "the hope of eternal life, which God, who cannot lie, promised before the world began," Tit. 1: 2. It is called the covenant of grace, not only as designing the glory of his grace in the saving of men; but as giving freely, and of mere grace and favor, whatever must bring about that salvation. For where else can lie the difference between the two covenants? It cannot be in respect of the easiness

and difficulty of the duties enjoined; for faith and repentance are much more above the compass of natural power,
than to forbear the forbidden tree: but the difference lies
in this, that the new covenant consists in better promises;
and this betterness, in the free, absolute, independent engagement of God, to invest his covenant ones with all things
conducing to the blessedness held forth; as well that to be
done on their part, as on his own upon their doing it. That
is, plainly, to give to them, and work in them, whatever in
this covenant he requires of them. The law shows matter
of duty, but gives not wherewith to perform it: the covenant of grace does both, by writing the law in the heart;
and without this, it would still have been but a covenant
of works, be the duties enjoined what you will. It therefore runs not upon conditional or fallible terms, " I will,
if ye will;" but absolute and sovereign, " I will, and ye
shall." This covenant does not only give life upon terms
of believing; but faith also and holiness, as the necessary
means of attaining that life: and this not upon your ingenious compliance, as some term it, or better improvement of what you have in common with other men, (such
allegations the Lord disallows, and often cautions against,)
but of grace. It is a covenant made up of promises; and
promise, by scripture intendment, is always free: both
freely made, and freely performed, without the desert or
procurement of men. Take Isaac for instance: Abraham's
body was now dead, and for Sarah, besides her natural
barrenness, " it ceased to be with her after the manner of
women," and yet Sarah shall have a son, Gen. 18: 11. 14.
But how? The promise had in it (though Abraham and Sarah had not) whatever might tend to Isaac's conception and
birth; and for this cause he was called " the son of the
promise," Gal. 4: 23, 28. as also believers are, Rom. 2: 8.
Gal. 3: 29. they are also termed " heirs of promise;" Heb.
6: 17. And on this account Christ is called the " promised
seed;" and the Holy Ghost the " Spirit of promise;" namely, to shew the independent freeness of those divine gifts;
the promise of sending them, their actual coming, and effectual operations, are all free, and free in all respects.
This " dew from the Lord waiteth not for men," Micah 5: 7.

For further illustration, the Jews are a pertinent instance,
as ye read in Jeremy, Jer. 32: 30—35. they had done no-

thing but evil from their youth up, and were a continual provocation; and when scattered among the nations, were no whit bettered; but caused even the heathen to blaspheme: and yet notwithstanding all this, the Lord will gather them, and "give them an heart to fear him for ever," ver. 37—44. and this, even while they were not moved "neither could they blush," chap. 8: 12. See also with what inexpressible freeness of grace the Lord deals with them in the 43d of Isaiah, "I, even I am he that blotteth out thy transgression,—and will not remember thy sins," Isa. 43: 25. But what is the introduction to this so great a promise? see it, and wonder at it! "Thou hast not called upon me, O Jacob, but thou hast been weary of me, O Israel: thou hast not brought me the small cattle of thy burnt-offerings: thou hast bought me no sweet cane with thy money; but hast made me to serve with thy sins, and wearied me with thine iniquities," ver. 22, 23, 24. "I, even I (whom thou hast dealt so ungratefully with and disingenuously, even I) am he that blotteth out thy transgressions, for mine own sake," ver. 25. And this was a great thing they looked not for: as, indeed considering themselves, and what their demeanor had been, they had no reason to look for it. From all which it is clear, that grace respects not the worthiness of men in what it does for them; nay, it must respect their unworthiness rather, as that by which grace is more illustrated, and the glory thereof more advanced: in that, "where sin abounded, grace did much more abound," Rom. 5: 20. And Paul proclaims it as verified on himself: "I was a blasphemer, and a persecutor, and injurious: but I obtained mercy; and the grace of our Lord was exceeding abundant," 1 Tim. 1: 13. and hereupon he falls to adoring that grace; "Now, to the King eternal, immortal, invisible, the only wise God, be honor and glory for ever and ever. Amen," verse 17.

The riches of mercy is made out by saving the chief of sinners, and in quickening them when dead, Eph. 2: 1. 4. and it is very observable, that the apostles, whenever they mention the grace of God in saving, quickening, &c. give not the least intimation of men's worthiness, preparedness, compliance, or any such thing, but dead in sins, and quickening, come one on the neck of the other, as light does upon darkness, which in no sort induces the light, or pre-

pares the dark earth or air for it, as is abundantly evident
in all their epistles.   And how often does the Lord declare
against all the pretensions of men, as to their activity in
this matter, in Isaiah, Jeremiah, Ezekial, Hosea? &c. and
as a bar to those pretensions, the holy people he calls, " A
people sought out;" and proclaims, " I am found of them
that sought me not."   This I shall end with a very observable instance within my own memory; and I bring it not
in for proof, but illustration.   I knew a man, who when he
came under convictions, endeavored with all his might to
stifle them: his convictions grew stronger, and he hardened himself against them: he saw their tendency: but was
so opposite to it, that he resolved, in express terms, he
would not be a puritan, whatever came of it.   To the
church he must go, his master would have it so; but this
was his wont, to loll over the seat, with his fingers in both
his ears: here general or conditional grace was surely non-
plussed.   But a chosen vessel must not be so lost; now
steps in electing grace, and by a casual slip of his elbow,
drew out the stoppers, and sent in a word from the pulpit,
which, like fire from heaven, melted his heart, and cast it
in a new mould.   Surely, in this the Lord did not wait for
the man's compliance or improvements; his work was not
originated thence, nor dependant thereon.

Arg. II. If all that pertains to salvation were not given
freely, salvation itself would not be of grace, for " to him
that worketh, is the reward not reckoned of grace, but of
debt," Rom. 4: 4.   but salvation is of grace, Eph. 2: 5.
" By grace ye are saved."   And again verse 8.   " By
grace ye are saved, through faith:" where also, lest
the adding of faith should occasion a lessening of that
or grace, or seem to detract from the freeness of it, he cau-
tiously subjoins, that this faith is the work of that grace, "not
of yourselves, it is the gift of God."   For if grace be perfectly free in choosing, it must be answerably free in giving
and applying the means to bring about the end it hath chosen us to: for if the effect of the means should depend
upon something to be done by men, which grace is not the
doer of: then works would put in for a share in the glory of
men's salvation; and so the grace of God would be de-
throned, and be as if it were not; grace is no more grace,
as is argued in Rom. 11: 16.

Arg. III. Spiritual blessings must be given freely, and of pure grace, because the natural man cannot perform any such act as might be motive for such a gift. Things materially good they may do, as Cain in offering the first-fruits; but not acceptable, because not done in a due manner; that is, in faith; the want of which makes incense itself an abomination, Isa. 1: 13, 14. If without faith it be impossible to please God, then it must be impossible to do aught before you believe, that may move God to give you faith. Salvation is promised to faith, remission of sins to repentance, the blessed vision to purity of heart: but we find not these graces promised to any act or qualification inferior to, or going before the graces themselves; our holy calling, and the washing of regeneration, we are not entitled to by works of our own, 2 Tim. 1: 9. Tit. 3: 15.

Arg. IV. If any of the requisites to salvation should be given upon condition, reason would it should be that which in worth and virtue containeth all the rest, and without which the rest had never been, or been of none effect, and that is our Lord Jesus Christ; of whom it is said, that "all the fulness of the godhead dwells in him bodily," Col. 2: 9. "and that out of his fulness all grace is received," John 1: 16. the giving of whom was the most superlative commendation of God's love to men, Rom. 5: 8. and is therefore termed "the," or "that gift of God," John 4: 10. being such a gift as comprehends all others. And as touching the free and unconditional giving of Christ, see that ancient authentic record in Gen. 3: 15. "It shall bruise thy head:" wherein is contained an absolute free promise to send the Son of God, in human flesh, to be a Redeemer. And we evidently know, that his actual coming and performance thereof, was not suspended upon any desert or worthiness of men: how could it, when after the fall they did not, nor could do any thing but what might turn his heart more against them? For evidence hereof, we need not go out of the context: do but observe the first Adam's carriage, and the manner of it, a little before the promise was made: first, they believe the serpent rather than God; then they break the commandment of life, when they had neither need nor occasion so to do. This done, and finding themselves lost, they do not so much as seek after God for help, but rather to hide themselves from him; so far from confessing themselves faulty, that they charge God foolishly, and shift the blame of their miscarriage upon him; "The woman whom thou gavest to be with me, she gave me of the tree—and the serpent, which also is a creature of thy making, beguiled me," &c. Here is nothing in their deportment that looks like the motive of such a promise. But, though they run from God, he will not so part with them; yea, he follows them, finds them out, and, for a door of hope, freely pronounceth this gracious promise, of sending his Son to destroy this old serpent, the devil; and, consequently, the serpentine nature, that had now instilled and mingled itself with theirs. It is the first promulgation of the gospel, and and speaks with as much absoluteness as words can express, "It shall bruise thy head." This I insist the more upon, because it is the first that was made in time, and that out of which all following promises are educed.

The intent of this promise, was Adam's recovery and comfort; who, doubtless, at this time, was in a very disconsolate condition; as lying under a fresh sense of the happiness he had lost, and the woful estate he was now plunged into; and therefore it was necessary, if Adam shall have comfort by it, that the terms thereof be altogether free and absolute: for, suppose them to be conditional, as, namely, if Adam shall now repent and convert himself; if he shall better improve a second stock, or rather the cankered remnant of that he had at first, my Son then shall come into this lower world, to still that enemy and avenger: his life shall go for thy life; I will be friends with thee, and restore thee to thy former state. All this, and more of this kind, had yielded but little comfort of hope to a guilty and defiled conscience, who found itself not only naked, and wholly bereft of its primitive righteousness, but at enmity with its Creator, and a bond-slave to Satan: for such reasonings as these would have broken in like a flood, to bear down, and stifle all hopes of future success, especially, if when I was in so blessed a state, and endued with power to keep the law, upon so slight a temptation I yielded and fell; how should I rise now I am down, and my strength is gone? If when I had freedom of will, and stood upright, I so easily warped into crooked paths; how can I hope to return, and do better, now my will is so perverted and bent to a contrary course? If whilst I had eyes in my head, and saw things with clearness I yet lost my way, and wandered; how should I think to recover it, being now both sadly bewildered, and my eyes put out? How should I bring a clean thing out of an unclean, who kept not my heart clean when it was so? How should I gain more with fewer talents, who ran myself out of all when I had abundantly more? Grapes will not grow upon thorns, nor figs on thistles: nay, were my primitive state restored to me on the former terms, I could not expect to keep it, having this woful experience of so causeless and dreadful an apostacy, &c.

It was therefore importantly necessary, that this first promise, made upon so great and solemn an occasion, and bearing in it all the hopes and comforts of God's people to eternity, should be thoroughly free and absolute, and not depend, in the least, upon any good thing to be done by men as the condition of it. And if Christ be given freely, there is good ground of arguing thence, the free giving of lesser things: for, " he that spared not his own Son, how shall he not with him freely give us all things?" Rom. 8: 32. " Is not the life more than meat?" Matt. 6: 25. Is not Christ more than faith and all grace? Has God given us the flesh of his Son, which is meat indeed; and will he not restore our withered hand to receive it? It cannot be; especially considering, that this may be done with a word; and without this, the other would be lost, and as water spilt in the ground. But though this promise of Christ be virtually a promise of all grace; yet, because of our slowness of heart to believe, and to win us off from our legalizing notions, the Lord condescends to gratify his people in words, as well as substance: therefore,

Arg. V. To make it expressly evident, that all spiritual blessings are perfectly free, he hath put them into absolute promises. Not that all promises run in that tenor: many of them have conditions annexed; which also, in their place, have a very significant usefulness: 1. As proofs of our willing subjection to God, Gen. 22: 12. 2. As directives by what mediums we must get to the blessedness designed us, John 3: 16. John 14: 6. and how qualified for the enjoyment of it, Matth. 5: 8. 2 Cor. 7: 1. 3. As marks and evidences of our being in the way to it, and of

those to whom it doth belong, Mark 15: 16. Rom. 8: 1.
John 10: 9. But this annexing of conditions does not imply a power in men to perform them; though performed
they must be, before we come to the promised reward; nor
does the effect of those promises depend upon any act to be
done by us, which some other promise doth not provide us
with. But that great fundamental promise, on which is
founded our hopes of eternal life, was absolute; it was
given before the world, Tit. 1: 2. Though clearly conditional to him with whom the compact was made, yet perfectly free and absolute to us; and, therefore, the adding
of conditions to after-promises, may not be taken as invali-
dating that first promise, or as a defeazance to it. It is a
scripture maxim, that " the covenant which was before
confirmed of God in Christ, the law (which was four hundred and thirty years after) cannot disannul, that it should
make the promise of none effect," Gal. 3: 17. The like
may be said of promises made in time, namely, that the
conditionality of some does not make void the absoluteness
of others. As the law was to Christ, such are conditional
promises to the absolute; they show what we should be and
do; and, by consequence, that we can neither be nor do as
we should; and thence infer to us, the necessity of divine
grace to undertake for us; and then, indeed, and not till
then, is the freeness of grace adorable, which promiseth
help in terms of an absolute tenor. And accordingly we
find that whatever is in one scripture made the condition
of acceptance with God, and eternal life, in other scriptures those very conditions are promised without condition; some of which we have a prospect of in the following
balance, which being that of the sanctuary, may well be
allowed to cast it: nor would it be once debated, if men
knew their interest; for interest will not lie.

Conditional Promises	*Promises of the Condition*
" Wash ye, make you clean: cease to do evil; learn to do well: come now, and let us reason together; and though your sins be as scar-	" Then will I sprinkle clean water upon you, and ye shall be clean: from all your filthiness will I cleanse you," Ezek. 36: 25. " I will

Conditional Promises

let, they shall be white as snow," Isa. 1: 16, 17, 18.

" Repent and turn; so iniquity shall not be your ruin," Ezek. 18: 30.

" Make you a new heart, and a new spirit," Ezek. 18: 31.

" Hear, and your soul shall live," Isa. 55: 3. " If thou shalt seek the Lord thy God, thou shalt find him, if thou seek him with thy whole heart," Deut. 4: 29.

" Then shall we know, if we follow on to know the Lord," Hosea 6: 3.

" Circumcise, therefore, the foreskin of your heart," Deut. 10: 16.

" Return, O backsliding children," Jer. 3: 14.

" If ye be willing and obedient, ye shall eat the good of the land," Isa. 1: 9.

" I will yet for this be inquired of by the house of Israel," Exek. 36: 37.

" He that endureth unto the end, the same shall be saved," Matth. 24: 13.

Promises of the Condition.

forgive your iniquity; and your sin I will remember no more" Jer. 31: 34.

" I will put a new spirit within you," Ezek. 11: 19. " A new heart also will I give you, and a new spirit will I put within you," Ezek. 36: 26.

.." Thou shalt return, and obey the voice of the Lord," Deut. 30: 8. " They shall return unto me with their whole heart," Jer. 24: 7. " I am found of them that sought me not," Isa. 65: 1.

" Thou shalt call me, My Father, and shalt not turn from me," Jer. 3: 19.

" The Lord thy God will circumcise thine heart," Deut. 30: 6.

" I will heal their backslidings," Hosea 14: 4.

" Thy people shall be willing," Psal. 110: 3. " I will cause you to walk in my statutes," Ezek. 36: 27. Phil. 2: 13.

" I will pour upon the house of David, the Spirit of grace and supplications," Zech. 12: 10.

" They shall not depart from me," Jer. 32: 40. " Who shall confirm you unto the end," 1 Cor. 1: 8. Jer. 3: 10.

These are some of those many exceeding great and precious promises, by which we are made partakers of the divine nature, 2 Pet. 1: 4. and if duly considered would much conduce to establish the present truth, which affirms the absolute free giving of " all things pertaining to life and godliness," ver. 3. and this nothing more plainly contradicts, than to make the dispensations of grace to depend on the wills and improvements of natural men: to exclude which is a principal scope of absolute promises, " that no flesh should glory in his presence," 1 Cor. 1: 29. since it is God that worketh all in all, both to will and to do; and that of his own good pleasure, 1 Cor. 12: 6.   Phil. 2: 13. There are yet divers things alleged against this doctrine; which the holy scriptures, with reasons drawn from thence and sanctified experience, do afford a plentiful bar and answer to: and this service they have done us, to bring some things to mind (before omitted) which may prove to the further clearing and confirmation of the truth.

Obj. All men universally, others as well as those you call the elect, are endued with means sufficient for salvation.

Answ. It shall be far from us to lessen the means afforded to any; or their sin in not living up to what they have: they have all means to be better than they are; and yet we cannot assent that all men now (since the fall) have the sufficiency alleged; for, of all the rest, the name of Christ, and faith in him, must not be excluded; but these all men have not.   In a great part of the world Christ is not so much as named; and " how shall they believe in him of whom they have not heard?" Rom. 11: 14. and where the gospel is, " all men have not faith," 2 Thess. 3: 2.   For men to believe (or fancy rather) that some excellent person hath interposed an atonement, to keep off vengeance from sinful men (as some speak,) is not to believe on the name of the Son of God, but rather to erect an altar to an unknown deity, and to worship they know not what.   Our Saviour tells the Jews (who knew that Messiah cometh,) " If ye believe not that I am he, ye shall die in your sins," John 8: 24.   For other reasons also, we cannot admit the objection.   1. Because it sets man in the same state now as before the fall; then, indeed they had a sufficiency to retain their present state; but ever since, all are born children of wrath, and enemies to God.   2. Because the objection, while it seems to magnify common grace, nullifies the special; as if God no more regarded his own elect than other men.   3. Because it lays a foundation for self-boasting; for, if all have but the same means given from above, the betterness of any must be from themselves; men must make themselves to differ; which is contrary to all reason, since the same means can have but the same effect upon subjects alike qualified.   4. Because the scripture speaks expressly the contrary; and that of those who had the likeliest sufficiency of any others; and yet they " could not believe," John 12: 39. and of believers themselves, that " they cannot think," 2 Cor. 3: 5. and of Christ's own disciples (who, of all believers, had the highest means,) that " without him they can do nothing," John 15: 5. and if such as these can neither do nor think, where is the sufficiency boasted of? You say, they have the power to believe, if they will: not so, but if they will, they have power. Power and will, in this matter, are the same thing variously expressed: it is common to say, we cannot, when nothing is wanting but will.   And, for power to will (if such a thing could be) without a will to put that power into act, it would signify no more than an arm without strength (which makes a shew, but can do nothing;) like the feet and ankle-bones of him that was born a cripple.   But is not that a deplorable kind of sufficiency, which leaves " without hope, and without God in the world?" Eph. 2: 12. and yet such is the state of a very great part of mankind. You will say, perhaps, they had a sufficiency, but by mis-usage they lost it: and can there be a more palpable instance of a thing's insufficiency, than its inability to preserve itself, and the general successfulness of it? But means may be proper enough, and in their kind sufficient, towards the production of such an event, and yet that event never succeed, for want of something else which also was requisite for it. Some of the Jews, by the evident testimonies of Christ's divinity, were convinced that he was the Messiah, but it came not up to a perfect work; " they did not confess him," John 12: 42. and this because " the arm of the Lord was not revealed to them," Isa. 53: 1. that is, as Moses speaks, " the Lord had not given them an heart to understand," Deut. 29: 4.   Planting and watering are proper, and sufficient in their kind, as means and secondary causes; but nothing as to increase, without a blessing from God. Who could reason more strongly than Paul? or speak more eloquently than Apollos? and yet the success of their ministry was " as God gave to every man," 1 Cor. 3: 5. it is God that worketh both will and deed, Phil. 2: 13. it is he that openeth the ear to discipline, Job 36: 10. and sealeth instruction, chap. 33: 16. when his hand is set to, then it is authentic and powerful, and not before. Of this, those ancient Jews are a downright instance: they had means of being purged, and yet were not purged, Ezek. 24: 13. but afterwards, the Lord takes the work into his own hand; " I will sprinkle clean water upon you, and ye shall be clean; from all your filthiness, and from all your idols, will I cleanse you; a new heart also will I give you, and cause you to walk in my statutes," Ezek. 36: 25—28. by which it appears, that the Lord will not only afford them means, as aforetime, and leave the improvement thereof to themselves; for that he saw would not do; but now, he. will take the whole upon himself; not to exempt them from their duty, but enable them for it; adding also his own divine power to make the means effectual; as is plainly implied in that of the prophet Jeremiah, " I will bring it health and cure, and I will cure them," Jer. 33: 6. that is, he would give them an honest and good heart, which shall bring forth fruit to perfection, Luke 8: 15. These are the means proper and sufficient for salvation, and less than this will not do.

Object. They have as full a sufficiency as is meet and just for God to give.

Answ. 1. Is it meet and just to do good? Why not then the chiefest good that men are capable of, which is, to have their hearts perfectly turned to God, and united to him for ever? 2. The objection attributes more to man, in the business of his salvation, than to God: for, if all that God can justly or meetly do in order thereto will not save him, without something done by himself, which God is not the doer of, then man will be reckoned chief agent in the work; and so " the axe will boast itself against him that handles it," Isa. 10: 15. Suppose a plaster or medicine to be made up of twenty ingredients, and one of them to be of such sovereign virtue as to influence all the rest; all which, if that be wanting, will but ulcerate the wound, or heighten the distemper; that one must be counted the principal. 3. It is not to be supposed that the great and only wise God would set up a creature whose will he cannot justly and meetly overrule, especially in things requisite to the very end for which he was made: nor, that he should make him for such an end, as that any thing conducible thereto may not meetly and justly be done, in order to its accomplishment. 4. It would not answer the end of Christ's receiving gifts for men; yea, for the rebellious, to bring in whom, all power was given to him. Suppose a general should take in the lesser forts of a revolted city, but leave the fort royal, which commands all the rest, in the enemy's hand; shall he tell his prince they would not yield; and that, being men of reason, he thought it not fair to force them? would this be a fair account of his expedition? I trow not; for it would be to say, in effect, that he did not reduce them, because they were rebels. 5. It cannot be righteous or meet for men to affirm, nor for the honor of sovereign majesty, to admit, that the creature's will should limit, divert, or frustrate, the will and intent of the Creator. Shall it be at the will of one possessed, whether or no the devil shall be cast out? shall every base and pitiful lust have a negative vote to that which has passed the Trinity's fiat? It was religiously said of one, " I will not have him for my God, that hath not power over my will." And, *lastly,* Suppose a man crazed in his head, and you intend him an honor or office, which he never will be capable of without the full use of his reason; is it not meeter, and doth it not argue an higher degree of love, prudence, and justice, to cure his distemper, though in a way contrary to his present mind, than to wait his complying with your prescriptions, which (as he is) he will never understand? And what hinders, but that God may do so by his people; even give them a heart to know him, and to fear him for ever, save only that this boggy principle of human liberty will not comport with it?

Object. But if a sufficiency of means to repent and believe be not afforded to all, how shall God be just in punishing for neglects?

Answ. The justice of God will not need our salving, especially by a balm of our making: whether he judge or justify, he is just in what he doeth, though purblind reason sees not how. His judgments are a great deep; not to be fathomed by human comprehension. In sounding at sea, will it follow that there is no bottom, because your line will not reach it? God dealt not so (in respect of means) with any nation as with Israel: and the men going with Paul to Damascus, the Lord would not give them to see his face, nor to hear his voice; both which he vouchsafed to Paul, and yet he needs no vindication or apology for punishing their unbelief: "They that have sinned without law, shall perish without law," Rom. 2: 12. Besides, men are justly obnoxious to punishment for neglecting or not improving the means they have; although those means, when made the best of that nature can, will not save them: they are punishable for not feeding and not clothing; and yet by doing these, men are not justified. The least transgression lays men open to wrath; and we cannot, by keeping some commands, compensate the breach of others.

Object. Where it is said, "I will write my law in their hearts; and cause them to walk in my statutes," &c. there is no more intended by it, but the giving of things or means proper to such an end.

Answ. If one obliged to save your life should thus expound his engagement, you would not think it good payment, nor that he had dealt faithfully with you. The sense objected cannot be the mind and limit of that most gracious promise: for, 1. The promise must be as broad and large as the precept: it would else be too short to repose our confidence in. If, then, the precept intends as much as the words of it do literally import, then also doth the promise: but the precept not only requires a using the means that tend to the duty enjoined, but the perfect, effectual performance of the duty itself, both as to matter and form; therefore doth likewise the promise: and then it will follow, that to write the law in the heart, and cause us to walk, &c. is more than a means: it is the thing itself. 2. The doctrine is hardly bestead, and not much to be credited, which, for its support, must put such a construction on the highest and most absolute promises that God hath made, as would render them weak and fruitless things. 3. Where God hath absolutely said, that such a thing he will do, for men to put in conditions or limitations, is to raze or interline a record; which is a felonious act: and how he will deal with those who add to, or take from, the words of his prophecy, you have recorded in the last chapter of his book: (it is ill trifling with sacred things.) 4. A physician that undertakes to cure a man of his phrensy, and to keep him in his right mind, is not said to have done his work, or made good his word, whatever means have been applied to him, if the patient continue his former distraction, or relapse into it. 5. There is no need or reason why the Lord should promise, or make shew of promising, more than he intends to perform, for that would be as a broken staff: or why he should express himself in terms of a fuller or more absolute engagement than might in all points consist with his wisdom, justice, holiness, &c. 6. *Lastly,* The objection is further excepted against and rejected, not only as it makes man the chief agent in his own salvation, but as denying that God doeth any thing more for them that are saved, than for them that perish. If men make themselves to differ, the gospel design of magnifying grace is dashed at once. And, truly, it is matter both of wonder and grief, to see how industriously witty some men are to enervate the promises of God; as if they could not accept of salvation, unless their own wills may stand partners with his grace.

Object. But is it not said, " To him that hath shall be given?" Matt. 25: 29. that is, he that uses common grace well, shall have special.

Answ. 1. If that gracious promise, of writing the law in our hearts, intend only the affording of means, which is but common grace, where shall we find a promise of the special? The well using of common grace is indeed a duty incumbent upon all; but is in no way meriting, or moving God to bestow the special: he is above all human motives; and is not wrought upon by them, as men are. This is seen by Paul, whom special grace took hold upon, even while misusing that which is common: there was no space of time between his being a persecutor, and his obtaining mercy, 1 Tim. 1: 3. with Acts 9: 4, 5, 6. 2. What proportion is there, in value, between a handful of clay, and a talent of gold? Infinitely more is the disproportion between the grace of faith, and all that a natural man can do for obtaining it: " they that are in the flesh cannot please God," Rom. 8: 8. 3. Whatsoever is not of faith is sin; but a man's sin cannot be a motive for his good: to plead your improvements, is to make your filthy rags an argument why God should accept you. Remember the condition he was in that proffered money for the gift of the Holy Ghost, Acts 8: 18, 19. improvements for faith is no better. 4. It would not become the wisdom, power, or grace of God, to build on a foundation made ready to his hand: he needs it not, nor will it sort with his design; which is to have his grace acknowledged the alpha and omega of men's salvation. *Lastly,* A will to improve, is as much from God as the thing to be improved: " A man can receive nothing except it be given him from above," John 3: 27. the thing given, and power to receive and improve it, are both from thence: and things from above are not fetched down by men; but they come down when, and upon whom, the Father of lights pleaseth, James 1: 17.

Object. Men are commanded to make them a new heart, Ezek. 18: 31. which must imply an ability so to do: for how can it be just to require things impossible; and that under so severe a penalty?

Answ. Whatever is implied in the command, such allegations do surely imply that the framers of them are much unacquainted with the scriptures, or extremely rash in drawing conclusions from them. There are reasons enough, and holy ends, which do justly warrant such commands, without supposing those to whom they are given able now to perform them: as, 1. Perhaps the Lord speaks it ironically; deriding their vain confidence, as Elijah did the priests of Baal, when he bids them " Cry aloud, for he is a god," 1 Kings 18: 27. will you hence infer, that Baal was a god? or that idols can shew things to come, because the Lord bids them do it, thereby to evidence their godhead? Isa. 41: 23. or that Adam had advantaged himself by his fall, because the Lord says, " The man is become like one of us?" Gen. 3: 22. The like form of speech is sometimes used concerning Babylon; " Take balm for her pain, if so be she may be healed," even then when " his device was to destroy her;" Jer. 51: 8. with chap. 50. So, here, as upbraiding those carnal Jews with their fond opinion of self-sufficiency, freedom of will, and power to do great matters; " Make you a new heart, for why will ye die?" *q. d.* " You know that the end of these things is death:

you pretend to an high pitch of ability, that men may be good if they will, and turn when they please, and yet you go on in an evil way: if ye can make you a new heart, do it; why will ye, by neglecting so easy a matter, fall under a sentence of death?" 2. To let men know God hath not lost his right of commanding, though they have lost their power of obeying: time was when they had it, and power to keep it; but, having lost it, God is not bound to restore it, nor unjust in punishing those neglects which arise from the want of it. It is man's duty to seek after God, though it be a peradventure whether he shall find him or not, Acts 17: 27. 3. Hereby to convince them what was that one thing necessary, namely, the change of heart; as, without which, all labor is spent in vain upon them, as in the parable of the sower. The root must be holy before the fruit; grapes will not grow upon thorns; nor the stony, thorny, or highway ground bring forth to perfection, Luke 3: 12—15. when Ephraim was turned, then he repented, and not before, Jer. 31: 19. 4. That being convinced of the necessity of such a change, and finding their own endeavors wholly ineffectual, as Paul did, Rom. 7: 8, 9. 23. they might see also the necessity of free grace, and of the divine power to do it for them; and so have their eyes turned off from themselves, and drawn thitherwards, even towards those hills of strength, which the church had an eye to when they prayed, "Turn thou me, and I shall be turned," Jer. 31: 18. 5. If the giving a command from God infers in men a power to obey; then it will follow, that men have a power to keep the whole law, and that without turning aside to the right hand or to the left; and to make themselves holy, as God is holy; for these he commanded, Deut. 5: 32, 33. 2 Pet. 1: 15. But, 6. That the Lord intends not such a conclusion should be made upon his command, appears from the 17th of Jer. ver. 1. "The sin of Judah is written with a pen of iron, and with a point of a diamond graven on the table of their heart;" that is, so as not to be blotted out by human wit or strength: and therefore, 7. He tells them expressly, it is as impossible for them to make themselves a new heart, "as for the Ethiopian to change his skin," Jer. 13: 23. "For who can bring a clean thing out of an unclean?" Job 14: 4. "They that sanctify themselves, and they that offer swine's flesh, shall both be consumed together," Isa. 66: 17.

Object. Why then are men enjoined attendance on the means, if there be so little in them?

Answ. If there were no other reason or end, this were enough, that God had commanded it; that binds us to use the means, though not the means to effect the thing it is used for: nor is the means so much to be considered, as God's institution and appointment; nor the use thereof to be rested on, but the grace and power of God giving influence thereto; who himself is not bound to means or method: originally he is found in his own way, and out of it we are not to look for him.

Object. But to what end is the gospel preached in terms universal, and universally to all, if some particular and determinate persons only can receive it?

Answ. The counsel of God concerning election is secret; the minister knows not who are the objects of it; and therefore must preach to all, according to his commission. The Lord deals in this, as in the matter of lots: Saul was fore-appointed to be king; yet all Israel must come together, and lots must be cast on the whole nation, as if the person were yet undesigned, 1 Sam. 9: 16. with chap: 10: 20, 21. The falling of the lot was wholly contingent, as to men: another might have been taken as well as he it fell upon: but the Lord disposed it, and cast it on the right person, Prov. 16: 33. So, touching the gospel, it is sent to a place where, perhaps, but one, or very few elect persons, are, and those only shall be taken by it, and yet it must be published to the whole city promiscuously: but the Holy Ghost, " who knoweth the deep things of God," brings it to the hearts of those for whom it is prepared; and there it fixeth: which the jailer, Lydia, and other examples, make evident.

Object. Man is a rational creature, and accordingly to be proceeded with: but this way and manner of conversion destroys all freedom of will; and makes conversion a compulsory thing.

Answ. The will cannot be forced: the man may be forced to act against his will, but not to will against his will: or, he may will that to day, which yesterday he willed not:

but this change is so far from being an infringement, that it is rather an effect and demonstration of his freedom. There are three sorts of compulsion, violent, natural, and rational. 1. Violent; when a man is constrained to do that which his will is opposite to: thus the Israelites, to serve the Egyptians, and go into captivity: so also Paul, and other saints, are led captive to that they would not, Rom. 7: 9. but the will in conversion comes not under this kind of constraint, nor any thing like it. 2. There is a natural compulsion: thus men, and other creatures, are compelled to eat, drink, sleep, and breathe; there need no violent hand to impose it, nor arguments to persuade to it; they do it by instinct, which God hath endued them with for their own conservation: this kind of compulsion is proper to the soul converted, in reference to a spiritual life and actions. 3. There is also a rational compulsion, which is nearest the case in hand: this is when the understanding and judgment are convinced of the goodness, necessity, or expediency of a thing, which before he judged otherwise of. For this, see the prodigal's reasons for returning to his father, Luke 15: 17. and the lepers' for going to the Syrian's camp, 2 Kings 7: 3. 4. their reason told them, it was better to go where there was hope, than to tarry where there was none. See also the arguments for the saints' living to Christ; the love of Christ constrains them; they cannot but so judge, namely, that if Christ died for them, they are bound to live to him, 2 Cor. 5: 14. yet no breach of their liberty, although at other times they were otherwise minded.

The first of these, namely, that which is violent, our doctrine hath nothing to do with: it is true, there is a drawing in conversion; and there would be no conversion without it; " no man can come to Christ except he be drawn," John 6: 44. which drawing implies an averseness, or at least a disability in him that is drawn, and, consequently, a kind of force, or extrinsical power, put forth upon him. But let me say, it is such a force as the enlightened soul most gladly subjects itself unto, and would not be from under the power and blessed influence of for a world. Let it therefore be observed how the Father draws: it is in the most genuine and kindly way that can be conceived: he draws by teaching, John 6: 45. not as Gideon taught the men of Succoth, Judges 8: 16. nor as the task-masters drew the people to their burdens, Exod. 5: 16. but as Jacob was drawn into Egypt; who need not be forced to dislodge, and remove his tent, when he found himself surrounded with famine, and he heard there was corn in Egypt; that the king had sent wagons for him, and provisions for the way; telling him withal, that the good of all the land was before him; especially considering that his beloved Joseph was there alive, and in the greatest honor, ready to receive him, Gen. ch. 45. In like manner, when the soul hath a sight of the holiness of God, and of its own vileness, of the purity, straightness, and just severity of the law; with its own uncleanness, crookedness, guiltiness, and disability, either to keep it, or bear the vengeance of it; that in God alone is all its blessedness; and that yet it cannot possibly come at him, but as dried stubble to a devouring flame: and yet again, if he comes not, he dies in the place where he is, and must dwell with everlasting burnings; and withal hears of a Mediator, who came from heaven to save such as himself is; and who casts out none that come to him; and by whom he may come to God both safely and acceptably; there will need no violent hand on the will; even love to himself makes the soul wings. There is, indeed, a violent (or rather, almighty) constraint and casting out of him that did usury upon the will, and perverted it, by deluding the understanding with false glosses and carnal reasonings; which being dispelled by the true light's shining, the will falls in with it, and follows with perfect freedom. Christ offered no violence to the man when he cast out the legion; but thereby restored him to his proper freedom: for we presently find him at " Jesus' feet, clothed, and in his right mind," Luke 8: 35. desiring now to dwell with him, the sight of whom before was a torment to him; here no man will say the patient was wronged, though his will was crossed; if any do, there is cause to inquire whether himself be yet in his right mind. When the faculties are put in order by renovation, the understanding is the spirit of the will; which therefore looks and goes the same way as of course, as the wheels did after the living creatures, Ezek. 1: 19. without any foreign or violent constraint: it hath now a spring within it, by which it is moved and guided (itself being also renewed and sanctified) according to this renewed light; as a needle that is rightly touched needs not to be forced to look towards the pole; it will do it by sympathy: " If the eye be single, the whole body is full of light," Matt. 6: 22.

But suppose the thing objected to be true, namely, that in' conversion the will suffereth violence, it no way deserves to be styled cruel and tyrannical, as some, extremely tender in nature's concerns! do presume to speak, nor indeed to be complained of in the least, since the tendency and issue thereof is an infinite good. What father would not cross the will of his child, rather than see him destroyed by his fool-hardiness? Shall parents, as it were, force their children's will for their good, and be blameless; and shall not much more the Father of spirits, that we may live? Heb. 12: 9. Was it not a mercy to Jeremiah, that " the word of the Lord was as a fire in his bones, that he could not forbear speaking," Jer. 20: 9. rather than be confounded for holding his peace? How much better is it to enter into life halt or maimed, than go into hell with a whole skin! I hope there is none so much beside themselves as to judge otherwise of it; or complain of their being compelled to go to heaven, though it were by a whirlwind and chariot of fire. At first, I grant it is pure necessity drives to Christ: but afterwards, his personal excellency and loveliness constrain to abide with him; a sweet and blessed compulsion! and now you would not leave him again, although the first necessity of your going to him were quite at an end: but still we say, as before, that the will is not violated, but changed, and that in a due and orderly way, by being made subject to an enlightened understanding, than which there is nothing more pleasant and natural to it.

Inferences

The inferences from this doctrine I reduce to two sorts; 1. Cautionary, to prevent the misusing so great a truth: 2. Directive, to draw forth some of the spirits of it into practice: and of these, intermixedly and briefly, though capable of much enlargement. In general, take notice, that the scope and design of the doctrine, is not to foster remissness in duty, nor to countenance a stupid, or carnal quiet: but, to set forth the fulness, freeness, and prevalent efficacy of divine grace, with the creature's nothingness, as to any considerable act, in this matter.   More particularly:

Infer. I. Presume not yourself interested in the promise of eternal life, until you find in yourself those necessary evidential qualifications of faith and regeneration: or, least, a truly earnest and restless pursuit after them: " I will not let thee go, except thou bless me," Gen. 32: 26.

Infer. II. Let not the means be despised, or lightly regarded, because of themselves not sufficient to save. Where the means are, the Lord expects that men should use them; and we read not of any saved without, where they might be had.

Infer. III. Let no man sit still in the wilful or careless neglect of his duty, pretending, that if elected he shall surely be saved; if not, all he can do will not help him. Such a disposition argues a great height of pride, or sullenness of spirit, and enmity against God: fly from it as from hell; for it is truly that death which hell follows after: as, on the contrary, ye can hardly have a more hopeful symptom of your state, than a serious attendance upon God in his way.   And, in seeking to know your election, begin at the right end; give all diligence to make your calling sure; and the certainty of your election will fall in upon it.

Infer. IV. Take notice, from the import and tenor of the contrary doctrine, what standing need and usefulness there is of those often repeated cautions, to " try the spirits; search the scriptures; take heed how you hear;" and not be led by " fair shows in the flesh."   The more smooth and pleasing notions are to the carnal ear, the more to be suspected, and thoroughly examined before they pass.   Let the drift of the law and the testimony determine the question; and that will tell you, those doctrines are not to be held guiltless, that cry up that excellent creature man; with the strength and capacity of natural reason; the sufficiency of free-will grace; power of improvement, and truly I know not what, for they are not after the pattern of wholesome words; making these the great hinge whereon the design, that glorious design, of grace in election, the mediation of Christ, and the Holy Ghost's operations, must all hang and move; yea, be frustrate too, and come to nothing, except the reason of man will dethrone itself, and submit to that which it reckons foolishness. Godliness is a mystery, 1 Tim. 3: 16. and a great one, it is a spiritual mystery; which it could not be said to be, if reason could comprehend it. With all your care and circumspection, fly from that dangerous quicksand, which the Jews sunk into and perished, Rom. 9: 31, 32. and how many in our days are in danger of it! It hath slain its thousands, for others' single tens. As preventive of this, I would put in a three-fold memorial.

1. That there is a specific difference between moral virtues, and divine, or holiness of truth. True holiness has all morality in it; but all that is called moral may be without holiness, nor will ever rise to it; sublimation does not vary the kind; holiness must have a root of its own: he that best knew the nature of things, and what may be made of them, affirms it as irrational to think otherwise, as to expect figs from thistles, Matth. 7: 16. That they proceed from several heads, appears from their several ends. What rises from the divine nature, directs its course towards God, and ceases not until it arrive at him; and what rises in itself, terminates there; as a circle, wheresoever it begins, there it ends, fetch it ever so far a compass. Paul was a moralist of no ordinary size; his often quoting it, shows the esteem he had once had of it: but when it pleased God to reveal his Son in him, Gal. 1: 15. he counts it all but dung, Phil. 3: 8. Which he would not have done, had the new creature sprung out of the old: but thus far he was, when he knew better things from his former fondness; and so shall we. Think not, therefore, to find in yourselves the materials of gospel holiness, or to raise them out of the dust of your natural endowments: which, though of good use in their place, will not bear of the right kind, Matth. 12: 33. till headed by the ingrafted word, James 1. 21. He that thinks to draw saving graces out of natural principles, does but spin out of his bowels to die in his own web.

2. You may not think to obtain special grace upon your improvement of that which is common: he that does, builds on a wrong foundation, and is yet under a covenant of works; under which no man was ever saved, or shall be, Gal. 3: 10. This was the case with those who followed

after the law of righteousness, and did not attain to it: what was it that hindered? " They sought it (as it were) by the works of the law," Rom. 9: 31, 32. and yet the Gentiles, who sought it not, attained it, Rom. 9: 30. Where note, by the way, that those who do not at all seek after right-eousness and life, are as likely to speed, as those who seek it unduly; that is, by works of their own. In vain is sal-vation looked for from the hills of natural freedom, free-will-grace, human improvements, or whatever else is of highest esteem with men: none in such danger of being broken off, that is, of losing that they profess and seem to have, as those who are high minded, who stand on their terms, and will not yield without taking their baggage with them: it was the very same with those carnal Jews, " We have Abraham to our father; were never in bondage to any man," John 8: 33. " and are we also blind?" John 9: 40. If thy carnal heart hath been hankering that way, and is now bought off, bless the Lord for it; remember the danger thou hast escaped, and come no more there; bear in thy heart, as a frontlet between thine eyes, that good word recorded in Jeremiah, which shows the danger of making " flesh thine arm," and the blessedness of trusting only in the Lord, Jer. 17: 5, 6, 7. and this, I verily think, is the cause that some, who have made a fair profession, do fall off and wither; they make the promises of grace conditional, and the efficacy of them to depend upon their free-will's disposition, and treat them accordingly. Such faith is but of human extract; it is of men, and therefore it comes to nought; whereas, " if it were of God, it could not be overthrown." Acts 5: 38.

3. Human wisdom is no competent judge in this matter. Ye may as well try metals on a brickbat, or judge of co-lors by moon-light, as of spiritual things by natural reason; they are above it, though not contrary to it: nor will the clearness of light without help in this case; high noon and midnight are both alike to one that was born blind; the light of the sun, if seven-fold, would but more dazzle the sight that is not adapted for it. Divine things are not visible but by an organ suitably disposed; in the want of which the scripture itself is too often perverted; and the letter of it set up to obliterate its meaning. The very disciples of Christ knew not the scriptures, but as he opened their understand-ing, 1 John 5: 20. with John 20: 9. and Luke 24: 45. and

shone into it: and enabled by this, they looked upon and handled the word of life as such, 1 John 1: 1. they beheld his glory, the glory as of the only begotten Son of the Father, John 1: 14. when, at the same time, the learned scribes, with all their moral and literary endowment, saw no such thing; but counted him a deceiver, and one possessed, John 7: 12. 20. chap. 10: 20. "The things of God knoweth no man, but the Spirit of God," and he to whom the Spirit will reveal them: "but the natural man, (while such,) receiveth not the things of the Spirit," 1 Cor. 2: 14. "they are foolishness to him," 1 Cor. 1: 18,19. and Heb.1:5. "neither can he know them, because they are spiritually discerned," and not otherwise. "But, he that is spiritual, endued with power from on high," Luke 24: 49. "judgeth all things, yet he himself is judged of no man," 1 Cor. 2:15. no unspiritual man understands him, nor his principles; it is a "new name, which no man knows but he that hath it," Rev. 3: 17. Hence they are called unintelligible notions; and "what will this babbler say? when he preached Jesus, and the resurrection of the dead," Acts 17: 18. And for this cause the apostle still prays for those he writes unto, "that God would give them the spirit of wisdom and revelation, and enlighten the eyes of their understanding," Eph. 1: 17, 18. where note, that one of the great things they were to discern, was, the "exceeding greatness of the divine power put forth in them that believe," ver. 19. and, that "they might abound in knowledge, and in all judgment; and this, that they might approve things that are excellent," Phil. 1: 9, 10. or try things that differ, as the margin hath it. So, for the Colossians; "He ceaseth not to pray for them, that they might be filled with the knowledge of his will, in all wisdom and spiritual understanding," Col. 1: 9. Which scriptures plainly import, that there is not in every man this knowledge; nor yet enough in the best: for why should he pray so solemnly for that which is common, or easily obtained? so then, wisdom is the principal thing, Prov. 4: 7. and it must be wisdom from above, James 3: 17. without which the mind is not good, nor capable of right judgment, however garnished with human habiliments: but endued with this, those other will be serviceable handmaids: if the eye be single, the whole body shall be full of light. Those lesser lights are yet of use, and may serve to rule the night, which they were made for, but when the day-star is up, they vanish; then those wild beasts of human abilities, lie down in their dens, and man goes forth to his work, Psal. 104: 22. with another kind of skill and power than ever he had before, and with better success. Therefore get wisdom, and with all thy getting, get understanding," Prov. 4: 7. " It is a well-spring of life to him that hath it," Prov. 16: 22. the image of God and eternal life begin here, Jon 17: 3. Col. 3: 10. The first step towards it, is your sense of its want: " he that thinks he knows any thing, knows nothing yet as he ought to know," 1 Cor. 8: 2. The more ye know in truth, the deeper sense shall ye have of your scanty attainments. " He that will be wise, let him become a fool (in his own sight) that he may be wise," 1 Cor. 3: 18. " Whom God will teach knowledge, and make to understand doctrine, he weans from the milk, and draws from the breasts," Isa. 28: 9. of their mother-wit and carnal understanding. Your next step is, to seek wisdom where it is to be had, namely, at the fountain-head, " the Father of lights," James 1: 5. He that thinks to obtain of himself, a phrase too much in use with some, goes to a wrong door; and is but as likely to speed, as a beggar that asketh an alms of himself: and hence it is, that in so many seekers, there are so few that find. When Solomon, from a sense of his childhood in knowledge, sought wisdom of God, he obtained it; when of himself, though better stocked than before, he failed; " I said I will be wise, but it was far from me," Eccl. 7: 23. he seemed, at this turn, to be of the free-will persuasion, and he sped accordingly. He therefore puts upon this course a mark of ignominy; " He that trusteth to his own heart is a fool," Prov. 28: 26. I heartily wish it may not be said to any among us, " thy wisdom and thy knowledge it hath perverted thee," Isa. 47: 10. And having once got this spiritual faculty, preserve it like fire upon the altar; let it never go out, Levit. 6: 13. and for your growth in it, live up to what you know. " He that will do his will, shall know of his doctrine," John 7: 17. 2 Pet. 1: 5—8.

Infer. V. If the divine power be absolutely necessary; then rest not on means or ministry, though the best; use them as means, but still have your eye towards that power and grace which alone can make them effectual. Elisha smote the waters with Elijah's mantle but it was the God of Elijah that parted them hither and thither, to make a way over, 2 Kings 2: 14. Men rolled the stone from Lazarus's grave; but Christ was he who brought Lazarus forth, John 11: 41—44. so the minister preaches Christ; but it is God only that gives an understanding to know him. Our business is, to mind our duty, and to have our faith in God, as the principal part of it: for he it is, who is both the maker of our plaster, and the layer of it on; who also doth influence and manage it for us, from first to last; he is both the author and finisher, Heb. 12: 2. " It is God that worketh all in all," 1 Cor. 12: 6.

Infer. VI. In looking over the several parts of this great work, and parties concerned about it, let not the grace of Jesus Christ be overlooked; nor let it be lightly considered, how little, indeed, less than nothing, you or I have done to induce or help it on. See how manifestly our Lord and Redeemer approves himself the good shepherd: he is not satisfied to send his servants, but he goes himself; and such is his care and love to our souls, that he leaves no place unsearched; ranges the briers and thickets; avoids neither mountains nor valleys; no, not even the valley of the shadow of death; nay, he knows, that there he is most likely to meet them, and rests him not until he has found. He doth, as it were, forget the ninety and nine of his very sheep, that are already brought in, yet so, as not to leave them without a good guardian, and all to fetch in a straggler: which having found, he doth not yet think it found, till he have it at home in the fold. It is not enough with him to move, argue, persuade, threaten; and if they will not comply, let them take their course, and feed on the fruit of their doings: his mercies are not like our free-will mercies to ourselves: to see them but deeper plunged, by all he hath done for them, would not be to see of the travail of his soul and be satisfied. But if all this will not do, and he knows it will not, he apprehends his lost sheep, as he did Manasseh and Paul, or as an officer does a fugitive, lays it on his shoulders, and brings it home; which plainly shows the sheep's averseness to return: for, if it would either lead or drive, the shepherd would not trouble himself to bear it on his back. O that the love and faithfulness of

Christ might have its weight on our hearts, to love him highly, and ourselves only for his sake, who saves us at first against our wills, in saving us from self-willedness: and so making us willing to be saved indeed!

Infer. VII. If all that pertains to salvation be given in right of election, then let every soul that seeks for spiritual gifts, and would be sure to speed, apply himself to electing love: and let all your thankfulness for all that you have or hope for, be referred to that love: for that is the rock out of which they are hewn, the fountain and spring from whence they proceed. See the bounty and nobleness of it! electing love not only provides your home, but sends you wagons and provision for the way: regard not your stuff: whatever you have of your own, be it good, or be it bad; for, " the good of all the land is yours." Make mention of nothing that is properly thine, except the " greatness of thy sins," as David, Psal. 25. 11. the power of indwelling corruption, as Paul, Rom. 7: thy inability to serve him, as Joshua and Jeremiah, Josh. 24: 19. Jer. 1: 6. that without faith thou canst not please God, nor give glory to him; that without holiness thou canst not show forth his virtues, nor answer the end for which he hath chosen thee: and, finally, that thou canst be sanctified by that will only, which wills thy sanctification, Heb. 10: 10. When Moses would prevail for the gracious presence of God with that people, what does he plead for it? " Remember (says he) this nation is thy people; and wherein shall it be known, that I and thy people have found grace in thy sight? Is it not in this, that thou goest with us?" Exod. 33: 13. 16. Here, you see, he makes God's presence with them an evidence of his having chosen them; and from his choosing them, he draws an argument why he should be with them. Moses durst not say, " They are a people that keep thy commands; they are persons of a very honest, ingenuous disposition, (as some say,) a tractable sort of men, that have complied with thee, and better improved thy favors than their neighbors have done; therefore own them, and go with them:" no, but " consider, I pray thee, that they are thy people; thou hast chosen them above all people," Deut. 10: 15. and therefore deal with them above the rate of thy dealings with other men.

In like manner, having received any special favor from

God, sacrifice not to your better deservings; but as Daniel, who, though a man of singular wisdom, yet, says he, " This secret is not revealed to me for any wisdom that I have more than any living," Dan. 2: 30. Thus also we find David deporting himself when Nathan brought him that gracious message from God, how great things he would do for him, and for his house; what does David put upon it? " Thou, Lord God, knowest thy servant;" that is, thou knowest that I have done nothing which might move thee to this munificent bounty; but, " for thy word's sake, and according to thine own heart, thou hast done all these great things," 2 Sam. 7: 20, 21. this is the voice of the man after God's own heart.

Again, suppose you have done any signal service for God; retire into self-abasement, and magnify God that he was pleased to vouchsafe you that honor. Thus also did David, when setting his affection to the house of God, he had gathered that huge incredible mass of treasure for the building it: he wonders not so much at his having gotten it, though that might be well wondered at, as that he had an heart so freely to devote it to that sacred use: " Who am I (says he,) and what is my people, that we should be able to offer thus willingly? for all things are of thee," 1 Chron. 29: 14. He acknowledgeth their willingness to offer to be as much of God, as the offering itself. And Paul, having labored more abundantly than all the apostles, puts from himself the honor of it: " Not I, but the grace of God which was with me," 1 Cor. 15: 10.

Three or four things, in seeking for spiritual blessings, be sure to keep still in your mind.

1. That you must be nothing in yourself. New wine is not for old bottles; the bottles must be first undone, and made up anew; or else the wine will be spilt. and the bottles perish, Matt. 9: 17. All your imaginary righteousness, wisdom, strength, &c. must be parted from you; and it is as necessary, as to leave your made ground, to build on the firm rock.

2. That spiritual blessings are a gift, and will not admit of any plea which may seem to make them wages. Lazarus loved Christ, yet would not his sisters use that as their argument; but, " Lord, he whom thou lovest is sick," John 11: 3. What the scripture holds forth as a motive with

God, that you may plead, and that in his name; and, indeed, nothing else is pleadable at the throne of grace. Esteem not yourself the better for what you may carry with you: think not to be accepted because of your present; it is not your money, Isa. 55: 1. John 7: 37. nor your double money in your hand, that will fetch you corn from above, though it may from Egypt: silver and gold, your own works and worthiness, are of no value at the mint of free grace; but there it is, and thence you must have whatever may render you welcome at the court of heaven.

3. Be not over solicitous how you shall speed; nor think you shall fare worse for coming in so tattered and pitiful a condition. Free-grace is compassionate, rich, bountiful: you are not the less welcome because you bring nothing: the best qualification is to find yourself ill qualified, empty, hungry, poor, naked, blind, miserable. Electing love hath provided enough, and more: not bread and water only (though these are very welcome to an hungry and thirsty soul,) but wine and milk, " wine on the lees, a feast of fat things," Isa. 25: 6. not aprons made of fig-leaves, or coats made of beasts' skins; but " long robes of linen, fine and white," Rev. 19: 8. not money made of leather, or base metal, that burden one to carry a month's provision of it; but gold, and of that the finest, and tried in the fire, Rev. 3: 18. which hath nothing of dross or cankering rust adhering to it. And if thou have but little, look on that little as an earnest of more; " To him that hath shall be given:" although thou be but " smoking flax, he will not quench thee," Isa. 42: 3. But to make sure this important work,

4. Be sure you leave not out your Mediator, the Lord Jesus Christ. Electing love doeth all in him, and so must you: ask all in his name, and then say, " Lord, he is worthy for whose sake thou shouldest do this." And, withal, take heed of patching; join not law and grace together, lest the rent be made worse: the righteousness wherein you must appear before God is not made up of divers sorts and pieces, partly his, and partly your own; but a seamless vesture, wrought throughout of one kind of substance, and by one hand: in this you may approach with boldness, and touch the top of the golden sceptre.

Infer. VIII. Having so firm and impregnable a rock to found your faith upon; why should the greatest of difficulties, even the power of inbred corruption, discourage any soul from casting itself upon electing love, as that which is perfectly able; and the very design of it is, to subdue iniquity, as well as to pardon it? It chose us, not because we were, or would be holy, but that we might be so, Eph. 1: 4. and, to that end, undertakes the whole of our work for us. It is between us and sin, as it was between Israel and the Canaanites; until the Lord began to drive, they did not stir; they were giants, too big for grasshoppers to deal with; had iron chariots, and cities walled up to heaven: and yet that company of grasshoppers turned them out; and this, because the Lord, who gave them that land, was at the head of them; he went before them, and cut their way for them; while he drove, they were driven; when he ceased, the work stood still, Psal. 44: 23. Exod. 23: 28. nay, his own people were routed, and put to the worse, John 7: 4. And we shall find both Moses and Joshua still using arguments fetched from the covenant that God had made with them, by which always they were supported. Let us do likewise, make election our all; our bread, water, munition of rocks, and whatever else we can be supposed to want: here we are sure of supply and safety: it is a tower that is really walled up to heaven; a never-to-be emptied cloud of manna, and a Jacob's well that is never dry: it is deep indeed, and you have nothing (of your own) to draw with; yet be not disheartened; stay by it, and the well itself shall rise up to you, Numb. 21: 17. rather than you shall want.

Infer. IX. Having done all you can, and in the midst of your doing, walk humbly, as living on another's bounty. Assume not to yourself, but ascribe the whole of your salvation, and of all the conducements thereto, to electing grace, and hang on that root alone: even faith itself, as it is the believer's act, is not to be rested in, nor to share in this glory. We may say of faith, as he to Felix, whom Cæsar set over them, " By thee we enjoy much quietness;" but the honor chiefly belonged to Cæsar, who gave them that governor. Give unto faith its due; " accept always, and in all places, the benefits you have by it, with all thankfulness," Acts 24: 2, 3. for it does you many good offices, and you cannot indeed live without it; only in the throne, let grace be above it; for that is the potentate which puts faith in that capacity, and maintains it there; and the truth is, true faith is best pleased with its own place. To this end, the Lord tells his people, it was not their sword nor their bow that drove out their enemies: but, say some, it was the sword and bow which God put into their hands, and which they manfully employed: no, God will not have men arrogate so much to themselves; but to acknowledge, " It is God that subdues our enemies under us," Psal. 60: 12. The people with Gideon he reckons too many to give the Midianites into their hands; why? Lest they should vaunt themselves against him, Judges 7: 2. Faith, and other graces, are mighty only through God: as they are his workmanship, so it is he only can keep them going (as a watch, or other engine, cannot wind up itself.) To frame a perpetual motion, no man hath ever attained: no, not in trifling matters. As thou hadst no hand in changing thy heart at first, so, neither, of thyself, in carrying on the work afterwards: all our sufficiency is of God; even all the strivings of the saints are " according to the workings of God in them," Col. 1: 29. A good tree will bring forth good fruit; but not without sun, air, dew, and other heavenly influences; for if separate from these, the tree itself will die: so, without a continual communication of virtue from above, Cant. 4: 16. the new creature can neither act nor live. Depend, therefore, on that radical grace (that is, on the God of all grace,) for preserving and actuating the grace he hath given you: rest not in this, that you know God; but, rather, that you are known of him.

By this, I hope, the proposition is made evident, with something of its usefulness, namely, that whatever things are requisite to salvation, are freely given of God to all the elect, and wrought in them effectually by his divine power, as a part of that salvation to which they are appointed; and are all contained in the decree of election. And I cannot but reckon it one (and that a principal part) of those works of God that stand for ever; and is so perfect, that nothing can be taken from it, nor any thing added to it; and is a good introduction into, yea, and argument for, the final perseverance of believers.

PERSEVERANCE

OR THE INVINCIBLE PROGRESS OF BELIEVERS IN FAITH AND HOLINESS

For the firmer support and comfort of his people (notwithstanding the present weakness of their faith, and daily infirmities of the flesh,) as also to allure and bring in others who are hankering about the door, or yet in the highways and hedges, it hath pleased the holy and only wise God to indulge us with plain and positive assurance of the certain continuance, and going on, of all who have once believed and received the grace of God in truth, notwithstanding many concerned in this assurance attain not to it. That faith and holiness do inseparably follow election, is shewn before: our business now is to shew, that faith and holiness are of an abiding nature, and shall never be lost: and this is what we call perseverance; which being the crown and glory of all the former points, and that which secures to us the comforts arising thence, being also as much impugned as any of those, the proof and confirmation thereof is apparently necessary, and tending to profit. And, I trust, it shall not only appear that the doctrine is true, but also replete with arguments promotive of holiness, by which the contrary opinion will best be contradicted: for so it is, in the wisdom of God, that every truth hath that in it which properly tends to its own defence and establishment. It is the property of men truly wise, to enterprise only attainable things, and things worthy their wisdom, as also, so to frame and model the means, as not to miss their intent: much more must it become, and be incumbent upon him who is wisdom itself so to do. If then the ultimate end of all things is the glory of God; and the second great end the salvation of his chosen; it may well be concluded, that the properest means for attainment are pitched upon, and those, such as will compass his end. Hence also we may be satisfied that all intermediate occurrences, however improper in their own nature, and casual to us, were all foreappointed of God, and that by a decree most wise and fixed;

and consequently are, and shall be, so dispensed and over-
ruled as not to hinder, but help on, and bring about the
thing principally designed; which therefore shall not (cannot) miscarry, nor be finally defeated. However, therefore, men of corrupt minds may stumble at the word, change
the truth of God into a lie, and turn his grace into lasciviousness; and some others, not of design, but by mistake,
and unacquaintedness with the true state of the question,
may disapprove and object against it: yet may not the truth
be discarded, nor its friends shy to own it; but strive the
more industriously, by their sobriety, meekness, holiness,
and all good fruits, to make the world know, that " to the
pure, all things are pure;" while to other men, through the
impurity of their own spirits, all things are defiled, and
turned into sin; and, in particular, that the doctrine of
God's unchangeable love to his chosen, and their endless
abiding therein, is no way an inlet or encouragement to sin,
or remissness in duty; but the most powerful strengthener
against apostacy, and most effectual quickener to gospel
obedience.

The substance of what I intend lies in this proposition:
namely,

> That all and every one of God's elect, being once rege-
> nerate and believing, are, and shall be, invincibly car-
> ried on, to the perfect obtainment of blessedness and
> glory.

Towards the evidencing of this truth,

I. Let us take in things of a lower consideration than
that of eternal salvation, and observe how those persons,
formerly instanced, being destined of God to eminent service in the world, were carried through, and that com-
pletely, to the end of their work; notwithstanding the greatest of difficulties, and natural impossibilities, which stood
in the way to obstruct it: by which will appear the certain
effect of God's purposes; and will contribute not a little to
illustrate the point in hand.

1. I begin with Abraham's seed. In Gen. 12: 7. the
land of Canaan is given them by promise: Isaac, in whom
this seed should be called, was not yet born; nor yet, until
both his parents were past age, Gen. 18: 11. To help this,

the Lord brings back the sun many degrees; makes it a new
spring time with them, and gives them Isaac, chap. 21: 2.
When Isaac was married, his wife proves barren: after
twenty years waiting, the Lord, in answer to prayer, gives
her conception, chap. 25: 21. Now, two children they had;
the elder of which the Lord rejects, ver. 23. and the other,
to whom the promise belonged, in danger every day to be
killed by his brother, and so the line of the promise in
danger of failing, chap. 27: 41. Jacob, to save his life,
flies to Padanaram, chap. 28: 2. there Laban deals hardly
with him, chap. 31: 41. and when he made homewards,
follows him with evil intent: but the Lord, in a dream,
takes him off, ver. 23, 24. No sooner is he escaped from
him, but Esau comes against him with four hundred men,
full bent to revenge the old grudge, chap. 32: 6. the Lord
turns his heart in a moment, and melts him into brotherly
affection; that, instead of destroying Jacob, he proffers
himself to be his guard and convoy, chap. 33: 4. 12.

When Simeon and Levi had so highly provoked the Canaanites, that it was a thousand to one but they would come
and cut off Jacob's family at once, chap. 24: 25. the Lord
causes a terror to fall upon them, that they do not so much
as look after them, chap. 35: 5. When a seven years' famine was coming upon the land, likely enough to eat up
poor Jacob and his house, the Lord, by a strange providence, sends a harbinger to make provision for them in
Egypt, chap. 37: 28. with chap. 41: 54. When oppressed
by the Egyptians, and all means used to destroy them, and
that both with craft and cruelty, the Lord so orders the matter, that the more they were oppressed, the faster they
grew, Exod. 1: 12. and by an high hand brings them out
at last. In the wilderness, they carry themselves as unworthily towards God as ever people did; doing all that in
them lay to cut off the entail of that good land, by their
unbelief, and daily repeated rebellions; insomuch that the
Lord threatens to dispossess them: but, for his promise'
sake made with Abraham, withdraws his hand, and spares
them. I might instance also the great straits and dangers
they were in at the Red Sea, which the Lord divided for
them: afterwards for want of water, which he brings them
out of a rock: then for bread, which also he gives them
from heaven: how they were denied passage by some, and

waylaid by others; and yet carried on and delivered: and at last, how the Lord drove out those giants, whom they despaired of overcoming, and so gave them the land in possession, according to his promise hundreds of years before: " there failed not aught of any good thing the Lord had promised: it all came to pass," Joshua 21: 45.

2. Joseph. Little Joseph is one the Lord will honor; which in several dreams he intimates to him, Gen. 37: 7. 9. 11. his brethren therefore hate him: and to frustrate his dreams, which signified their subjection to him, they conspire to kill him, ver. 18. and how shall Joseph escape? they are ten to one, and he the least.   Reuben, who, being the eldest, was most concerned, in point of honor, to hinder Joseph's advancement, he shall relent at the very moment of taking him away; and, out of respect to his father, shall deliver him, ver. 22. Well, though they will not presently kill him, they will cast him into a pit, where, in all likelihood, he must perish: but, in the good providence of God, the Ishmaelite merchants pass by in the very instant, ere any wild beast shall have found him, or his brethren determined worse against him, ver. 24. 28. to them they sell him, and by them he is brought into Egypt (far enough out of Jacob's inquiry,) and sold to the captain of Pharaoh's guard, a person likely enough to deal roughly with him. But here the Lord owns him, and, to bring him into favor, makes all that he doeth to prosper; which his master observing, puts the management of all his estate in Joseph's hands, chap. 39: 3. 4. Now there is fair hopes of his coming to honor; but how soon is it dashed! Joseph being a goodly person, his lascivious mistress tempts him to folly; which the fear of God keeping him from, she misreports him to his master, charging her own wickedness upon him. Hereby Potiphar's favor is lost, and Joseph cast into prison, and laid in irons, Gen. 39: 7. 9. 17. 20. Psal. 105: 18. Now all hopes of preferment are gone, and what will become of his dreams? yet still the counsel of the Lord, that shall stand; and this downfall of Joseph shall prove another step to his rising: and to make way for it, two of Pharaoh's servants shall fall under their lord's displeasure, be put in prison, and committed to Joseph's keeping: here they shall dream, Joseph shall interpret, and the event shall answer it.   Now the day begins again to dawn upon Joseph, and,

by the chief butler's restorement, some hopes of his enlargement: but this again is soon overcast; for the butler forgot him, Gen. 40: 23. notwithstanding all which, the providences of God do still pursue his decree, and cease not until Joseph is lord over Egypt, and his brethren bow down before him, chap. 41, and chap. 42: 6. and chap. 50: 18.

3. David. God promised David to give him the kingdom, and anoints him to it, 1 Sam. 16: 12. What, notwithstanding all possible interveniencies? Yes, for the promise is absolute: hath the Lord said it, and shall he not do it? If, therefore, Saul cast a javelin at him (unsuspected,) to nail him to the wall, a sharpness of eye, and agility of body, shall be given him to discern and avoid it, chap. 18: 11. If he determine evil against him, Jonathan shall advertise him of it, chap. 19: 7. If he send messengers to Naioth to apprehend him, they shall forget their errand, and fall a prophesying: and if he send others, and others after them, they shall do likewise; yea, Saul himself shall turn prophet for a day and a night together, that David may have time to escape, ver. 20—24. If he be in a city that will betray him, and not a friend among them to advise him of it, the Lord himself will be his intelligencer, and send him out, chap. 33: 12. If Saul's army have encompassed him, and no way left to escape, the Philistines shall invade the land, and tidings shall come in the very instant, and take him off, ver. 26, 27. If an host do encamp against him, he will not be afraid, Psal. 27: 3. Why so? The Lord had made an absolute promise; and, therefore, if no help on earth, " he shall send from heaven, and save me," Psal. 57: 3. Yea, David's wavering at times, and the weakness of his faith, shall not hinder it, and the reason of all was this, the Lord took him to be ruler over his people, and therefore he was with him wheresoever he went, 1 Chron. 17: 7, 8.

4. Josiah. " A child shall be born in the house of David, Josiah by name, who shall offer the bones of Jereboam's priests upon his altar," 1 Kings 13: 2. If, therefore, Athaliah determine to destroy all the seed-royal, Joash shall be stolen from among the rest, and preserved, 2 Kings 11: 2. and by him David's line shall be continued: and Hezekiah, though sick unto death, he shall not die, but be

healed, as it were, by a miracle, and fifteen years added to his life, rather than Manasseh, who must be Josiah's grandfather, shall be unborn, chap. 20: 6.

5. Paul. Paul was a chosen vessel, appointed to preach Christ to the Gentiles, and at last, to bear witness of him at Rome: and this must be done, although bonds, imprisonments, and death itself, do attend him in every place. If, therefore, they lie in wait for him at Damascus, and watch the gates night and day, to kill him, he shall be let down by the wall in a basket, and so escape them, Acts 9: 2—25. If all Jerusalem be in an uproar to kill him; the chief captain shall come with an army, and rescue him, Acts 21: 31, 32. though no friend to Paul, nor to his cause. If more than forty men have bound themselves with an oath, that they will neither eat nor drink until they have killed him, his kinsman shall hear of it and by his means the chief captain shall be his friend again, and grant him a sufficient convoy, chap. 23: 14—23. and this attempt shall be an occasion of sending him to Rome, where his last testimony is to be given. If Jews and Gentiles make an assault together, to use him despitefully, and to stone him, he shall be aware of it, and by fleeing save himself, chap. 14: 5, 6, 7. by which means also the gospel shall be further spread. But suppose he be left in their hands, and they so far prevail as to stone him, and drag him out of the city, ver. 19. then, sure, his work is at an end: no, all this shall not hinder; death itself shall nor separate Paul from his work. It is not his being once stoned, nor his thrice suffering shipwreck, nor his being in deaths often, nor any thing else, that shall make void the purpose of God for his bearing witness of Christ at Rome, as is abundantly evident by the stories of him, and the event at last.

Other instances might be produced to the same effect; but by these we may take an estimate of the thing under proof, and rationally infer, that if the Lord be so exact and punctual, in performing his word, touching these lesser things, carrying on his work through such a press of natural oppositions, much more will he be, in securing and bringing about the eternal welfare of his chosen: that as he dealt by his people of old; "he bore them upon eagles' wings," Exod. 19: 4. above the reach of danger, and "kept them as the apple of his eye," with all possible care and ten-

derness, " until he had brought them to himself," Deut.
32: 10. so will he carry it towards his elect; for he values
the world but little, save with respect to them.

II. Now for a more direct proof of the proposition;
though two or three witnesses might suffice to establish
it; yet, since the scriptures do abound with testimonies for
it, the collection whereof may be very useful to us, for the
help of our faith, in a time of temptation, as, also to fortify
our souls against the assaults of such as teach final apostacy,
I shall somewhat enlarge in reciting them, with some of
those genuine deductions that flow from them.   In the Old
Testament are many petitions and resolves made by holy
men, which import the truth of this doctrine, as, that " the
Lord will perfect that which concerns them: that he will
not forsake the work of his own hands," Psal. 138: 8. " that
he will guide them by his counsel, and after receive them
to glory," Psal. 73: 24. and that in the mean time, " none of
their ste ps shall slide," Psal. 37: 31. and this, because it
is God that "girdeth them with strength, and will make their
way perfect," Psal. 18: 32. with abundantly more; as also
in Paul's Epistles.   In every of which is implied a promise
of the thing prayed for, or concluded upon; without such a
promise, they could not have done it in faith, nor justly
have given them down as matter of instruction to others.
But we know they spake as they were moved by the Holy
Ghost, 2 Pet. 1: 21. who knowing the deep things of God,
what his decrees were, and what was contained in the
" promise of eternal life before the world began," Tit. 1:
2. drew out their hearts to believe, and formed their prayers accordingly.

But, besides these, we have many express promises and
affirmations of it.   In the tenth of John, our Saviour says,
" his sheep shall never perish," ver. 28. which is, in effect,
their faith shall never fail; for, safe they cannot be from
perishing, without the securement of their faith.   Again,
speaking of the Spirit of holiness which believers receive
from him, John 4: 14. he saith expressly, " whosoever
drinketh thereof, shall never thirst: but it shall be in him
a well of water, springing up to everlasting life," then it
shall not be dried up, Prov. 10: 30. " The righteous shall
never be removed," that is, they shall never fall back into
their former state; and the reason is, because " the way of

the Lord is strength to the upright," ver. 29. Whether by
" the way of the Lord" be meant his way or manner of dealing with upright persons, which is to increase their strength,
according to Job, 17: 9. or, of the genuine property of God's
ways, which is to afford that peace and satisfaction to those
who walk in them, that they are daily more habituated and
connaturalized to them, and estranged from all ways else;
they are both to the purpose in hand, Prov. 24: 19. " A just
man falleth seven times, and riseth up again;" he falls not so
as to lie where he fell; he falleth not into mischief, as the
wicked do; yea he rather gets ground by his fall, as ver. 5.
" A man of wisdom increaseth strength," from a sense of
his own weakness, he is led to strength everlasting, as
was Paul, 2 Cor. 12: 10.

Prov. 12: 21. " There shall no evil happen to the just,"
then, not the greatest and worst of evils, which is, to " depart from the living God:" verse 3. " The root of the
righteous shall not be removed;" his fruit may sometimes
be blighted, or blown off, his branches tossed with a tempest; but still his root is where it was; his life is hid, and
free from all commotion, and shall therefore renew both his
fruit and branches; " he that trusteth in the Lord, shall
not cease from yielding fruit," Jer. 17: 7, 8.

Jer. 32: 40. " I will put my fear in their hearts, that
they shall not depart from me." This, say some, is the
promise of affording them means, but not of effecting the
end; therefore see chap. 3: 19. " Thou shalt call me, My
Father, and shalt not depart from me:" and this, because he
worketh effectually in them that believe, 1 Thess. 2: 13.
as at first in causing them to believe, so now, in maintaining and perfecting their faith.

Psalm 84: 11. " The Lord withholdeth no good thing
from them that walk uprightly:" and if so, then continuing
to walk uprightly shall not be withheld from them; which
deduction is also warranted by this; " that the righteous
shall hold on his way, and he that hath clean hands, shall
be stronger and stronger," Job 17: 9. as also from Prov. 4:
18. " The path of the just is as the shining light, which
shineth more and more unto the perfect day." And David further backs it, where, from his present faith, he concludes his future progress, " I have trusted I shall not
slide," Psal. 26: 1. and this, because the Lord holdeth his

soul in life, and suffereth not his feet to be moved, Psal.
66: 9.

Mark 16: 16. " He that believeth shall be saved:" and
John 11: 26. " Whosoever liveth and believeth in me
(says Christ) shall never die," that is, he that once has faith
shall never lose it (as some would give the sense) had
been a comfortless and empty notion, and injudicious way
of speaking.   This is yet further confirmed by John 5: 24.
" He that believeth is passed from death unto life, and shall
not come into condemnation:" the reason of which is this,
that their faith is founded on a rock; which winds and
waves may beat and break themselves against; but never
the rock itself nor that which is built upon it, Mat. 7: 25.
" He that trusteth in the Lord, is as mount Zion, which
cannot be removed," Psal. 125: 1. no, not so much as one
of the stakes of that tabernacle shall be removed, and that
for ever, Isa. 33: 20. 1 Pet. 2: 6. " They shall not be ashamed nor confounded, world without end," Isa. 45: 17.

It would very much allay that superlative cause of rejoicing, that our names are written in heaven, if possibly
they might be blotted out again; since we find in ourselves
so great a proneness to revolt, which every one acquainted
with his own heart must acknowledge: but we are sure
Christ would not propound to us a fallible ground of rejoicing: for that kind of dependance he is evermore calling us
from.   Believers are indeed sometimes foiled, but never
overcome: though they fall, and that seven times in a day,
(as was said,) as often do they rise again: and it is no disparagement to their leader: nay, it is the glory of a general,
to give his enemy advantages, and take them again at his
pleasure, to his enemy's greater confusion and overthrow.
Satan got nothing by his winnowing Peter: Peter lost some
of his chaff, which well might be spared, and the tempter lost many an after-advantage; for the world of believers
have been the warier ever since.   To this I shall only add
that of the holy apostle, in Rom. 8: he was persuaded, that
is, he was thoroughly swayed in his faith, to believe it for
himself, and deliver it down to the ages to come, as a truth
infallible, that " neither height, nor depth, nor any other
creature, shall be able to separate from the love of God,
which is in Christ Jesus our Lord," ver. 38, 39.   He reckons up all that can be named; and, lest any thing might

have slipt him, he brings in height and depth; as being those two extremes that take in all, and more than men can think; and then resolves, that even these shall not be able to do it. And, surely, if the super-celestial height of God's holiness, nor the infra-infernal depth of sinful sin, shall not separate from that day of glory, which the sons of God were predestinated to, and for which they were both made and redeemed, called into, and groan for, then are believers roundly secured against final apostacy.

III. A third sort of evidence for confirmation, are certain arguments or reasons why the saints must needs persevere in faith and holiness.

By needs must, I understand no other kind of necessity, than well consists with perfect freedom; such as was upon Paul to preach the gospel, which was a work he rejoiced in; and such as was upon Jesus Christ to bring home his sheep, and to lay down his life for them; he "must needs suffer," Acts 17: 3. " Yea, he was straitened till it was accomplished," Luke 12: 50. That it was written in his heart, was no hindrance to the freedom of his will.

Arg. I. The first argument, in proof of perseverance, is founded on the saints' extract or original, "they are born of God," John 1: 13. and this hath the force of a double argument.

1. As God is their father and eternal root. Our Saviour holds forth this relation as the ground of our faith in prayer, Matt. 6: 9. and he begins with it himself, when he prays for his own glory, and that his disciples might be partakers of it, John 17: 1. to the same end, he frequenty useth that style of Father in the gospel of John; as taking delight in mentioning that relation, " the Father himself loveth you," chap. 16: 27. and " I ascend to my Father, and your Father," chap. 20: 17. It is to strengthen our faith in God, (through himself) on the account of his fatherhood to us. " The father loveth the Son," chap. 3: 25. and he loves his believers, as he loveth Christ himself, chap. 17: 23. on which ground the apostle concludes, that " he cannot but give us all things else," Rom. 8: 32. Believers are the product of his love, both in respect of election and regeneration; and being so, he cannot but have a paternal affection for them; to administer to them whatever tends to their sustentation and growth, and to

keep off whatever would intercept or weaken his gracious influences towards them: " having once loved them, he loves them for ever," John 13: 1. They may therefore be confident, that " what he hath begun in the spirit, he will not let end in the flesh:" that " having begun a good work, he will also perform it," Phil. 1: 6. for, as they have their spiritual being from him, as the Father of it; so it is as natural to him to diffuse his virtues into them without intermission, as for a vine to send up its sap into its own branches, or the sun to cherish the plants of its own production. All the natural affections that are in creatures towards their own, are but drops of his immense fulness: a mother may possibly forget the child of her womb; but the Lord cannot forget his offspring; " that none may hurt them, (nor they themselves,) he will keep them night and day, and water them every moment," Isa. 27: 3. they are born by him from the belly, and carried from the womb; and even to their old age he will carry them, and deliver them, Isa. 46: 3, 4.

2. The new creature, as it comes from God, so it exists in him, and lives upon him, and it is natural to it to seek its nourishment where it had its original: nothing can satisfy it, but that great deep from whence it sprung: as a new-born child, that has not the use of reason, will hunt for the breast by natural instinct, and not be quiet without it. As soon as ever Paul was converted, " Behold he prays," Acts 9: 11. Having once received the Spirit of Christ, they cannot but incline after him, as Elisha did to Elijah, upon the casting of his mantle upon him, 1 Kings 19: 19, 20. it is natural to them, as for sparks to fly upwards. They are said to be " baptized with fire;" not only because of its purifying nature, but in respect of its aspiring quality; it will be mounting, and not rest till it comes to its own element. Obstructions many it meets withal; but still it presseth onwards, and by degrees bears down all before it, and carries that with it in which it dwells, to the place of its birth; as the dove could not rest till she came to the ark whence she set out. This is set forth in a lively manner by our Saviour, in John 7: 38. " He that believeth in me, out of his belly shall flow rivers of living waters;" rivers that bear down all opposition; and rivers of living waters, not land floods, which are of but short continuance; or

standing pools, subject to drying up; but rivers, and those such as have an immortal head. We see how all things tend to their centre: " The wicked sleep not unless they do evil," Prov. 4: 16. They can bear the want of things most necessary to their being, rather than cease from sin: they are of the serpent's brood, and " the lusts of their father they will do," John 8: 44. Judas was a devil, and that carried him headlong to his own place, Acts 1: 25. And if being born of the devil, habituates men with so strong and restless a bent to devilish lusts, the divine nature must needs work as efficaciously towards God, and godlike actions: his love constrains them, 2 Cor. 5: 14. And if it were not so, the ingrafted word had never borne a human stock to heaven: the first fruits of the Spirit possess them with an earnest expectation and longing for the harvest, Rom. 8: 23. It is true, the remainders of the old man will be opposing the new, and many contests there are between them: but grace (like him that is advocate for the king) will ever have the last word, and will also go out victor. Ye may see it in Jeremiah, the word of the Lord was made a reproach to him; he therefore resolves to stifle it, and will no more speak in his name. But how succeeds this carnal resolution? " The word of the Lord was in his heart, as fire shut up in his bones, he was weary of forbearing, he could not hold," chap. 20: 8, 9. And Jonas, when he thought himself cut off, and in the belly of hell; " yet (saith he,) will I look again towards thy holy temple," Jonah 2: 2. 4. Psal. 84: 6,7. (as the needle, that is rightly touched, never rests, but in pointing towards the pole;) and when obstructed in their course, they cry the more earnestly, " O, when shall I come and appear before God?" Psal. 42: 2.

Arg. II. Another argument is taken from the graces themselves, which are the subjects of perseverance; namely, faith and holiness: which, let us consider first, as they are a gift, then in the genuine use and property of them.

1. As they are a gift. They are of those good and perfect gifts which come down from above, from the Father of lights, with whom is no variableness, nor shadow of turning," James 1: 17, 18. This attribute of God's unchangeableness is fitly and significantly added, to show, that as good and perfect gifts are from God, and from him

only; so that he never changeth in his purpose concerning those to whom he once gives them; they are of those gifts which are without repentance: as also, that these gifts do partake of his own unvariableness; they cannot die, nor turn to be any other than what they were at first, save only in point of perfection. There can happen no after-unworthiness in those he gives them to, which he did not foresee when he gave them, (which seems to be implied in the following words, "Of his own will begat he us,") and so, no cause why he should withdraw them, which would not as well have hindered his giving them at first. As the word of God is not yea and nay, so neither are his gifts. They are also God's workmanship; and "we know, saith Solomon, that whatsoever God doeth, it shall be for ever, nothing can be put to it, nor any thing taken from it," Eccl. 3:14.

2. Let faith and holiness be considered in the genuine use and property of them. Nothing so endangers the soul as self-fulness; faith, therefore, was ordained to nullify that, and devolve the soul on another, namely, Christ; which the more it does, the safer it is; and having once done it, it never undoes it again. Faith also is an active grace, and diligent, and therefore thriving; he that hath it, shall have more of it, Luke 19: 26. then sure he shall not lose that he hath! it is always travelling and never tired; 1. Because it travels in the strength of Omnipotence, "which never faints, nor is weary," Isa. 40: 28. and, 2. Because it works by love, Gal. 5: 6. which is the most kindly and efficacious principle of service and great acts. Love is an endless screw: it has truly attained the perpetual motion; it enables to endure all things, and faileth not, 1 Cor. 13: 7, 8. All that God doeth for his people is from love, John 3: 16. and all that they do for God grows from the same root; they love him, because he loved them first, 1 John 4: 19. Love is that which renders a work both pleasant to the agent, and acceptable to the object of it; faith, therefore, working by love, shall never be weary of its work, nor fail of its end; " it is of faith, that it might be by grace," and consequently sure, Rom. 4: 16. And as for holiness, (which is a disposition according to God, and capacitates for the blessed vision,) a little of it, in truth, is of infinite value; the very smoke of it shall not be quenched, Matt. 12: 20. and it would be strange, if a thing so precious should be liable to

putrefaction; but it is not; yea, it changeth other things, but is itself never changed. It is of a spreading nature; compared therefore to leaven put into dough, and hid there, till the whole lump be seasoned. It is of an assimilating property; there is an heavenly tincture in it, which sanctifies all that it touches; " to the pure all things are pure," Tit. 1: 15. It also meetens for converse with God, and it draws and engages the soul to him; there it is in its proper element, and out of which it cannot live; and by this converse it is both increased and sublimated.

A natural body, once in being, can never be reduced to nothing; how then should things of divine substance? They are " born of incorruptible seed, which liveth and abideth for ever," 1 Pet. 1: 23. and as the seed is, such will be the fruit; the older it grows, the firmer it is; " he that hath clean hands shall be stronger and stronger," Job 17: 9. They are the holy seed; and, therefore, though they cast their leaves, at times, " their substance is in them," Isa. 6: 13. by which they are still renewed. Holiness is the seed of glory; and holy persons are in glory, as to its kind, and the certainty of their obtainment; although it has no glory at present, in comparison with that which shall be, as the seed of the rose or lily, compared with the flowers they will grow into, and which are virtually in them. According with this is that of our Saviour, " He that believeth, hath everlasting life," John 3: 36. it argues the certainty of their perseverance, " the law of his God is in his heart; none of his steps shall slide," Psal. 37: 31. and therefore he saith, " Destroy it not, there is a blessing in it," Isa. 65: 5. 8.

Arg. III. Another proof arises from the nature, extent, and design of providence; or from the intent and purpose of God, in that great variety of things which believers are exercised with in the world. There are three things to be considered to make out this argument.

1. That there is a divine providence which governs the world; as in dividing to the nations their inheritance, and bounding their habitations, at first; so by continuing them in possession, or removing them, at his pleasure; and this, sometimes, by very unlikely means, and over-ruling things accordingly. Seir being given to Esau, and Ar to the children of Lot, and their term not yet expired, the Lord inclines them to let Israel pass through, and to give them

meat for their money: whereas the Amorites, who were destined to destruction, " he hardens their spirits, and makes them obstinate," Deut. 2: 29, 30. that they deny them passage, and come out against them in battle. So, when he would translate the Chaldean monarchy to the Persians, he enfeebles the one, but stirs up the other's spirits, and " girds them with strength," Jer. 15: 11. Isa. 45: 1— 5. How often doth the scripture repeat, " that the Lord reigneth: that he puts down one, and sets up another," Psal. 93: 1. 97: 1. 75: 7. " that he doeth according to his will in the armies of heaven, and amongst the inhabitants of the earth," Dan. 4: 35. How evident is it in his humbling of Pharaoh, Nebuchadnezzar, and others? This providence reacheth to all manner of persons, times, and things, and circumscribes them: it leaves not the least things to a contingency; even ravens, sparrows, and lilies; yea, and the hairs of your head are all numbered, and under the conduct of the providence of God, Matt. 6: 26.

2. That the design and course of God's providence is to accomplish his purpose. As providence governs the world, so purpose is the director of providence. He is a provident man that orders his affairs prudently; that is, so that nothing is wanting, nor any thing spent in waste. Both these are in the providence of God eminently: for, 1. It is all-sufficient; supplies all needs; gives all things pertaining to means and end. 2. It does nothing in vain, nothing superfluous or impertinent to his purpose. Things most casual to men are levelled at a set and certain end: " what the Lord speaks with his mouth, he fulfils with his hand," 1 Kings 8: 24. and his act shall not vary a tittle from his decree: for, known unto God are all his works from the beginning of the world. Whence was it that Esau tarried so long at hunting that he was over faint? that Jacob was making pottage just when Esau came in, which set his appetite on edge after it, but that the purpose of God, according to election, might stand? the elder must serve the younger, which now came to pass, by the sale of his birthright? and thus the providence of God makes even the profaneness of men subservient to his end. The Lord had determined to cast Judah and Jerusalem out of his sight for their obstinacy; and to this end (that is, to make way for it,) " It came to pass, that Zedekiah rebelled against the

king of Babylon," 2 Kings 24: 20. it was to fulfil the word
of the Lord before declared, 2 Chron. 36: 21. though that
was far from the rebel's intent. So he gave Cyrus all
the kingdoms of the earth, that he might build his temple
at Jerusalem; and it was to fulfil his purpose before also recorded, as is evident, ver. 22, 23. In like manner, Herod,
Pilate, and the Jews, all conspire the death of Christ,
and each party on a several account; not thinking in the
least to fulfil the determinate counsel of God: yet that was
it which providence intended, as is plain by Acts 2: 23.
As also the soldiers, in parting his garments, and piercing
his side: it was their barbarous rudeness which put them
upon it; but providence designed to make good a prophecy;
" these things therefore the soldiers did," John 19: 24. All
that God does in the world, is the transcript or impression
of his ancient decrees.

3. That the providence of God never fails of its end. If
he will work, who shall hinder it? for " our God is in heaven,
and doeth whatsoever he will," Psal. 115: 3. And what
will he work? " the things that are coming, and shall come,"
Isa. 44: 7. " he hath both devised, and done it," Jer. 51:
12. His purpose is to preserve his people; and, therefore,
" no weapon that is formed against them shall prosper: whosoever gathers together against them shall fall for their
sakes," Isa. 54: 15: 17. " for as he hath purposed, so it
shall stand," chap. 14: 24. The scriptures abound with
instances of this kind: as, on the contrary, when the Lord
will execute judgment, the thing shall be done, be the
means ever so weak and improbable; " though the army
of the Chaldeans were all wounded men, yet shall they
burn Jerusalem with fire," Jer. 37: 10. Shamgar shall kill
six hundred men with an ox-goad, Judg. 3: 13. and Samson a thousand with the jawbone of an ass, chap. 15: 15.
These things considered, and laid together (though mostly
referring to temperal things,) do strongly enforce the argument for things of spiritual concernment: inasmuch as
things of eternal moment are worthy of more peculiar regard and security.

Now, all a believer's exercises, which may seem to endanger him, are either from the guilt of sins committed;
from the power of indwelling corruption; from Satan's
temptation, or persecution from the world: none of which

come on them accidentally, but as things fore-appointed of God, and for a good intent. It is " for the elect's sake that all things else have their being," 2 Cor. 4: 15. " and are all caused to work together for their good," Rom. 8: 28. as, namely, to humble them for sin; to wean them from the world; to endear Jesus Christ to them; to shew them the usefulness of ordinances; to exercise and try their graces; to purge out their dross; to enable them to succor others; to demonstrate the wisdom, power, and faithfulness of God towards them; to meeten them for glory; and to make them groan and long to be clothed upon with their house from heaven; as might plentifully be made out by the scriptures, and the visible effects thereof upon those who have been exercised thereby. To instance a few particulars: David, after that great miscarriage in the matter of Uriah, with his broken bones upon it, walked the more humbly and warily all his days: he was also the more intent on that great duty of " teaching sinners the way of God," Psal. 51: 13. Peter, he also got ground by denying his master; thereby he came to see his own weakness, the need he had of Christ's support, and continual prayer for him; and we hear no more of his carnal confidence after that: but what a clamor and outcry does he make against our adversary the devil! 1 Pet. 5: 8. to warn others by his own example, what danger they are in by a carnal confidence. And, doubtless, whatever the tempter got by Peter's fall, he lost twice as much by the after watchfulness of others; for that is the designed end, to strengthen, establish, and settle them, ver. 10. Luke 22: 31. Paul had a messenger of Satan let loose upon him, to buffet him; the end of which was, to humble him, and to shew him the sufficiency of the grace of Christ. It is likely, also, that he got as much by that thorn in his flesh, as by his rapture and revelation: to be sure, they did well together, and poised him the better for his work. The like effect upon Job, Job 23: 10. with chap. 40: 4. and chap. 42: 6. Mary Magdalen, the remembrance of the seven devils which once possessed her, and of that love which cast them out; how did it heighten her love to Christ, and keep her heart in a melting frame! " she loved much, because much was forgiven her," Luke 7: 47. The people's forty years' travel through that great and terrible wilderness, among fiery ser-

pents and scorpions, it was to prove them, and to do them
good in the latter end, Deut. 8: 15, 16. They were also
sent into captivity for their good, Jer. 24: 5. this was all
the fruit intended, to take away their sin, Isa. 27: 9. to
make them partakers of his holiness, Heb. 12: 10. These
things, indeed, at present, are physic, which nature desires not: yet they are as needful, in their season, as our
food; and in very faithfulness we must have them; which
also is evident by the scope of the new covenant; as will
appear afterwards. Now, these things considered and laid
together, I think it may be well inferred, that " all these
things worketh God with man," not to destroy him, but to
bring back his soul from the pit," Job 33: 29, 30. they are
all made to turn to their salvation; they have always triumphed over them, and been " more than conquerors,
through him that loved them," Rom. 8: 37. and ever shall.
And if this be the fruit of all that doth or can befal a believer, while in this world, and there is no more of evil or
danger when this is done, then welcome let them be, by
the grace of God, as another demonstration of their invincible perseverance. " Whoso is wise, and will observe
these things, even they shall understand the loving kindness of the Lord," Psal. 107: 43.

   Arg. IV. A fourth argument for the saints' perseverance,
is built on their union with Christ, which is of that inti-
mateness, that the scripture sets it forth by terms of the
nearest relation, as foundation and building, vine and
branches, father and children, husband and spouse, head
and members, yea, they are both called, interchangeably,
by the same name; he is called Jacob, and they are called
Christ, Psal. 24: 6. with 1 Cor. 12: 12. And, which is
more, if more can be, he communicates to them that title
which one would think incommunicable, namely, " The
Lord our righteousness," Jer. 23: 6. with 33: 16. And this
union is such as can never be dissolved: there is the like
oneness between Christ and them, as between the Father
and Christ, as is plain by that passage of his prayer in the
17th of John, 21. " That they all may be one" (how one?)
" as thou Father art in me, and I in thee, that they may be
one in us." They are so near to him, that they are said to
be " of his flesh, and of his bones," Eph. 5: 30. as, also,
that they are " one spirit," 1 Cor. 6: 17. He and they are

actuated by the same Spirit, as the head and members of the same body are by one soul.

And this is the reason why believers cannot walk after the flesh. "The Spirit of life which is in Christ Jesus (as their root) rules in them," Rom. 8: 2. They are preserved in Christ, Jude ver. 1. as Noah was in the ark; or as branches in their own stock: for this difference is still to be noted, that believers have not this life in themselves, as Christ hath; but they have it in him, which is better for them than if in their own keeping: for, being in him as in a root, it is natural to him to communicate to them; and as natural to them, by virtue of the divine nature communicated to them, to derive from him: and, consequently, "because, and while he lives, they shall live also," John 14: 19. "he that hath the Son hath life," 1 John 5: 12. and they have it in a way of right; as he that is possessed of the soil has right to all that grows upon it. All that is Christ's is theirs; there is a happy commutation of interests; their debts, with the consequences thereof, are devolved upon him; and all that was his imputed and communicated to them. And his care of them is such, that he will be able to say at the latter day, "Of all that thou hast given me, I have lost nothing," John 17: 12. he will not leave a hoof behind. The signet on his right hand (men of shining outsides) may possibly be plucked thence. Jer. 22: 24. but the least joint of his finger shall not; no man that is *compos mentis* will suffer the meanest part of himself to gangrene and perish, if it be in his power to help it; how then should our Lord Christ? who, besides the natural affection he hath to those of his own body, Eph. 5: 25. hath also received a commandment from the Father to keep them safe, John 6: 40. and is perfectly qualified in all respects to make it good. On this account, as well as others, they are "complete in him," Col. 2: 10. Believers are so one with Christ, that whatsoever he did, they are said to do it with him; circumcised with him, ver. 11. crucified with him, Rom. 6: 6. buried with him, ver. 4. risen with him, ver. 5. ascended with him, Eph. 4: 8. and they sit in heaven with him, chap. 2: 6. It is no more possible for believers to miscarry finally, than for Christ himself to be held under the power of the grave; there is one law for them both: it is a faithful saying, "If we be dead with him, we shall also live with him," 2 Tim. 2: 11. "If we suffer with him, we shall be glorified together," Rom. 8: 17. As Christ once raised, dies no more, chap. 6: 9. so none of those raised with him, shall return any more to corruption: for he gave himself for his church; not only to sanctify and cleanse it once, but once for all; and to "present it without spot or wrinkle," at the last day, Eph. 5: 25,26,27. by that "one offering, he perfected for ever them that are sanctified," Heb. 10:14. These are those "sure mercies of David," recorded in the fifty-fifth chapter of Isaiah, and explained in the thirteenth chapter of the Acts.

It is not for nothing that our blessed Lord and Saviour so often repeats that good word and promise concerning believers, which surely he did as being greatly pleased with the thoughts of it; "I will raise him up at the last day;" and "I will raise him up at the last day," John 6: 39, 40. 44. 54. *q. d.* "I will be with him unto the end of the world, and see him safe in heaven;" and this may be said of it, as by Joseph to Pharaoh, "the thing is doubled, because it is established of God, and he will bring it to pass," Gen. 41: 32.

Arg. V. Another argument for believers' invincible perseverance, is, that all the attributes of God do stand engaged for it. Virtue invincible has undertaken it; therefore it must needs succeed.

1. Power. In Jer. 32: 27. God's sovereign power over all flesh is laid down as the ground of their faith, touching their return from captivity, and his giving them a new heart; and for his so keeping them, that they "should not depart from him any more," as they had done, Jer. 32: 36—41. So, when he would strengthen his fainting people, he styles himself, "The everlasting God, the Lord, the Creator of the ends of the earth, who fainteth not, neither is weary," Isa. 40: 28. and which is yet more, his right hand, and the arm of his strength are engaged by oath, chap. 42: 8. In 2 Tim. 1: 12. the apostle argues the certainty of his salvation from the power of God; which he could not have done with any good reason or comfort, had not that power been engaged for it. "I am not ashamed—for I know in whom I have believed, and that he is able to keep that I have committed to him against that day." And he gives the like counsel to others, where he points at the "power of God,

to make all grace abound in them," 2 Cor. 9: 8.   The call-ing also of the Jews, and grafting them into Christ, is laid on the same rock, for " God is able to graft them in again," Rom. 11: 23. Col. 1: 11.   In Eph. ch. 6. he tells them what kind of enemies they were to wrestle with, namely, " prin-cipalities and powers, and spiritual wickednesses in high places," Eph. 6: 12. a sort of adversaries too potent for spirits housed in clay: but, to harness them fit for the bat-tle, he shows them a power that is higher than those, and, indeed, much more above them, than they above us; and with this he would have them to invest themselves.   " Be strong in the Lord, and in the power of his might," ver. 10. this is an armor complete; aptly termed, " the whole armor of God," ver. 11. and in this strong tower believers are safe. So likewise in Eph. ch.1. to confirm them, touching the hope of calling, he brings in the mighty power of God, even " that exceeding greatness of his power, by which he raised Jesus Christ from the dead, and set him at his own right hand, far above all principalities and powers, and putting all things un-der his feet," ch. 1: 19—22. wherein he sets forth Christ as a pattern of what God will do for believers; they shall be rais-ed and set above all, as he was. And though they sometimes fall, (" for there is no man which sinneth not," 1 Chron. 6: 36.) let it make them more wary, but not discourage them, " for they shall not be utterly cast down," Psal. 37: 24. and this, because " the Lord upholdeth them with his hand." The archers may shoot at them, and sorely grieve them; yet shall their " bow abide in strength, and the arms of their hands be made strong by the hands of the mighty God of Jacob," Gen. 49:23,24.   And well it is for us that the di-vine power hath undertaken this difficult work, and that the scriptures do so clearly avouch it; for nothing less could be a buttress sufficient to stay our faith upon, touch-ing our holding out to the end; but because " he is strong in power, not one faileth," Isa. 40:26.

2. Wisdom. This is an ability to fit and direct means to their proper end. In matters of less concern, we find the Lord so laying his work that it cannot miscarry. If, therefore, it be his good pleasure to ordain men to salva-tion, his wisdom requires that it be in such a way as is sure to succeed, and that all sorts of impediments be either prevented, or so over-ruled as not to interrupt, but become

subservient to this great end. Having counted his cost, and paid it off, and also begun to build, it behooves his wisdom to see that his work be done, and brought to perfection, Luke 14: 29, 30. and accordingly to provide suitable instruments, such as he knows will do, and yet not overdo the thing intended; much like to the husbandman sorting his seed to the nature of the soil, and threshing instruments to the capacity of his grain; he will not use a wheel, where the rod will serve; nor a rod, where the wheel is needful: and this he hath from his God, "who instructeth him to discretion," Isa. 28: 25. 28. So, the Lord "stayeth the rough wind in the day of the east-wind," chap. 27: 8. he does not only design the end of a man's journey, but every step in it is of his ordering, Psal. 37: 23. Job 31: 4. " the Lord preserveth his going out, and his coming in," Psal. 121: 8. In Isaiah 26: 7. the Lord is said "to weigh the path of the just," which is not meant only of his observing their works, and dispensing to them accordingly; but as pre-pondering what they are to do, and what is requisite for their doing of it, and apportioning their faith and assistance answerably. As at the making of the world " he weighed the mountains in scales, and the hills in a balance," Isa. 40: 12. that its parts might be of equal weight; or, as one that is to run in a race, and must carry weights about him, will be wise to have them equally poised; so the Lord sets one thing against another in our souls' concerns. Paul, therefore, brings in this wisdom of God, as well as his power, to help their faith touching their establishment, Rom. 16: 25,27. and the apostle Jude, in the close of his epistle, gives glory to God, " as the only wise God," upon the account of " his keeping them from falling; and presenting them faultless before the presence of his glory," Jude ver. 24, 25.

3. Honor. The concernment of God's honor, is also an important argument for proof of his doctrine: the Lord's manner of dealing with his people of old, and the reason of it, is an instance above contradiction. The promise of giving them Canaan was not more absolute than the promise of salvation to believers; nor was it less clogged with conditions, threatenings, and cautions, which were afterwards added; but, the promise being once made absolute "To thy seed will I give this land," Gen. 12: 7. chap. 15: 18.

the Lord held himself obliged in honor to make it good. How often did he seem to be pouring out his wrath to destroy them? first in Egypt, then in the wilderness, &c. Ezek. 20: 8.--40. And what kept it off, but the interest of his honor? this put him upon finding out ways to deliver them; " I wrought (says he) for my name's sake," ver. 14. The Lord did, as it were, labor to suppress his righteous fury, incensed by their intolerable provocations, his name and honor were concerned, and that held his hands; he had once made an absolute promise, which therefore must be made good; though they made themselves ever so unworthy of it. We likewise find, in the 48th of Isaiah, that they had dealt very treacherously, than which nothing is more provoking; but says the Lord, " For mine own sake will I defer mine anger:" and again, " For mine own sake, even for mine own sake, will I do it; for how should my name be polluted?" Isa. 48: 9. 11. The Lord will overlook a thousand transgressions, rather than expose his name and honor to reproach, as once it was by a temporary suspension; to recover which, and that his name might be sanctified, he will bring them home again; yea, though it be in the eyes of men a thing impossible; and they themselves do think so likewise; for, " our hope is lost and we are cut off," Ezek. 37: 11. and, again, my " hope is perished from the Lord," Lam. 3: 18. Whether at home, or abroad, they still caused his name to be profaned; and for this his holy name, he had pity on them, Ezek. 36: 20. for if he should have cast them off for ever, it would have been said, that he did not foresee how unworthy a people they would be; or, he was not able to keep them in their own land, nor to bring them back again; or else, that he was changeable in his purposes, and not true to his word, &c. Some reflection or other they would cast upon him, which he would not bear. All which, and much more of a like kind, is applicable to believers with respect to their perseverance.

4. Justice, or Righteousness. There can hardly be found a firmer support, or more full consolation to believers, than that the justice of God is engaged to save them; " for, the righteous Lord loveth righteousness," Psal. 11: 7. and "cannot deny himself." He would not justify any, no, not his very elect, but in a way consistent with his justice: for which cause, he sent forth his Son a propitiation for

sin. Surely, then, having received the atonement, he will not expose his justice to censure, by leaving them in any-wise obnoxious to condemnation. Salvation now is their due, his grace hath made it so, by both giving and accepting such a price for it, as engageth righteousness itself to save them; for, " who shall condemn, since it is Christ that died?" Rom. 8: 34. it is as righteous a thing with God to give rest to his people, as tribulation to those that trouble them, 2 Thess. 1: 6, 7. Paul therefore builds his expectation of the crown upon this attribute, as well as any other; " henceforth is laid up for me a crown of righteousness, which the Lord, the righteous Judge, shall give me at that day," 2 Tim. 4: 8. The righteousness of God secures to them their holding out, " to finish their course, and to keep the faith," as well as the reward when their work is done. " God is not unrighteous to forget his people's labor of love," Heb. 6: 10. much less Christ's. This gave the apostle to be persuaded better things of those he writes to, than to be subject to falling away, Heb. 6: 9. The blood of the everlasting covenant, is engaged to make them perfect in every good work, to do his will, chap. 13: 20, 21. Yea, they shall bring forth fruit in their old age, Psal. 92: 14. and this, to declare that the Lord is upright, and no unrighteousness in him, verse 15.

5. The faithfulness, or truth of God, is also concerned in the final perseverance of believers. For, having drawn them from all created bottoms, to a total reliance on himself he cannot but give them that they have trusted him for. The Lord will not be to his people, as that broken staff Egypt was to the Jews, to fail them at their greatest need; which is, when they are lost, driven away, broken, and sick, and perhaps have no mind to return; as Ephraim, who " went on frowardly," Isa. 57: 17, 18. then is the fit time for the faithfulness of God to discover itself, by seeking them out, bringing them back, binding them up, healing, and comforting them, Exek. 34: 16. To heal their back-slidings, as it shows the freeness of God's love, so his faithfulness. " The Lord will not behold iniquity in Jacob," Numb. 23: 21. that is, he will not take notice of it, so as to recede from his word; for he could not but see their perverseness and murmurings; for which he punished them severely; and sometimes made as if he would disin-

herit them: but still he remembered his covenant, and that restrained it; the Lord had blessed, and therefore men could not reverse it; neither themselves, by their insufferable contumacy, nor Balaam with his enchantments, verse 20. "The Lord loveth judgment" that is, truth and faithfulness, and "therefore he forsaketh not his saints, they are preserved for ever," Psal. 37: 28. The saints are in league with God, "they have made a covenant with him by sacrifice," Psal. 50: 5. and it is a league of his own propounding, by which he hath obliged himself to protect them. And though men may break their compacts, the holy One of Israel will not; "he is not a man, that he should lie, nor the son of man, that he should repent," Numb. 23: 19. David having made God his fortress, concludes from thence, that "the name of God was engaged to lead, and to guide him," Psal. 16: 1. with Psal. 31: 3, 4. Those Corinthians were as liable to temptations, as other men who fell by them; for they had strong remainders of corruption, as appears by both the epistles, and a subtle adversary to observe and draw it out; besides, they were highly gifted, and so the more ready to think themselves above the rank of ordinary christians; than which nothing could more expose them to danger: but notwithstanding all these disadvantages, they shall be kept; the faithfulness of God, that secures them, and "shall confirm them unto the end," 1 Cor. 1: 8, 9. for "God is faithful, (says he,) by whom ye were called;" it is as if he had said, God would never have called you into the fellowship of his Son, if he had not resolved to keep you there. So, again, he tells them, "God will not suffer them to be tempted above what they are able," 1 Cor. 10: 13. and he brings it in as an inference from the faithfulness of God. He likewise lays the stress of his confidence for the Thessalonians' being preserved blameless unto the coming of Christ, upon the same attribute; "Faithful is he that called you, who also will do it," 1 Thess. 5: 23, 24. And when he would move the Hebrews to purpose, to hold fast the profession of their faith without wavering, he uses the same engine, "faithful is he that promised," Heb. 10: 23. Peter, also directs the saints to "commit their souls unto God, in well doing, as unto a faithful Creator," 1 Pet. 4: 19. Now, the scripture always propounds to us,

such attributes and motives as are proper to the matter in
hand; and, therefore, in styling God, here, a " faithful
Creator," it is as much as to say " he that hath wrought
you for this self-same thing is God," 2 Cor. 5: 5. who is
faithful to his purpose, or first intent of his work, and will
therefore perfect it, notwithstanding the fiery trial you are
to pass under, 1 Pet. 4: 12. you may therefore build upon
it, and commit yourselves to him accordingly; for "his
faithfulness shall not fail," Psal. 89: 33. and, consequently,
not yours.

6. **Mercy.** This attribute also freely contributes to
the saints' perseverance. Mercy respects men in distress,
to support and bring them out, not having of their own to
help themselves: this, none are so sensible of as believers;
them, therefore, will mercy especially provide for; Hos.
14: 3. "In thee the fatherless find mercy." Psal. 59: 10.
" The God of mercy shall preserve me." Mercy is the
name of God, and his glory, Exod. 34: 7. Mercy is
his way, "and all the paths of the Lord are mercy," Psal.
25: 10. and it is his pleasant path, called, therefore, his
delight, Micah, 7: 18. it pleaseth him above any thing;
yea, " he takes pleasure in them that hope in his mercy,"
Psal. 147: 11. We may say, in a good sense, " his throne
(that is, his glory in the world,) is upholden by mercy,"
Prov. 20: 28. It is mercy that makes men to fear him,
Psal. 130: 4. The 136th Psalm throughout, is an enco-
mium of mercy, as that which doeth all for us; and this,
because it " endureth for ever." In the 138th Psalm, the
prophet grounds his confidence, touching his perseverance,
upon this attribute expressly, namely, that God would perfect that which concerned him, " because his mercy,
(which began the work,) endureth for ever." The great
covenant is founded in mercy, and is therefore styled, " the
sure mercies of David," Isa. 55: 3. I shall not add more
touching this attribute: for if all the rest be on our side,
(as you see they are,) the mercy of God must needs be for
us; for it is that, indeed, which hath engaged and brought
in all the rest.

Arg. VI. The saints' perseverance may also be argued
from the ends of their being, with the author of those ends:
this the scripture puts weight upon. Their ends are to
glorify God, and to be glorified with him; but neither of

these can be attained without persevering; not the first; for nothing so dishonors God as apostacy: not the latter, because such only as endure to the end shall be saved. They must, therefore, persevere, or those ends will be frustrated; which will not stand with the author's interest or authority. That these were the ends of their being is evident, Isa. 43: 21. "These people have I formed for myself;" and verse 7. "I created him for my glory." The apostle also is very express for it, in 2 Cor. chap. 5. where, speaking of that divine building in the heavens, prepared for believers, he tells us, "they were wrought for that self-same thing." The manner of expression is worthy of re-mark: it is not barely said this end or this thing, we are made for; but in effect, this very thing, and nothing else, to be sure nothing less, was the scope and end of our cre-ation, both old and new, even of all God's workmanship upon us. And as evident it is, that God himself is the author of those ends, and that therefore they cannot mis-carry. Upon this ground the Lord would have his people to found an undauntable confidence; as may well be gath-ered from his so frequent indicating of it. In Isa. 43. he thus fortifies them against the sorest of evils; "fear not, for I have redeemed thee; I have called thee;" and ver. 7. "I have created him; I have formed him; yea, I have made him, I, even I the Lord," verse 11. and chap. 41: 10. "Fear thou not, for I am with thee: I will strengthen thee, I will help thee, yea, I will uphold thee:" the emphasis lies in the person active, I, that is, I the Lord, a note of infinite signifi-cancy and security to believers! the apostle also in 2 Cor. 5. that believers might know themselves invincibly secu-red, points us to God, as the great author of those important ends, and almighty undertaker for their accomplishment; "he that wrought us for the self-same thing is God." It is as if he had said; it is impossible we should lose the thing we were wrought for, because it is God that wrought it for us. It is not the designment of an idol; that is, of some ignorant, rash, fallible, or mutable agent, such a one as may possibly be surprised by unlooked-for accidents, circumvented by a sublimer understanding, over-borne by a power above him, or recede from his purpose through levity and fickleness of his nature, &c. But it is God, who is "wise in heart, and mighty in strength," Job

9: 4. It is he from whom all things that are have their
being, and are perfectly under his rule and obeisance.
He had eternity before him, to lay his design surely; and
accordingly, " he declared the end from the beginning."
It is therefore as impossible for him either to do, or neglect to do, or suffer to be done, any thing whereby his
purpose might suffer disappointment; as it is impossible
that God should lie. He would never have set up those
ends as the sum and substance of his design, if he had not
determined to see them made good. And therefore, as
says the apostle, " We are always confident, that when
absent from the body, we shall be present with the Lord,"
2 Cor. 5: 6. 8. This is also further confirmed by that compendious promise, Jer. 31: 33. " I will be their God, and
they shall be my people:" every word here hath a peculiar
emphasis; 1. That he will be a God to them; 2. Their
God; and, 3. for ever: this *I will*, imports both a fixed
resolution, and time without limit. It is as if he had
said, though other lords have had the rule over you, and
you have still a proneness to revolt to them, it shall not be; I
will not be excluded any more; I will heal your backslidings, and be your God still; I will carry it towards you,
as becomes a God to do; and I will make you such a people,
as becometh God to own: " I will not be ashamed to be
called your God," Heb. 11: 16. It would indeed be
both a disparagement and dissatisfaction to God, if his
people should fail of that he made them for; which certainly cannot be, because God is theirs; and if God be theirs,
all things are theirs, both this world and that to come,
1 Cor. 3: 22, 23.

Arg. VII. *Lastly.* For the final perseverance of believers, a principal argument is derived from the sovereign decree of election. I call it sovereign, partly because
it is the highest manifestation of God's absolute dominion
over his creatures, in choosing whom he would, and passing by the rest: partly, also, because all sorts of things whatsoever are subjected to it, and made subservient to its final
accomplishment. And this I take for a principal reason
why election is so frequently placed in eternity, or before
the foundation of the world, namely, to show, that the very
fabric of the world and all occurrences therein, were so
contrived and framed in God's decree, as having election

for their primary scope and end: that this first cause is the supreme moderator of all intermediate causes, and is itself subject to none.   It was not any loveliness in elect persons which moved God to love them at first; so neither shall their unlovely backslidings deprive them of it, though it may be eclipsed by their own default, to the breaking of their bones.   The Lord chose them for that blessed image of his own, which he would afterwards imprint upon them; and this he still prosecutes through all dispensations.

That elect nation was the Jews; they apostatized from God, and did worse than any other; yet would not the Lord utterly cast them off.   In Samuel's time their wickedness was very great; yet, saith he (to stay them from total apostacy,) " The Lord will not forsake you:" but what is the ground of that his confidence, and grand warranty? The very same that now we are upon: " The Lord will not forsake you, because it hath pleased the Lord to make you his people:" not because they remembered their duty, and returned to God; but because " he remembered them for his covenant:" in pursuance whereof he long maintained their title, notwithstanding their often repeated forfeitures; and, when in captivity, brought them home again.

And, indeed, there is nothing so melts the hearts of those in covenant with God, as that " the Lord should be pacified towards them after all their abominations," Ezek. 16: 63.   The manner of God's dealings with his people is especially instructive to help the faith of the spiritual election upon all occasions, as holding forth the special regard the Lord has for them, because of his covenant: that though he may and will punish their iniquities, yet his loving kindness he will not take from them.   And he puts it still upon his having once chosen them, as ye have it in Jeremiah 41: 9. " I have chosen thee, and not cast thee away."   This latter clause, " and not cast thee away," seems added to shew, that his choosing them was an act unrepealable, q. d. I knew beforehand what thou wouldest do, and how thou wouldest prove; and if I had meant ever to cast thee off; yea, if I had not resolved against it, I would not have chosen thee at all: but, since I have, be sure I will stand by thee; " I will strengthen thee; I will help thee; yea, I will uphold thee with the right hand of my righteousness."

It is true, the body of that nation, for their unbelief, are

now broken off; there is a suspension of the outward part
of the covenant: not that God intends an utter rejection of
them: for such as have part in the special election are always saved, Rom. 11: 7. and the time will come when all
Israel shall be saved; for as touching the election, they are
beloved still, though yet unborn.   For their sakes it was,
that " those days of tribulation were shortened," Matt. 24:
22. which answers to that in Isa. 65: 8. " Destroy it not,
there is a blessing in it."   The Lord will not so much regard what they have done or deserved, as what his covenant
is concerning Abraham's seed; which minding of his covenant, is from the unchangeableness of his purpose; and,
therefore, though broken off at present, " they shall be
grafted in again," ver. 24. though driven into all lands;
scattered into corners; mingled with the heathen; and become so like them, as not to be known asunder; yet being
his chosen, and within his covenant, he will bring them out
of their holes, and gather them one by one, Isa. 27: 12. he
will do it so accurately, exactly, punctually, that none shall
be wanting, " though sifted among all nations, " not one
grain shall fall to the earth," Amos 9: 9.   The reservation
mentioned in Rom. 11. was God's omnipotent safeguarding
his elect, when the rest of the nation fell to idolatry: they
had gone all, as well as some, had not election held them
back; it is therefore said to be according to the election of
grace: election was the pattern, and reservation the copy of
it.   And that this was not a single case, or restrained to
that present time, is evident from Matt. 24. where our Saviour foretels, that the subtlety of deceivers, and temptations of the times, shall be such, and the torrent rise to that
strength, that it will be next to impossible not to be carried
away by it; but for the elect, they are safeguarded: how?
By the coming in of the first and sovereign cause, by the
virtue of which, the whole force and influence of those second causes shall either be prevented, or removed, miti-
gated, inverted, shortened, or over-ruled, Matt. 24: 22. and
the faith of his sealed ones so confirmed, that they shall not
be hurt by them, Ezek. 9: 6.   Rev. 7: 3. yea, and which is
more, those very things which are destructive to others shall
work life in them.   This turned Balaam's curse into a blessing to Israel, Deut. 23: 5. and Paul's afflictions to his salvation, Phil. 1: 19. they are to them a cause of " lifting up

the head," Luke 21: 28.   And if it were not so, the apostle could not exhort us to " count it all joy when we fall into divers temptations," James 1: 2. but that in the midst thereof " he keepeth the feet of his saints," 1 Sam. 2: 9. for, says God, " they are my people; children that will not lie," Isa. 63: 8. *q. d.* They are of those I have chosen, and set apart for myself, and therefore they shall not frustrate my purpose in choosing them; which seems implied in the word *so,* " so he was their Saviour;" I will save them, because I have made them my people.

And, further, it is worthy your notice, that this sovereign decree is always regnant; a kingdom that beareth rule over all, and shall never be broken, Dan. 2: 44. Psal. 89: 34. " My covenant will I not break, nor alter the thing that is gone out of my lips: my covenant shall stand fast with him," ver. 28.   It is meant of the covenant made with David and his house; or rather with Christ and his spiritual seed, of whom David was a type.   And that we might have strong consolation, the Lord is pleased to bind it with an oath; " once," (that is, once for all, and once for ever; it was so full, perfect, and absolute, that it needed no alteration, amendment, or repetition,) " once have I sworn by my holiness, that I will not lie unto David," ver. 35.   And how impossible it was that this covenant should be broken, appears by Jeremiah, who, speaking in the name of the Lord, delivers it thus; " If you can break my covenant of the day, and my covenant of the night, that there should not be day and night in their season; then may also my covenant be broken with David, my servant," Jer. 33: 20, 21.   Here note, by the way, that day and night take their turns; but still it is in their season.   And David himself says of it, that " it is a covenant everlasting, ordered in all things, and sure," 2 Sam. 23: 5. that is, whatever might possibly fall in to interrupt it, there was that order observed in the composition of the covenant, and such a power laid up within it, as should certainly overrun and bear down those impediments, triumph over all, and hold on its way; as all the tempests and tumults that happen in this lower world can in no wise obstruct the course and harmony of the superior orbs.   He therefore declares in high, yet humble expressions, that he desires no other or better security for his salvation.   And it is not unlikely that Da-

vid and Solomon were both of them left to those great and
grievous backslidings, to give proof of the sureness of this
covenant, which indeed was sufficiently done by them, and
tried to the uttermost: for they both broke the covenant on
their part, and yet the covenant was not nulled: no thanks
to them, but to that sovereign grace, that had laid in provision before to prevent it, by making it absolute and unrepealable.   Yet will not the Lord connive at their miscar-
riages; but " if his children forsake my law, and break
my statutes, I will visit their transgressions with the rod,
and their iniquity with stripes: nevertheless, my loving
kindness will I not utterly take from him, nor suffer my
faithfulness to fail," Psal. 89: 31, 32, 33.   There was, indeed, at times, a seeming to make void this covenant, ver.
39. and great complaints are made upon it, as well there
might; but it revives, and looks fresh again; joy comes in
the morning; as is evident by the close of that Psalm,
" Blessed be the Lord for evermore, Amen, and Amen!"
Its return was the more welcome for its temporary absence;
and therefore he meets with a double gratulation, Amen,
and Amen! It was but in a little wrath that he hid his face
from them, and that but for a moment of time! " but with
everlasting kindness will I have mercy on thee, saith the
Lord, thy Redeemer.   The mountains shall depart, and the
hills be removed;—but my kindness shall not depart from
thee, neither shall the covenant of my peace be removed,
saith the Lord, that hath mercy on thee," Isa. 54: 8. 10.   In
Jeremiah another impossibility is instanced, to shew the
eternal validity of this covenant; " Thus saith the Lord, if
heaven above can be measured, and the foundations of the
earth searched out beneath, I will also cast off all the seed
of Israel, for all that they have done, saith the Lord," Jer.
31: 37. the Lord, you see, has made himself both the alpha
and omega of this great sentence; to shew that both ends
of the covenant are in his own hands.

By these scriptures, with many others, it is apparent,
there shall be no failure on God's part, and consequently
none at all, because he hath taken on himself the performance of the whole; not so as to exempt us from our duty,
but to reduce us to it, and carry us through it: believers,
therefore, shall be invincibly secured to the end of their
faith, the salvation of their souls.

Yet doth not this doctrine go free of contradiction; and, truly, considering how plain and pertinent the scripture is for it, it may well be conjectured, that if the first impugners of perseverance had not found themselves in a toil, and necessitated to oppose it, for the maintenance of other principles they had before espoused, and which would not stand with this, they would never have set themselves against it. But errors (like truths in that) do hang together, or as links in a chain; the first mover draws the rest after it: but I trust, through help from above, all the objections that are laid against this doctrine shall, by one hand or other, prove to its farther confirmation. The chief that have occurred to me are these that follow; and if I had met with any more considerable, I trust I should not have shunned their trial.

Object. The doctrine of absolute perseverance deprives men of the sharpest bit which God hath given them to curb the unregenerate part of the soul; we mean the fear and dread of eternal fire.

Answ. The law is good, if lawfully used; so is fear, in its time and place; but out of that, it is as a bone out of joint. The law works by fear, as a schoolmaster unto Christ: it is ordinarily the first occasion of our motion towards believing. The heir, whilst a child, may be under the tutorage of fear: but when faith is grown up, then cast out the bond-woman and her son; fear shall not be heir with faith; for, though it be a good servant, it is an ill master. For fear to predominate over faith, is for " servants to ride, while princes walk on the earth, which is an error the earth cannot bear," Eccl. 10: 5. 7. with Prov. 30: 21, 22. Believers, especially such as know themselves so to be, " receive not the spirit of bondage again to fear," Rom. 8: 15. they are actuated now by another principle, as a horse that is thoroughly broke and well tempered, is better managed by a gentle hand than a biting curb. Faith works by love: it is not henceforth the fear of wrath, but the sense of Christ's love, in delivering from wrath, that both curbs the unregenerate part, and carries to higher acts of obedience than fear is capable of, although, at times, all sorts of motives may be needful to keep us going; and the Lord, for exercise of our graces, and other holy ends, may let the dearest of his children long conflict with their fears, under which he yet supports them, and brings them forth like gold at last.

See Ethan's complaint, and the close he makes, in the 89th Psalm: see also that excellent treatise, " A Child of Light walking in Darkness," &c. by Dr. Goodwin.

There are two sorts of fear; of God, and of the creature. Creature-fear believers are still called from, and with good reason, as ye will find after. Godly fear is quite another thing; it is a grace of the largest import: no saving grace, but this fear is put for it, or joined with it; which juncture shows its import in that place. It is sometimes put for faith, Gen. 22: 12. with Heb. 11: 17. sometimes for love, Psal. 130: 4. with Luke 7: 47. for reverence also, Psal. 89: 7. Lev. 19: 3. Heb. 12: 28. for vigilance and circumspection, 2 Cor. 7: 11. for subjection, or observance, Mal. 1: 6. Holiness also is coupled with fear, 2 Cor. 7: 1. So is meekness, 1 Pet. 3: 15. So also is knowledge, wisdom, and good understanding, Prov. 1: 7. Psal. 111: 12. Sometimes the whole of religious worship is intended by it, Judges 6: 10. Isa. 8: 13. Job 1: 1. and 8. This fear ariseth from the sight of God's holiness, greatness, just severity against sin, with the freeness of his grace, sureness of his covenant, fulness that is in Christ, and our interest in him, wherewith that slavish fear of hell will not consist. On this account, the Lord our God is said to be a " fearful name," Deut. 28: 58. that is, it is the only object worthy of our faith, love, reverence, and religious worship: and, according to this sense of the word, " Blessed is the man that feareth always." But, touching the fear of hell, as supposed the best to curb sin, and promoter of perseverance, it ought to be rejected. How far it may influence an unregenerate person, as a curb to his lusts, is not the question here; but if Saul and Judas ran headlong to hell, with this bit in their mouths, then the sharpest bit is not the most effectual curb. Arguments against it are obvious; 1. That by which God purifies the heart, and whereby believers are strengthened to a concurrence with him in that work, is surely the properest curb to sin: that also which weakens and tends to destroy the root, must needs be more effectual than that which only hinders some puttings of it forth: but all this is done by faith; this lays the axe to the root: " By faith God purifies the heart," Acts 15: 9. and " every one that hath this hope, purifieth himself, as he is pure," 1 John 3: 3. There is no such virtue ascribed to the fear of hell; but, plainly, the spirit of fear is opposed to the spirit of love, of faith, and of a sound mind, 2 Tim. 1: 7. 2. That which has the place of an end in Christ's delivering from enemies, can be no let to perseverance; but, that we might serve God "without fear," has the place of an end in that deliverance, Luke 1: 74, 75. 3. That which the scripture holds forth as an help to perseverance, cannot be an hindrance to it; but the scripture holds forth faith and confidence in God as a principal help to perseverance, Rom. 6: 12. 14. Heb. 3: 14. chap. 10: 35. 4. That which irritates the unregenerate part, cannot be said to curb it: but this does the fear of wrath; " When the commandment came, sin revived," Rom. 7: 9. that is, it took occasion, by the law's restraint, to rise the more powerful against it; and so, the " law worketh wrath," chap. 4: 15. as a torrent stopped in its course, grows more impetuous. Cain was an instance of this, Gen. 4: 5. and even Paul, in his unregeneracy, Rom. 7: 10, 11. when thoroughly convinced of sin, if grace step not in as its guardian, the soul is undone. That scripture, Matt. 10: 28. gives the objection no countenance; the fear there intended, is that which hath faith and love in it: " Fear not them which kill the body, but fear him that is able to destroy both soul and body in hell." The two objects of fear he puts in the balance; to shew how little reason we have to shun our duty for fear of men, whose power can but reach to a bodily death; and how much more to fear him, that has the keys of death and of hell; that is, who hath power to cast into hell, might justly have done it, and yet hath saved us from it: and this fear is love; as is evident by Matt. 10: 37. where speaking of the same thing, namely, cleaving to Christ, parting with all for him, it is expressly called love: " He that loveth father or mother more than me, is not worthy of me:" and, for aught that appears to the contrary, it might be the fear of hell that made the slothful servant to hide his talent; " I knew thee, that thou art an hard man; and I was afraid, and went and hid thy talent in the earth," Matt. 25: 24, 25. It is also to be observed, that before the great tribunal, the fearful and unbelieving stand linked together, Rev. 21: 8. But whatever influence the fear of hell may have upon persons unregenerate, as a curb to their lusts, the doctrine of perseverance deprives not of it, for this concerns only believers.

The objection is further excepted against,

1. Because it puts an indignity on the wisdom of God, as if he had taken from believers some expedient help to perseverance, by giving them absolute promises; whereas, we should rather suspect our own understandings, and renounce those opinions, which necessitate such unnatural deductions to support them: for, do but separate the promises from their absoluteness, and their strength is gone; they would prove, as the law, " weak, through the weakness of the flesh," Rom. 8: 3.   The Lord knows that believers have the most difficult work, and deepest sense of their own insufficiency, and that nothing more weakens their hands, than doubting and fears, and for that very cause hath made his promises absolute.   Thus he armed Joshua to the battle; " There shall not a man be able to stand before thee all the days of thy life: I will not leave thee, nor forsake thee;" and thence draws him an argument, to be " strong, and of a good courage," Josh. 1: 5, 6.   Thus also Samuel, in the place before-mentioned, when the people were greatly perplexed because of God's displeasure towards them: to confirm them in their duty, he comforts them against their fears; " Fear not, ye have done all this wickedness, yet turn not aside from following the Lord," 1 Sam. 12: 20.   And what is the strong reason by which he fixes them? " For the Lord will not forsake his people," ver. 22. Paul, likewise, exhorting believers to that great duty of keeping down sin, that it might not reign, because the sharpness and heat of the conflict might otherwise make them recoil, he gives them, as an high cordial, assurance of victory; tells them expressly, that " sin shall not have dominion over them," Rom. 6: 14.   Of the same mind were Peter and John; the one directs " to give all diligence to make our calling and election sure;" and this, as a principal means to " keep us from falling," 2 Pet. 1: 10. and the other makes it the very scope of his whole epistle, that believers might know they have eternal life, and that they might " go on in believing," 1 John 5: 13.   Which kind of arguments had been very improper, and unduly applied, if giving them assurance, touching the event, had not been

a strengthening of them in their duty, and much more, if it would have proved an indulgence to the flesh.

2. Let fear be considered in its ordinary and natural effects; and it will easily appear, that nothing is less pleasing to God, or more unapt for the service of perseverance. As a man's principle is, such will be his obedience; slavish observance is the best that slavish fear can produce, which is no way acceptable to an ingenuous spirit: God loves a cheerful giver, not Samaritan worship, " for fear of lions," 2 Kings 17: 25. Such service will also be weak and wavering; for nothing so unsettles the mind as fear; it enervates the soul, and takes away its strength: " Nabal's heart died within him for fear," 1 Sam. 25: 37. and the soldiers that kept the sepulchre were as " dead men for fear," Matt. 28: 4. the obedience, therefore, which comes from thence can be but a dead obedience; the effect cannot rise higher than the cause. Pharaoh let Israel go because of the plagues, which being a little removed, he repents his obedience, and chides himself for it, Exod. 14: 5. and those hypocrites, though fearfulness had surprised them, remained hypocrites still, Isa. 33: 14. This fear will also consist with the greatest impieties: those very Samaritans, who thus feared the Lord, did also worship their graven images, 2 Kings 17: 41.

3. Fear puts upon using unlawful means: Isaac to deny his wife, Gen. 26: 7. David to lie, and feign himself mad, 1 Sam. 21: 13. Peter, and other holy men, to dissemble, Gal. 2: 12, 13. It sends men to Egypt for help, as it did the Jews, Isa. 30: 2. Hos. 7: 11. yea, to hell, as it did Saul, 1 Sam. 28: 7. Therefore, both Satan and wicked men are still endeavoring to put God's people in fear, as they would Nehemiah, whereby his work had ceased, Neh. 6: 13, 14. 19. And Satan stood at Joshua's right hand to resist him, that is, to accuse him; and so to put him in fear, because of his filthy garments, thereby to discourage him in the work of his office, Zec. 3: 1.

4. Let fear be compared with its contrary, which is faith, this removes the mountain, while fear fixes it, yea, makes it seem to be where no such thing is. Fear made the unbelieving spies to bring up an evil report of the good land, and to fancy impossibilities of obtaining it, Numb. 13: 31. faith made Caleb and Joshua magnanimous; " Let us go

up at once (say they) and possess it, for we are well able to overcome it," ver. 30. " yea, they shall be bread for us," chap. 14: 9. These two who feared no miscarriage under an absolute promise, were carried in; all that doubted were shut out. Peter, while confident, walked on the waves; when he began to doubt, he began to sink, Matth. 14: 29, 30. It was faith made those worthies valiant to fight, enabled one to chase a thousand, Josh. 23: 10. When fear caused a thousand to flee at the rebuke of one, yea, at the shaking of a leaf, Lev. 27: 36. A handful of obedience, springing from faith and confidence in God, is more acceptable to him, than sheaves and loads arising from fear of wrath. If Paul, for fear of hell, had given his body to be burned, it had been nothing, 1 Cor. 13:3. but faith and love render small things of value with God, even the widow's mite, and a cup of cold water. And it is worthy of remark, that when the fruits of the Spirit are reckoned up, this fear is not so much as named among them, Gal. 5: 22, 23. And certain it is, that the more sensible and lively our love is to God, the less will be our fear of hell; for perfect love casts out fear.

5. If fear were such an effectual curb to sin, or help to perseverance, there would not be such promises of delivering God's people from their fears, nor would they so affectionately bless God for their being delivered, nor so resolutely set themselves against it; neither would there be so many commands and injunctions laid upon them, not to be afraid.

(1.) For commands against fear. " Fear not thou, O my servant Jacob,—for I will save thee: fear thou not,— I will correct thee in measure," Jer. 46: 27, 28. that is, meetly and proportionably, according to the scope of my covenant, which is to save thee. The Lord would not have us think ourselves in danger of being cashiered when we are chastened; which seems the import of that in Isaiah, " I have chosen thee, and not cast thee away; fear thou not," Isa. 41: 9, 10. So, to the Hebrews, "Cast not away your confidence," Heb. 10: 35. and Christ to his disciples, Let not your heart be troubled, neither let it be afraid," John 14: 27. nothing brings such perturbation of mind as fear. And, " Fear not little flock;" why? " it is your Father's good pleasure to give you the kingdom," Luke

12: 32. Innumerable are the injunctions laid upon God's people against fear, Isa. 35:4. ch. 43:5. ch. 44:2. Jer.30:10. Joel 2: 21. Zeph. 3: 16. Hag. 2: 5. Zach. 8: 13. 15. Matt. 10: 29. Acts 27· 24. Rev. 1: 17. &c. Therefore freedom from this fear is no impediment to perseverance.

(2.) Promises of delivering from fears. "Jacob shall be in quiet, and none shall make him afraid," Jer. 30: 10. "He shall not be afraid of evil tidings," Psal. 112: 7. "He shall be quiet from fear of evil," Prov. 1: 33. The promise is not made to fear and fainting, but to faith and confidence; "Be of good courage and he shall strengthen thy heart," Psal. 27: 14. If it had been the mind of Christ, that believers should still be under this fear, he would not have told them, they are passed from death unto life, and shall not come into condemnation, John 5: 24. that they shall sit upon thrones, Matth. 19: 28. that their inheritance is reserved in heaven for them, and they kept for it; and that by the mighty power of God, 1 Pet. 1: 4, 5. The result of all which is, that "having these promises, we should cleanse ourselves from all filthiness of flesh and spirit; perfecting holiness in the fear of God," 2 Cor. 7: 1.

(3.) Examples of Christian resolution not to fear. "Yea, though I walk through the valley of the shadow of death, I will fear no evil," Psal. 23: 4. Isa. 50: 7. "Therefore (that is, because the Lord God had promised to help him; therefore) have I set my face as a flint, and I know that I shall not be confounded," Psal. 56: 4. "I will not fear what flesh can do unto me." And Psal. 49: 5. Wherefore should I fear in the days "of evil, when the iniquity of my heels shall compass me about?" These, if any thing should have put him in fear; but his faith resolves against it, according to Isa. 12:2. "I will trust, and not be afraid," that is, he would not willingly admit the least mixture of fear with his faith; and good reason for it, since "the joy of the Lord was his strength," Neh. 8: 10.

(4.) Instances of thankfulness for deliverance from fears. "O magnify the Lord with me, and let us exalt his name together." But what is the occasion of this joyful triumph? "I sought the Lord, and he heard me, and delivered me from all my fears," Psal. 43: 3, 4. and therefore will I offer in his tabernacle sacrifices of joy;" and the reason of it was, that "God would hide him in his own pavilion," Psal. 27:

5, 6. that is, he would secure him from danger, and set him above all fears; which he could not, with any good reason, have rejoiced in; nor have prayed that God would "restore him to the joy of his salvation," if the dread of eternal fire had been so good a friend to perseverance. Scriptures might be multiplied; but, besides these, it is evident in experience, that nothing so elevates the spirit and courage of a man in great undertakings, as assurance of success: but while he is wavering, and doubtful how he shall speed, especially while he meditates terrors, and of them the dreadfulest, his hands are enfeebled, nor has he his wits about him (as we use to speak) to discern and improve them, as otherwise he might. That which tends really to make a man "steadfast, immoveable, and always to abound in the work of the Lord," is not the fear of miscarrying, and losing all at last; but "faith and a certain knowledge that his labor shall not be in vain in the Lord," 1 Cor. 15: 58.

Object. If a man once believing cannot lose his faith, why is it said, "Let him that standeth take heed lest he fall?" and, "Look to yourselves, that ye lose not the things we have wrought?" If there be no possibility or losing, what need of such cautions and such great circumspection?

Answ. The maker of this objection hath elsewhere granted, that the obtaining of Canaan was sure to Abraham's seed, so as their unworthiness could not deprive them of it: and yet we find their induction and actual possession yoked, afterwards, with as many conditions, cautions, and limitations, as the promise of salvation to believers any where is; and yet, nevertheless certain. But, for more particular answer,

1. That a righteous man may fall, is evident; and as evident it is, that he cannot fall finally; for though he fall seven times in a day, as often does he rise again, Prov. 24: 16. and this, because the "Lord upholdeth him with his hand," Psal. 37: 24. and again, the "Lord upholdeth all that fall," Psal. 145: 14. that is, either he stays them when they are falling, or so orders and limits the matter, that they fall not into mischief, as others do; and to be sure he will set them on their feet again. The absolute promise cannot be nullified or made uncertain by cautionary words elsewhere delivered. It cannot, therefore be meant of a

total and final falling away, which the scripture current expressly runs against.

2. There are considerations of great weight to make believers beware of falling, without supposing their final apostasy, (as the danger of breaking a man's bones, is ground sufficient for caution, though sure that his neck shall be safe,) the dishonor done unto his Father; the shame that is put upon Christ; grieving the Comforter; scandalizing the good ways of God; stumbling the weak; strengthening the wicked; unfitting him for his duty; interrupting his peace and communion with God, and so forth: every one of which will weigh deep with a soul that is born of God.

3. The Lord does ordinarily bring about his purposes by means, of which cautions are a part, and by which, as a means, he keeps off the evil cautioned against. In 1 John 2: 28. the apostle exhorts them to "abide in Christ," whom certain professors had relinquished, verse 19. And, as purposely intending to obviate this objection, he tells them "that they shall abide in him," verse 27. whereby he strenghens them to their duty.

For the other place objected,—namely, "Look to yourselves, that you lose not the things we have brought,"—it is one thing to lose for a time the sense and comfort of our state, as David, Heman, and others did, and another thing to lose the state itself; which a believer shall never do, as is shown before. Of much like import is that in 2 Pet. I: 5—9. where he exhorts them to "give all diligence to add one grace to another;" and, to help them in their work, he tells them, 1. What advantage they shall have by so doing: they shall not be unfruitful in the knowledge of Jesus Christ; that is, it shall evidence to them that the knowledge they have is a real knowledge, which cannot be known from that which is formal only, but by such an effect. That also by this means it shall be increased; the using of things well, and to their proper end, being the readiest way to their improvement, according to John 7: 17. "He that will do my will shall know of my doctrine." 2. He then sets before them the loss they shall have in case of neglect; they will become blind, unable to see afar off, and forget that they were purged from their old sins; remissness will bring obscurity; that which was clear before, will now become clouded, and be as if it were not: it may seem to them, that they are short of that rest, which yet is sure to them; and so they will be put to begin their work anew; whereas, " if they do these things, they shall never fall:" that is, they shall not fall from their steadfastness, nor lose that clear sight and assurance which they now have, touching their good estate, namely, as being partakers of the divine nature, and purged from their old sins, which these neglects might put out of their sight, and so lose them the sense and comfort of what they had wrought.

Object. We read in John 6: 66. that many of Christ's disciples forsook him; in Timothy, of some who, as concerning the faith, had made shipwreck; and of Simon Magus, who once believed, and was afterwards found in the bond of iniquity.

Answ. The objection has an answer sufficient made ready to its hand, in 1 John 2: 19. " They went out from us, because they were not of us: for if they had been of us, they would no doubt have continued with us." Seeming faith may really be lost, as theirs was; and real faith may seemingly be lost, as was the apostle's, Luke 24: 21. Seeming faith is lost really, because it was but seeming; real faith cannot be lost, because it is real. Yet we shall find, that that which is but seeming, is frequently called by the name of that it seems to be; as in Matt. 13: 12. it is said, " that which he hath:" in Luke 8: 18. (speaking of the same thing) it is rendered, " that he seemeth to have:" so those who forsook Christ, they were disciples but in shew; they never believed in truth; as appears by John 6: 64. " Jesus knew from the beginning who they were that believed not:" and this (namely, because it was but a seeming faith they had,) he gives as the reason of their now forsaking him. And for Simon Magus, the answer is as clear concerning him: where let us consider,

1. That a man may be said to believe, and yet not be a believer; as a righteous man to sin, and yet not be a sinner, 1 John 5: 18. To be a believer, is to be thorough-paced in faith, to believe all that is to be believed, and to have the heart united to it: thus Simon believed not; and if he had, could not have thought the Holy Ghost vendible for money.

2. His faith seems to be only such a belief concerning

Philip, as the Samaritans lately had concerning Simon, namely, that he was "the great power of God." For finding himself overmatched by Philip, who cast out the spirits, which he, perhaps, had possessed them with, he could not now but give the precedency to Philip, as having a greater power than himself; and, therefore, he "continued with Philip, wondering at what he did."

3. Simon's believing seems to be no more than an outward professional faith, taken up for by-respects, to preserve his interest and repute among the people, who now began to fall from him, and to follow Philip, whose disciple he himself will profess to be, rather than to be quite cashiered. Besides, this profession of his might, in his conceit, be a step towards " purchasing the gift of the Holy Ghost," which, if he could obtain, he had been again in as good a condition, both for reputation and profit, as before.

If any shall say, we read not of this distinction of faith, into true and false—I answer, the scripture frequently speaks of persons and things according to vulgar esteem, or what they professed themselves to be. Ahaz is said to " sacrifice to the gods of Damascus that smote him." 2 Chron. 28: 23. and yet neither were they gods, nor did they smite him; but it is spoken according to his own superstitious opinion of them. So those four hundred men, who prophesied before Ahab, are called prophets, 1 Kings 22:6. not that they were prophets indeed, but because they so professed themselves, or because so reputed by Ahab and the people. A prophet is one that is inspired by the Holy Ghost; which those men were not, but by a lying spirit, ver. 22. Now, Simon Magus was no more a true believer, than those true prophets; nor his faith any more of the right kind, than their predictions true prophecies. We also find, that the Scripture makes the coming to pass of the thing foretold, to be the evidence of a true prophet: according to which rule, perseverance to salvation must demonstrate the truth of faith; and wheresoever this follows not, there faith was but pretended; "They profess to know God, but in works deny him," Tit. 1: 16. as of the Samaritans, beforementioned, it is said, " They feared the Lord;" and presently after, that "they feared not the Lord," 2 Kings 17: 32. 34. they feared him in show, but not in truth.

4. " The foundation of God standeth sure; having this seal, the Lord knoweth them that are his," 2 Tim. 2: 19. He brings it in to comfort believers, touching the sureness of their standing; when others, of as glorious outsides, make shipwreck of the faith: it sands sure, because " the Lord knoweth them that are his:" he knows whom he hath chosen; for whom he hath received the atonement; whom he hath called, and caused to " take hold of his covenant;" and these shall surely be kept, notwithstanding the woful backslidings of others.

Object. If one that believes not now, may have faith hereafter; then one that is now a believer, may lose his faith, and turn apostate.

Answ. It follows not, that because Christ can bind Satan, and cast him out; therefore Satan can do so by Christ. He can come into the devil's nursery when he will; take a crab-stock, and transplant it, and graft it with a noble cion; but Satan cannot come into God's vineyard, which is a garden enclosed, and take thence what he pleaseth. One, who is now dead in sin, may be quickened; but, being once alive, can die no more: it is Christ's own assertion, " He that liveth, and believeth in me, shall never die," John 11: 26. which cannot be meant of any other but a spiritual death, which is all one with his losing his faith.

Object. A righteous man may turn away from his righteousness; and that so, that he shall die for it, Ezek. 18: 24.

Answ. There is a two-fold righteousness; 1. Moral; such as Paul had before his conversion; this a man may continue in to the last, and yet be not saved, 2. There is a gospel-righteousness; (1.) Imputed; this is the righteousness of Christ, by which we are justified. (2.) Infused; this is the divine nature communicated by the Spirit of Christ, whereby we are sanctified. These two go inseparably, and can never be lost. But the righteousness spoken of in the place objected, seems to be of the former sort; namely, moral or outward righteousness; for outward conformity to the law, was the condition of their possessing the land of Canaan, with long life and prosperity in it. This, if retained, gave them a legal right to those promises; if they turned from it, they ran into a forfeiture: and lose it they might, for they had no promise that they should abide in it. But the new covenant undertakes for that, as is evident, by comparing Jer. 31: 31, 33. with chap. 32: 43. But if any will yet suppose the righteous man spoken of in the 18th of Ezekiel, to be meant of a true believer; there is, I trust, in the answers foregoing, sufficient to solve it.

But suppose a believer be taken away in his sin, as perhaps Josiah was, and hath not time to repent of it? 1. It cannot be proved that this was the case with Josiah: he had time sufficient between his wounding and his death; as is evident by the story, 2 Chron. 35: 23, 24. But, 2. There was that in him that would have repented, and God reckons of a man according to what he would do. It being in David's heart to build him a house, it was accepted as if he had done it. The root of the matter is in every regenerate person, which, if it had time, would put forth itself in fruits: and therefore they shall not be dealt with as barren trees, which have not that substance in them.

Object. The promise of perseverance is not made to faith, that that shall not fail; but in reference to the favor of God, namely, that if men go on to believe, they shall abide in his love.

Ans. Thus to give the sense of the promise, is to enervate it, and make it speak but according to the covenant of works: it bereaves it wholly of that superiority the Scripture ascribes to it, in Heb. 8: 6—10. It also renders the promise as speaking fallaciously; making show of that it intends not: it would be as if he had said, You shall keep the favor of God, if you do not lose it. Besides, faith is the soul's coming to God; unbelief, its departing from him: the promise, therefore, that secures against departing from God, secures your continuance in believing: he that undertakes you shall be crowned, doth virtually undertake for your holding out to the end of your race.

Object. Others, again, in interpreting the promises recorded in the 36th of Ezekiel and 32d of Jeremiah, touching men's not departing from God, restrain them to the Jewish nation, and to the last days.

Ans. To this I shall only say, that although some particular times and persons are more immediately concerned in the promises of the Old Testament, especially such as refer to temporal things; yet is there not one promise, but, in the spirituality of it, belongs to every one that belongs

to Christ; that is, Jews in spirit.   No scripture is of private
interpretation; and therefore not to be confined to those particular times or persons, when and to whom they were delivered: they were written for the use of all, 1 Cor. 10: 11.
and we find them accordingly applied in the New Testament.   The promise made to Joshua, touching the success
of his warfare in Canaan, is, by the apostle, applied to believers in general, as an argument against overmuch careful-
ness in a married estate, and for contentedness with our
present condition, Josh. 1: 5. with Heb. 13: 5. So, likewise,
the prophecy of Isaiah, touching the hypocrites of his time,
is by Christ applied to the Pharisees, Isa. chap. 19. with
Matt. 25: 7, 8. and the promises made to the Jews in Isa.
54: 13 are applied to the Gentiles in John 6: 45.

  Object. The doctrine of absolute perseverance lays the
reins of security on the neck of the flesh, and of the old
man, in believers.

  Answ. For answer, 1. This objection, is, in effect, the
same with the first, only it speaks broader; which shows,
that the farther men go in opposing the truth, the worse
language they give it.   That many, who disbelieve the
doctrine of perseverance, have given the flesh its full range
and liberty, needs no proof: but, that any believer hath
made that impious use of it, will never be made out.   2.
The objection deserves no quarter, because it highly reproaches the goodness and faithfulness of God, as if for a
fish, he had given a scorpion; for so it would be, if his
giving them absolute promises would prove an indulgence
to the flesh.   3. It also contradicts the known and constant way of holy men's arguing and inferring from absolute promises, and the highest assurance: see a few
instances of this: " When Christ our life shall appear,
then shall ye also appear with him in glory:" the result of
it is, " mortify, therefore, your members which are upon
the earth," Col. 3:4, 5.   Again, " we know that when he
shall appear, we shall be like him:" and what is the fruit
of this knowledge?   " Every man that hath this hope in
him, purifieth himself, even as he is pure," 1 John 3: 2,3.
The like ye have in the Corinthians: " For we know, that
if our earthly house of this tabernacle were dissolved,
we have a building of God, an house not made with
hands, eternal in the heavens."   Now see the effect of

this assurance; " Wherefore we labor, that whether present or absent, we may be accepted of him," 2 Cor. 4: 5. 9. in the next chapter, he repeats the sum of the new covenant; " I will be a father unto you, and ye shall be my sons and daughters, saith the Lord Almighty," 2 Cor. 6: 18. Observe now the use he makes of it, and all believers have the same mind: " Having, therefore, these promises, (absolute promises,) let us cleanse ourselves from all filthiness of flesh and spirit, perfecting holiness in the fear of God," chap. 7: 1. Job knew that his Redeemer lived, and that he should live with him; and yet, as to holiness and integrity, not a man like Job in all the earth. And that holy man Asaph, was fully assured of persevering infallibly; " Thou shalt guide me by thy counsel, and afterwards receive me to glory," Psal. 73: 24. this did not loosen the reins, but made him cleave closer to God, renouncing all but him and his service; " Whom have I in heaven but thee?" And, " it is good for me to draw nigh to God," ver. 25. 28. The like frame of spirit we find in David, " Surely, goodness and mercy shall follow me all the days of my life:" his result also is " I will dwell in the house of God for ever," Psal. 23: 6. And, that these were not temporary fits and flashes, but from a settled principle, is further apparent by his manner of reasoning; " In time of trouble, he shall hide me in his pavilion, (no safer place on earth nor in heaven,) and now shall my head be lifted up above mine enemies round about me," Psal. 27: 5. But what follows upon this mounted assurance? "Soul, take thine ease, eat, drink, and be merry?" O! no: but, " therefore will I offer sacrifices of joy; I will sing, yea, I will sing praises unto the Lord!" Psal. 27: 6. he was now upon his high places, out of the reach of danger; but did not grow remiss upon it, restrain prayer, and give over calling upon God; but falls the more fervently upon that which shall be the object of all in heaven: he would rather have been remiss without this assurance, as he himself presently acknowledgeth: " I had fainted, unless I had believed to see the goodness of the Lord in the land of the living," ver. 15. So Paul's assurance of obtaining what he ran for, was a mighty strengthening to him in his race: who so crucified to the world as Paul? so abundant in all kind of service, or more ready to die for Christ, than he? who

yet had the fullest assurance of holding out, and of receiving the crown of righteousness at last; and that nothing
should separate him from it. By these ye may gather,
that believers are of a nobler extract, than to love God the
less, because he loves them so much; and that it is no trivial
slander, to insinuate that believers, especially such as have
assurance, are most exposed and given to backsliding;
which is, sure, an unnatural consequent of their being
" sealed to the day of redemption." Such objections do
also argue the authors of them, not well acquainted with
the goodly ways of God, nor with that spiritual obliging
sweetness that is found in them: which any one, who hath
tasted thereof in truth, would not turn from, although his
future happiness were not concerned in it. Nor do they
consider the frame and nature of the new creature, which
hath spiritual senses, fitted to discern what makes for its
own preservation, and what against it. Had you fifteen
years added to your life, and a certainty of it; would you
therefore forsake your food, and disuse the ordinary means
of preserving life? The Jews had an absolute promise,
that God would save Jerusalem from the king of Assyria,
who then besieged it: did they set open their gates, and
draw off their guards upon it? Sense and reason would
teach them otherwise, which grace does not destroy, but
perfect. It is a spark of that heavenly fire, which cannot
live out of its element, nor can all the waters under heaven
quench it. It is a participation of the divine nature, and
so loves and hates, as the Father of it doth; and it will
cleave to him in every state: " If he save me alive, I
will serve him; if he kill me, I will yet trust in him;"
in life, and in death, I will be the Lord's. This is the
natural disposition of the new creature, it savors only the
things which are of God: and the higher tasted they are
by assurance, the more is he aloft, and above the lure of
carnal divertisements, not to be governed or led by them.
Therefore, let God be true, and his prophets and apostles
be reckoned for faithful witnesses, and every one that
speaks otherwise a liar.

The next thing in course is, to consider what improvement may be made of this doctrine; which one would surely
conclude of very great usefulness, since the scriptures are
so greatly concerned about it. In general, it affords matter

of eminent support to believers; especially in difficult cases: it also evinceth matter of duty on the believer's part; and from the examples fore-quoted, something of direction in reference to both; which I shall here put intermixedly.

Infer. I. Stand still, and behold the salvation of the Lord! and at the sight of this great thing, say in your hearts, with a holy astonishment, " What hath God wrought!" Let your souls be filled and enlarged with everlasting admirings of that grace (that sovereign grace) which has so impregnably secured the salvation of his chosen, that no manner of thing, whether within them or without them, shall be able to defeat it, or hinder them of it; " no, not the gates of hell:" nay, not so much as one of the stakes thereof shall be removed, and that for ever. Shaken you may be, and tossed with a tempest, but not overturned, because ye have an eternal root. Electing love is of that sovereignty, that it rules and overrules all, both in heaven and in earth: Christ Jesus, our Saviour and Lord, the Holy Ghost, our sanctifier, counsellor, and comforter, in all they have done, do, or will do, do still pursue that scope. All ordinances, providences, temptations, afflictions, and whatever can be named, whether good or bad in itself, life, death, things present, and things to come, are all made subservient to the decree of election, and do all work together to bring about its most glorious designment. If the course and conduct of common providences were lively delineated, it would yield an illustrious prospect: how much more the conduct, order, and end, of those special providences, which are proper to, and conversant about election! when all the pieces thereof shall be brought together, and set in order, how beautiful will it be! angels and men shall shout for the glory of it! then it will be evident God hath done nothing in vain, or impertinent to your blessedness: that whatever hath befallen you here, however contrary to your present sense and opinion of it, was dispensed in very faithfulness to you: that if any of those manifold, and seemingly cross occurrences, you have been exercised with, had been omitted, it would have been a blank in your story, a blot in your escutcheon of honor. When you shall see what contrivances have been against you; what art, subtlety, malice, and power, they were agitated with; how unable you were, of yourselves, to foresee,

prevent, avoid, or repel them; and how all the attributes of
God and his providences, each one in its time and place,
which was always most seasonable, came in to your rescue,
retorting on your adversaries, and safeguarding you; yea,.
how that which was death in itself, was made to work life
in you; how amiable and admirable will the story of it be!
that when your faith was weak, the Lord did not withdraw
from you; that when it was at its height and strength, he
then did for you above all you could believe or think, and
through an unspeakable press of difficulties and contradictions, he carried on his work in you; even bearing you on
eagles' wings, until he had brought you to himself: how
will you magnify his work, and admire it then! Begin it
now.

Infer. II. Let us study more the knowledge and con-
tents of this great truth of believers' invincible perseverance; the rise, progress, and tendency of it, and what advantages it yields to us; which are indeed many, and very
considerable.

1. As it is a part of the doctrine of election which teacheth, that nothing in us, but grace and love in God, was the
only original cause of our salvation; the knowledge whereof
will work in the soul an holy ingenuity and love towards
God, whom nothing offends but sin.   Simon answered right
when he said, " He that had most forgiven him, would love
most," Luke 7 : 45. whence it follows, that he who believes
the free remission of all his sins, from first to last, must
love God more than he who believes only the pardon of
those that are past; and that so, as that they may all be
charged upon him again: or if not, that yet he may possibly
perish for those to come, perhaps in the last moment of his
life: for he is not sure, nay, it is very doubtful, if dependant
on his own natural will, that faith and repentance shall be
his last act.   Now this grace of love being the strongest
and most operative principle, he that is led by it must act
accordingly; that is, vigorously, and without weariness, as
Paul did.   And Joseph, having received large tokens of
God's love to him, and expecting more, yet argues against,
and, with an holy disdain and slight, puts by the temptation: " How can I do this, and sin against God," who hath
dealt, and will deal, so bountifully with me! Divine love is
of infinite efficacy.

2. As it teacheth the soul to depend upon God for its keeping, as having his almighty power absolutely engaged for it. Whereas, if the efficacy and event of all that God doeth for me, should depend upon something to be done by myself, who am a frail creature, and prone to revolt, I should still be in fear, because still in danger of falling, and losing all at last: and this fear being an enfeebling passion, must needs render my resistance, and all my endeavors, both irregular and weak; whereas a magnanimous and fearless spirit, who sees himself clothed with a divine power, shall have his wits (as we say) more about him, to discern dangers and advantages, and, consequently, how to eschew the one, and improve the other.

3. As it gives assurance, " our labor shall not be in vain." This made these believing Hebrews to " endure that great fight of afflictions, and to take joyfully the spoiling of their goods; because they knew they had in heaven a better and more enduring substance." All manner of accomplishments put into one, and made your own, would not so invincibly steel your foreheads, and strengthen your hearts, as to be sure of success, and to come off conquerors at last: the apostle, therefore, brings it in as the highest encouragement in our christian warfare, Rom. 6: 14. chap. 8: 37. And our blessed Lord himself, who, of all others, had the hardest task to perform, it made " his face as a flint, because he knew he should not be confounded," Isa. 50: 7.

Infer. III. Make it one, and that a main part of your business, to foil and disprove the objections that are brought against this doctrine; and your nearest way to it is, by " growing in grace," 2 Pet. 3: 18. with chap. 1: 5—10. 1. Lay aside, and cast away every weight; especially the sin that doth most easily beset you; your bosom sin, whatever it be; cast them to the moles, and to the bats; they are not fit mates for daylight creatures, 1 Thess. 5: 5, 6. It is a noble prize you run for; therefore clog not yourself with any thing that may hinder or retard your pace. 2. Keep yourselves in the love of God; maintain a spiritual sense of his love to you, and a lively answer of holy affections towards him. Whatever may tend to obscure or lessen your sense of it, have nothing to do with it; keep yourself from idols; let nothing have an interest in your love but

God, and all things else, but in subordination, and with respect to him only. 3. Watch against the beginning and very first motions of sin; nip it in the bud; abstain from all appearance of evil; and walk not on the brink of your liberty. It is easier to keep out an invader, than to expel him when entered, to keep down a rebel, and prevent his rising, than to conquer him when he is up. Great and black clouds have small beginnings; the bigness of your hand, at first, may rise and spread so as to cover the whole heavens; therefore, keep off sin at staff's end. 4. Be diligent and industrious in it. Think not, because it is God who performeth all things for you, that therefore you may sit still, or be remiss in your duty; your arms and armor were not provided to rust in your tent. There may be, indeed, such a juncture in providence, that it may be your duty, and, consequently, your strength, to sit still, as was theirs at the Red Sea, Exod. 14: 13. this is, when all further motion is shut up to you; and then the Lord will do his work without you: but usually there is something to be done on our part. Though the Lord would go forth before David, and smite the Philistines, yet David must bestir himself, 2 Sam. 5: 24. This thing is constantly to be affirmed, that " they who have believed in God, be careful to maintain good works," Tit. 3: 8. and do it the rather, to " cut off occasion from them which desire occasion; that wherein they glory, they may be found even as we," 2 Cor. 11: 22. 5. Cleave to Jesus Christ, and to him only; and trust not to your holding of him, but to his holding of you. This did David, when he says, " Thou holdest me by my right hand," Psal. 73: 23. Follow him, as men follow the court, whose dependance is upon it. While following him, you cannot do amiss; nor want any good thing, whether for counsel, strength, or otherwise. 6. Forget what is behind, and press on towards perfection; that, if possible, you may attain to the resurrection of the dead, that is, to be perfectly holy. Though perfectness, in the perfection of it, is not attainable here; yet the higher you aim, the higher shall your attainment be, and the farther off from losing what you have got. Keep the mark still in your eye, and shun whatever might intercept your sight of it. These are some of the ways to make your calling and election sure: and if ye do these things, ye shall prove this doctrine to be true; and either prevent or retort those carnal and groundless calumnies that are brought against it.

Infer. IV. Since there are such arguments for believers' perseverance, let us all so demean ourselves, that we may have them all stand on our side, for proof and evidence that we are of that happy remnant, whom the great God hath set apart for himself, and whom he hath made and wrought for this self-same thing: and as it was his purpose, so let it be our spirit and practice, to glorify the riches of his grace. 1. If born of God, let us shew forth the virtues of our Father, and bear ourselves as his children, both towards him, and towards the world. Let us live upon him, and live to him; rejoicing always before him; first, for his own blessedness, and then for ours, as derived from his, and by him reserved in heaven for us; and all, as designing to honor him as our Father. 2. If we have faith, let it appear by our works. It must be some singular thing that must distinguish us from other men: it is not profession, nor words, nor actions neither (as to the matter of them, and so far as visible to men,) that will approve us believers; but the principle whence they grow, and the end they drive at: the result of Abraham's faith was, " to give glory to God," and so will ours, if Abraham's seed. 3. Let us carry ourselves, under all dispensations, not only quietly, but thankfully, and so as to answer God's end: walk humbly; hate the thing that is evil; have the world under your feet; esteem preciously of Christ; honor his ordinances; let every grace have its perfect work; and rejoice in hopes of that glory, which all these things are preparatory to. 4. If one with Christ, and he our Mediator, then let us walk as he walked, who held his own will always subject to his Father; reckoning it " his meat to do his will, and to finish his work:" let us also wait his advice and counsel in every business, and follow it; commit our cause to him, and interest him in all our concernments. 5. Apply yourselves to every attribute of God, according to the present occasion; and dwell upon them, and leave them not until you have the grace and help intended by them. They are all made over to the heirs of salvation, to live upon: let it not be said, that in the midst of our abundance we are in straits! 6. If made for the glory of God, make good your end: he is glorious in holiness, and by holiness only can you glorify him. Bear, therefore, on the forehead of your designs and conversation, that royal inscription, Holiness to the Lord: by this, you will set to your seal, that " God is true," and approve yourselves to be " children that will not lie." It will also be of singular use and service to yourselves, as to that other end of your being: that you have " glorified God on the earth," will be a substantial argument that " he will glorify you" in the world to come, John 17: 4. For, though your personal righteousness be not your title to the heavenly inheritance, yet your constant progression in holiness will be your best evidence, next to the immediate witnessings of the spirit, that you have a title, and that your title is good. Since, therefore, we were made for, and expect such things, " what manner of persons ought we to be, in all holy conversation and godliness?" 2 Pet. 3: 11. 7. If under the covenant of grace, let us reckon ourselves strengthened with all might, and hold to it, as having all our salvation in it; both keeping, support, recovery, and settlement, grace and glory: not minding so much how any thing looks or feels at present, as the end it tends to; for if the end be good, the means (as such) cannot be otherwise. And, truly, we cannot have a better evidence of our interest in this covenant, than a total devolving and casting ourselves upon it, Isa. 56: 4. 6.

And well it is for us (who find in ourselves so great a proneness to backslide,) that our eternal condition doth not depend on ourselves, but upon that foundation of God mentioned in Timothy, where the apostle, speaking of some who had made shipwreck of the faith (lest true believers should faint in their minds at the sight and apprehension of it,) he tells them, that nevertheless (that is, notwithstanding this woful backsliding of some, perhaps of eminent profession, yet) " the foundation of God standeth sure;" q. d. That they who are on this foundation are sure to be kept: and he confirms it with this seal, " The Lord knoweth them that are his:" he knows whom he hath chosen, and concerning whom he hath covenanted, that " they shall not depart from him;" and therefore he will not let them go; they shall be kept as those seven thousand were, from bowing the knee to Baal; adding this caution withal, " That every one which nameth the name of the Lord should depart from iniquity," 2 Tim. 2: 19. which, as it is a means of God's appointing, to keep from apostacy, so it shall be to them an evidence that they are of that foundation, and shall be kept. For it being his scope to comfort believers against their misgivings, which arise from a sense of their own weakness, and a like aptness in themselves to revolt, he needs must use an argument suitable to such an end: and, therefore, in saying "the foundation of God standeth sure," he must intend, believers standing sure upon it; for the standing sure of the foundation would be small comfort to us, if yet we might be blown off it, or sink besides it. Does God take care for sparrows? for oxen? for ravens? much more for believing souls, who have committed themselves to his keeping. Let the fowler do all he can, not a sparrow shall fall to the ground: you will say, Without the will of God they cannot: and the will of God is, that they shall not. "A thousand may fall at his side, and ten thousand at his right hand, but it shall not come nigh him," Psal. 91: 7. He that determined such a sparrow shall not fall, determined also to prevent that which would cause him to fall; and, therefore, either the fowler shall not find the bird, or the bird shall discern his approach, or smell the powder, and be gone; or if he shoot, he shall miss his mark; or if he hit, it shall light on the feathers, that will grow again, or on some fleshy part, that may be licked whole; or, perhaps, it shall open an ulcer, that could not otherwise be cured: a believer's heel may be bruised, but his vital parts are out of reach, and therefore safe.

Infer. V. Let this doctrine, of believers' invincible perseverance in faith and holiness, strengthen our hearts against all sorts of doubts and fears which may arise from the presence of indwelling sin, with its frequent and sturdy insurrections; since "he that hath begun, will also perfect his work with power," Phil. 1: 6. Judge righteous judgment: of ourselves, indeed, we cannot think worse than we deserve, but of our state we may: therefore, for help in this case, consider,

1. That though the new nature shall certainly expunge the old, at last, the work is not perfected here. But take this for your present relief, that the best principle is still predominant, and getting ground, and the old party shall never recover its wasting condition: for the kingdom of God once in the heart, will surely work and spread itself

till the whole lump is savored by it, Matt. 13: 31. 33. " To him that hath shall be given," chap. 25: 29. " He that hath life, shall have it more abundantly," John 10: 10. As it was God who girded you with strength, so he will make your way perfect, Psal. 18: 32. Though faith and holiness be, at present, but as two little flocks of kids, and sin, like the Syrian's army, fills the country, be not dismayed; the king of Israel will clear the country of them; his " Spirit shall lift up a standard against them," Isa. 59: 19. " And though they come in like a flood, by him shall their proud waves be stayed," Job 38: 11. The Lord says to you in this case as he did to Jeremiah, " I have made thee a defenced city, an iron pillar, and brazen walls, against the whole land: they shall fight against thee, but they shall not prevail against thee," Jer. 1: 18, 19. or, as once to his people, concerning the giant Og, " Fear him not, for I will deliver him and all his people into thy hand," Deut. 3: 2.

2. This sickness is not unto death. The conflict is not to weaken or destroy, but for trial and improvement of your faith, and other graces; the very trial whereof is precious, 1 Pet. 1: 7. and shall be found so at last, both to the glory of him that tries you, and yours, who are tried. Abraham, David, Job, and others, are pregnant examples of this; they came forth like gold, more pure, solid, and flexible. David, indeed, though he held fast his confidence a great while, yet being still pursued and overprest, every day involved in danger anew, and having once admitted carnal reason into his council, he began to flag in his faith; " I shall one day perish—and all men are liars," 1 Sam. 27: 1. Psal. 106: 11. but it was in his haste, not considering the sureness of an absolute promise; and, therefore, when he had better weighed it, he confesses his fault, and recovers from it; and his faith was improved by his trial: for, being come again to himself, he comfortably concludes, that " goodness and mercy shall follow him all the days of his life; and, notwithstanding his present exile, he shall dwell in the house of the Lord for ever," Psal. 23: 6.

3. Be it always remembered, that God reckons of a man according to what his mind is; and you ought so also to reckon of yourself. This was Paul's course, in Rom. 7. where he thus reasoneth; " Now if I do that I would not,

it is no more I that do it, but sin that dwelleth in me," Rom. 7: 20. before conversion it was Saul, but now it is sin. Believers may be led captive, at times, even after they have sworn fealty to their true Lord: but still they are his in their mind, and that is their mark. It is the same with that in John, " Whosoever is born of God doth not commit sin; and he cannot sin, because he is born of God," 1 John 3: 9. that is, he does not, nor he cannot sin, as the devil's children do; for their wills are in it, which also is their mark, according to John 8: 44. " The lusts of your father ye will do;" but a regenerate person, " the evil he doeth, he allows not." And this is a staying consideration, that if " with our mind we serve the law of God," it shall not ruin us, that " with our flesh we serve the law of sin," Rom. 7: 25. but how shall I know it? If you be forced, you will cry out; and if you cry, it is a rape, and shall not be charged to your account; ye have the law for it, in Deut. 22: 25, 26, 27. So, he that kills a man against his will is not reckoned a murderer, nor worthy of death; although the act itself be the same that another man, whose will was in it, shall die for, Exod. 21: 13. with Deut. 19: 4. 6.

4. Believers are " trees of righteousness, and of the Lord's own planting; and therefore they shall not fear when heat cometh," Jer. 17: 8. They have their autumns indeed (too often,) and blighting winds (perhaps in the spring time too;) and also luxuriant branches and suckers, proceeding from the old stock, which rob the good ones of their sap, and make their fruit less, both in bulk and beauty: but still their substance is in them, and therefore they revive, and flourish again. And while those suckers are nipped and pruned off, the true branches are preserved and cherished, John 15: 2. " They shall bring forth fruit in their old age," Psal. 92: 14. They that are now (that is, once, they that are once) the children of God, shall never be otherwise, save only in a greater likeness to their Father, 1 John 3: 2. 9. chap. 2: 27. 2 John ver. 2. And though their living on him, and their likeness to him, be very weakly sometimes (as the natural life of infants is,) yet, being born, they must be kept; and the will and care of their Father is, to nurse them up to a perfect man, Eph. 4: 13.

You will say, perhaps, that never had any such cause of complaint as you! and possibly it may be so; to be sure you know not that they had; and those you compare your-self with, may have said as much of themselves; and they had the like cause, for your hearts are fashioned alike, only each one best knows the plague of his own. Agur, a man of great wisdom and holiness, says of himself, that he was "more brutish than any man," Prov. 30:2. But sup-pose it be true, that others' corruptions have not broken out as yours have done; yet may not this put your faith to a stand, much less make you weary, recoil, or to faint in your minds; for the same grace that prevented them, can pardon you, and will, if you cast yourselves upon it. Ye may, indeed, be allowed to complain of your sins, for no-thing else have ye to complain of; therefore complain and cry out as loud as you will, "O wretched man that I am! who shall deliver me from this body of death?" But withal, betake to you the same refuge that he did, and abide by it, "I thank God, through Jesus Christ, our Lord!" Rom. 7: 24, 25. Here you may triumph over all, both complaints and causes of them.

It must always be granted, that to deal with sin, combi-ned, intrenched, fortified as it is, is a great undertaking, and yet may be undertaken, and gone through with too; there is no retreat to be sounded, nor armor provided for your back; every child of Adam must either kill or be killed in this combat; there is no compounding the dif-ference, nor discharge in this warfare, until the day be perfectly won: but what a recruit is there levied, and always ready, as a sure reserve, that though the conflict be sharp, the success is sure! And, in order thereto, amongst other rules and articles of war, bear in mind these few following. 1. Entangle not yourself, but shun and avoid whatever may prove a clog, or unfit you for duty. 2. Exercise yourself in handling your spiritual arms, es-pecially that of your faith. 3. Stand on your guard watch-fully, that ye be not surprised by sudden excursions, or under pretence of friendship. 4. Arm yourself with the same mind that was in Christ; set your face as a flint, and conclude that ye shall not be confounded. 5. Submit to the place your general hath set you in; it must have been somebody's lot, and why not yours? and the hotter it is, the more honorable; remembering withal, that when tempt-ation was appointed, then also was ordained a way of escape; and this you are told of beforehand, that "you

might be able to bear it," 1 Cor. 10:13.   6. Look that ye
fight with proper weapons, which are only to be had at the
covenant of grace, and cross of Christ, and there they are never wanting; and be sure you go not down to the Philistines,
either to forge or sharpen.   7. Fight not as one that beats
the air, but as having, indeed, a sturdy adversary to deal
with, whom yet you are sure to overcome.   8. Look still
on your Captain, to observe what he says and does, and
do likewise.   To take up the cross, and endure hardship,
are necessary accoutrements for a soldier of Christ.   9.
Wait on the Lord to renew your strength, who then bestirs
himself most when your strength is gone; he then lays hold
upon shield and buckler, and stands up for your help, Psal.
35:2.   10. Lastly, and to influence all, mind the Lord of
his covenant; even then, when you yourself, perhaps, think
on it with trouble, as doubting your interest in it.   Pray
to him to remember it for you, and with the same goodwill
wherewith he made it.   Beseech him to look on his bow in
the cloud, which himself hath set there, as a sure sign between him and you; that though the skies be red and low-
ering, the clouds return after rain, and the billows go over
your head, you shall not be deluged by them; by this it is
that ye are hedged about, and walled up to heaven.   Therefore stand not like men in suspense, as unresolved to fall
on, or doubtful how to come off; but on, on; the day is
your own; the Lord of hosts pursues them, and " let all
the sons of God shout for joy."

Infer. VI. Since believers only are interested in the covenant, and faith is a necessary instrument, which the covenant will not work without, and without which you cannot
work with it, look well to your faith; first, that it be of
the right kind, such as renounces self and lives upon grace;
and then, having found it such, be sure you keep it well,
and improve it to the utmost.   Two uses, especially, are
to be made of it: 1. As your shield, to supply the place of
all other pieces of your armor, when broken or loose, as
well as to safeguard them when they are whole and tight
about you.   If your helmet be out of the way, and fiery
darts come pouring down, hold up your faith between your
head and them: faith is the truest quench-coal to the fire
of hell.   If your sword be forgot, or laid aside, or wants
an edge, and so forth, your shield, if well applied, will
retort your enemy's weapons on his own head.   2. Faith

is your spiritual optic, which shows you things of greatest moment, and not otherwise visible; even chariots and horsemen of fire, are not discernible without it. If temptations from the world do endanger you, turn your faith that way, and through it view and consider how shallow and short-lived the pleasures of it are, and how momentary your sufferings. Then look at the world to come, the glory of it, and your interest in it, and how much your crown will be brightened by the trials you have passed under here, and dwell on the contemplation of it. Bend not your eye so much on the peril and length of your passage, as on the longed-for shore that lies beyond it; and reckon the surges of that dreadful gulf which is yet between you and it, but as so many strokes to waft you thither. This was the course that Moses took, Heb. 11:26. and Christ himself, chap. 12:2. Nothing so blunts the edge of Satan's temptations, or the world's, as this faith of God's elect. Therefore, see that you hold fast your faith; keep it as your life; keep that and it will keep you; and let it not go until you die. Then, indeed, it will leave you, because then it will have done all the service it can, even the whole of what it was ordained for. But shall faith then be dissolved and go to nothing? I would rather express it, as the apostle does the state of the saints that shall be found alive at Christ's coming, " they shall not die, but they shall be changed," 1 Cor. 15: 51. Faith shall then be turned into sight, and we shall have the real presence, full possession, and perfect fruition of that blessedness we have believed and hoped for. And then shall we say to our glorious Redeemer, thou art the God that hast fed me all my life long; thy flesh has been meat indeed, and thy blood drink indeed; many a good meal have I had upon it in the valley of Baca, even feasts of fat things, and wine upon the lees; other bridegrooms and saviours have done worthily, but thou excellest them all; they set forth their best at first, but thou hast kept back the good wine until now!

Infer. VII. Gather hence both the reason and rationality of the saints' desires to be dissolved, Phil. 1:23. They knew, that when this earthly tabernacle went down, they had a better and more capacious building in heaven, 2 Cor. 5:1,2. They also found, that spirits, dwelling in flesh, are too much straitened and infirm, either to bear the glory they were made for, or to express an answerable thankfulness for it; and for this they groaned; not to be unclothed, as weary of their present state, but to be clothed upon with their house from heaven, ver. 4. They were now the sons of God, 1 John 3: 2. but what they should be, and fain would be, did not appear to them, nor could, until the vail was rent, which hung, as yet, between them and the holy of holies. The first fruits of the Spirit, Rom. 8:23. 2 Cor. 1:22. which were both an earnest and foretaste of future glory, Eph. 1:14. inspired them with fervent desires of liberty, that glorious liberty which belonged to them, as being the sons of God, Rom. 8:21. They had, by faith, laid hold on eternal life; this they had still in their eye, and earnestly pursued; and so intent were they upon it, that they forgot what was behind, Phil. 3:14. though very memorable in its time. The much they had attained, they counted for nothing, to what was coming; nor reckoned for any cost, to gain that inestimable pearl, namely, the prize of the high calling of God in Christ, Phil. 3:13. This they knew was a thing too big for mortal senses, though as highly refined and sublimated as capable of while mortal, and therefore longed for that day, when immortality should be their clothing. The love of God shed abroad in their hearts, Rom. 5:5. had given such a divine tincture, and so transformed and widened their souls, as nothing could satisfy, but that immense deep from whence it came. They knew, that when Christ, their life, should appear, they should be like him, and should see him as he is, Col. 3:4. not under shadows, as of old; nor in a state of humiliation, as when upon earth; nor, as since, under memorials and representations; but in his state of glory, the sight of which would transform them into his image indeed, and until then they could not say, it is enough. They knew, that the very quintessence of heavenly beatitude consists in the vision of God, and that heaven itself, with all that innumerable company of angels, and spirits of just men made perfect, though a very glorious and desirable society, would not satisfy heaven-born souls, if the Lord himself were not there in his glory; hence those holy exclamations and outcries, " whom have I in heaven but thee!" Psal. 73:25. and " when shall I come and appear before God," Psal. 62:2. Good Jacob would go and see his beloved

Joseph before he died; and these would die to go and see theirs. Thus does the kingdom of heaven, as it were, suffer violence a second time from the heirs of salvation; they know it is theirs, and that they were wrought for that self-same thing, and, being theirs, they might lawfully take it, by force upon all carnal impediments, Matt. 11: 12. 2 Cor. 5: 5.

Infer. VIII. To close all: you have seen what Paul and others did; go you and do likewise; " hasten to the day of God," 2 Pet. 3: 12. and wait for it, as they that watch for the morning. 1. Affectionately, as a thing greatly desirable, especially after a dark and toilsome night. 2. Patiently, and with quietness; not precipitating, but as knowing it will come, and that in the fittest time. 3. Attentively, as not willing to lose the smallest sound of your master s feet. 4. With diligence also, and preparedness; that neither oil nor lighting may be to seek when the cry is made. Be always ready, and then groan: groan (I say) for that day of glory, when life and immortality shall be brought to light in perfection: when yourself, with all the elect of God, meeting in that great and general assembly, the " church of the first born which are written in heaven" Heb. 12: 23. may be entirely, universally, and everlastingly taken up in admiring electing love which so gloriously and happily shall have wrought all our works for us and brought us to the ultimate end it designed us for, which was, to be ever with the Lord; to see him as he is and to experience the sum of that great petition in the 17th of John, " that they may be in us," John 17: 21, 26. And in your way thither, carry this assurance still before you; that the same hands which laid the foundation, will also lay the top stone, and that with shoutings; and you shall lift up, to eternity, that loud and joyful acclamation, " Grace grace unto it," Zech. 4: 7, 9. " Happy art thou, O Israel; who is like unto thee, O people saved by the Lord, the shield of thine help, and the sword of thine excellency! all thine enemies shall be found liars unto thee; and thou shalt tread upon their high places!" Deut. 33: 29. 2 Sam. 22:1. &c, and which is more than angels and men can utter besides, " God shall be all in all!" 1 Cor. 15: 28. to proclaim which, was the end of this work. Amen